# Acting Now

D0802439

# Acting
# Now

CONVERSATIONS ON
CRAFT AND CAREER

**Edward Vilga**

RUTGERS UNIVERSITY PRESS
New Brunswick, New Jersey, and London

Library of Congress Cataloging-in-Publication Data

Vilga, Edward, 1963–
Acting now : conversations on craft and career / Edward Vilga.
p.   cm.
Includes bibliographical references and index.
ISBN 0-8135-2402-4 (alk. paper). — ISBN 0-8135-2403-2 (pbk. :
alk. paper)
1. Acting. 2. Actors—Interviews. 3. Acting teachers—
Interviews. 4. Theatrical producers and directors—Interviews.
I. Title.
PN2061.V56   1997
792′.028—dc21                                    96-39285
                                                              CIP

British Cataloging-in-Publication information available

Manufactured in the United States of America

This book is dedicated

to all actors

who bare their hearts

courageously to the world

and

to N.W.V.

whose courageous heart

has taught my own so much.

# Contents

# *Preface*

Simply put, I came to do this book as a way out of my own confusion.

After I graduated from Yale as an English major, I moved to New York City and began working for Helen Whitney, a well-known documentary filmmaker attempting to expand into fiction narrative. Pursuing a career for myself as a writer-director of film, I knew I needed to understand something of the seemingly elusive process of acting so that I could work with actors most knowledgeably and effectively. I very much wanted to learn the essence of what good actors did that made their work particularly compelling. I sought an understanding of a great actor's "magic," insights into the secrets that allowed him or her to breathe life and mystery into words on a page. In my quest, I audited various acting classes, participated in numerous weekend workshops, and spoke at length whenever possible with actors whose work I respected.

Turning to the public library to peruse the available literature, I found myself overwhelmed by all that had been written about acting, yet also dismayed by how little existed about what I most wanted to know. I couldn't find a book that told me how modern actors really worked or one that contrasted different methods of training. I did find numerous historical treatises on dramatic literature, several seminal sources from great individual acting teachers, and a smattering of minor authorities. Indeed, many of these books were helpful and often quite marvelous but something like Michael Chekhov's *To the Actor,* and even the seminal works of Stanislavsky, could not anticipate the diversity of modern opinion that exists today. None of these books addressed issues of acting in the modern world, nor could they, having been written before the media of film and television came to dominate the finances of the acting profession.

The closest book to the one I sought was *Actors on Acting,* edited by Toby Cole and Helen Krich Chinoy, which proved an invaluable source of historical information.[1] That book presents the writings of actors on their craft beginning with the ancient Greeks, continuing through the Middle Ages, and ending in the late 1960s. The editors' universal concerns are indeed similar to my own. In their introduction they voice their guiding questions: "How does the actor transform himself?" What is "the personality of the actor?" "Is the actor an original creator or does he merely embody the playwright's text and vivify the director's perceptions?"[2] Like all writers on acting, we share a fascination and frustration with the difficulties inherent in examining the art form. The transitory nature of performance, and the extraordinary relationship between the artist and his or her instrument, namely himself or herself, make acting a singularly difficult art to analyze.

Yet there were many things not addressed in *Actors on Acting* that were of great interest to me. Beyond its datedness, most particularly I missed any discussion of how the harsh realities of the actor's world and the practical difficulties of the career and the modern entertainment industry shape his or her artistic path. The problem with this book, as with many others, is that it is out of touch with its audience. For example, the type of lengthy, exploratory rehearsal process described in these texts simply does not exist for much of the modern actor's employment in film, television, and often even theater. Most classic writings on acting maintain the repertory theater as the necessary developmental standard for the actor. Unfortunately, while this ideal of lifelong artistic growth amidst a supportive community is still often lauded by modern, dedicated actors and directors, it is increasingly disappearing in the contemporary world. Many individuals I spoke to insisted that even the notion of a career sustained by theater is utterly archaic; for all but the merest handful of actors, it is simply impossible to survive, much less support a family, based on theatrical employment alone. To be a working actor today means something very different than it did in the past, even during earlier decades of our own century.

Neither *Actors on Acting* nor any other book I could then find satisfactorily reconciled the clashes of opinion (often fueled by personality conflicts) within the post-Stanislavsky generation of great teachers: most particularly, Stella Adler, Sanford Meisner, and Lee Strasberg.[3] Adler, Meisner, and Strasberg each wrote a modern classic text on acting that differs greatly from the other two in both its areas of concern and its fundamental philosophy of how actors should train and approach their craft. After their bitter parting of ways, neither in person nor in print was there ever any serious discussion among them about their work and individual discoveries. As one noted critic said to me off the record, it sometimes seems as if they each read a different chapter of Stanislavsky and were determined to vehemently defend their fragment as the "complete truth." (At the risk of clichéd oversimplification, Strasberg stresses emotional memory, and Adler highlights the imagination, while Meisner focuses on responding to other actors by being truthful in the moment. I present this reduction here less because of its accuracy than its purveyance: even accomplished, knowledgeable actors would sometimes summarize other methods of working into these rough categories. I found that while certain actors drifted back and forth between great teachers—

more or less mentoring à la carte—many fine actors often doggedly stayed with one teacher alone, largely ignoring other viable methods of training.)

Knowing that the conflict among these theorists ranges from the deeply profound to the superficially personal, and also knowing that part of this volatile debate often serves a thought-provoking and stimulating purpose, I did not feel it was my duty to resolve their differences. Rather, the challenge, as I saw it, was to present multiple contrasting viewpoints juxtaposed so that the reader could make his or her own comparisons, conclusions, and syntheses. This is something no other book I found attempted to do.

The need for this book was quite clear to me. The timing was also right. Artistically, a new generation of actors had emerged from modern, post–Group Theatre teachers who often combine methods less rigidly than their predecessors did. Eva Mekler in *The New Generation of Acting Teachers* depicts this new breed, but I feel that things have progressed much further.[4] Today's actors are subject not just to a new generation of acting teachers but to a new era of technological innovation. Paralleling the present generation of film school students brought up on videotapes and VCRs, a media-savvy group of aspiring actors enjoys the historically unique advantage of being able to study decades of great performances preserved on film. If Blockbuster is not a great teacher of acting, it certainly serves as a great library of many of its treasures. Good, bad, and indifferent, the average individual's exposure to acting—even if only by watching the national average of twelve hours of television a week—has broadened and increased dramatically.

In the same way, employment for actors has changed drastically. While legitimate New York theater on Broadway has shriveled, new opportunities have sprung up in regional theaters across the country. Furthermore, over the past few decades, independent filmmaking has emerged not only as an alternative to Hollywood styles and entertainment values but also as an exciting venue for young, unknown actors to showcase cutting-edge, fully professional performances. Exemplifying this new breed is Lili Taylor, an actress whose credits and critical acclaim stem almost entirely from roles in independent, low-budget films. The proliferation of short industrial training films (known as "industrials") have created countless new employment possibilities for young performers, and the rising salaries for actors in television commercials and soap operas have allowed them to explore less profitable venues simultaneously. With the evolution of acting training and with new kinds of opportunities being created as others are dying, the time seemed doubly ripe for this account.

Having decided to embark on this project, I clarified my intentions. First and foremost, I wanted to present an open interchange of modern ideas about acting, acting training, and the actor's career that addressed artistic challenges in the real world. Second, amidst the diversity of opinion, I hoped that some general conclusions might be reached that would prove useful for actors, other artists, and the general public. Finally, I hoped to present a chronicle of the late 1980s to mid-1990s in American theater and film, an exciting period of great challenges, expansion, and changing opportunity. While I have endeavored to detail information vital to a historical context within the endnotes, my intention has never been to present a summary of acting theories or to offer an overview of acting history in this volume. That information can be found elsewhere. Rather, I wanted to capture something of what being an actor today truly means. Although I initially envisioned a collection of essays, I realized that the most effective way to achieve these goals was to present the wisdom of a diversified group of knowledgeable professionals from the acting world in interview format.

To this end I conducted over thirty-five interviews over a period of five years. Of these, my editor and I selected a representative fifteen interviews to appear in this volume. Most interviews lasted one to two hours; the shortest was forty-five minutes, the longest three and a half hours. Each interview took place in the subject's office or rehearsal room, with the exception of Stella Adler, who invited me to her home in Los Angeles, and Robert Falls, Juliet Taylor, and Henry House, each of whom I spoke to on the telephone. All interviews were taped at the time and later transcribed. They have been edited for clarity and accuracy, and all subjects were forwarded copies before publication so they could correct any inadvertent mistakes.

Admittedly highly subjective, the process of subject selection was governed by my desire to find a diverse and representative sampling. I began by approaching the post-Stanislavsky master teachers: Stella Adler, Anna Strasberg as Lee Strasberg's representative, and Harold Baldridge, the director of the Neighborhood Playhouse, which Sanford Meisner founded. I then spoke to the generation of teachers who follow closely a legendary teacher's methods. For example, Marilyn Fried, a well-known acting coach and Actors Studio board member, only teaches exactly what she learned directly from Lee Strasberg without any embellishment or innovation of her own.

Next I spoke to teachers at well-known universities and other established training institutions, such as Robert Brustein at the American Repertory Theatre in Cambridge, Frank Corsaro, the director of the Actors Studio, and Bob Moss, the director of the teaching program at Playwrights Horizons. After this I interviewed well-known actors who also teach, including Austin Pendleton, Ellen Burstyn, Olympia Dukakis, and Joanna Gleason.

Next I explored the world of the theater director, seeking individuals who had some experience of acting themselves. I spoke to André Bishop at Lincoln Center and such New York Off-Broadway luminaries as Tanya Berezin, then at Circle Rep. I continued with more Off-Off Broadway theaters, represented in this collection by the artistic directors of two very young and successful theater companies: Neil Pepe at the Atlantic (founded by David Mamet) and Nela Wagman at the Watermark Theater in SoHo. I completed my exploration of theater today by speaking to numerous regional theater directors across the country: Robert Falls at the Goodman in Chicago, Daniel Sullivan at the Seattle Rep, and Garland Wright at the Guthrie in Minneapolis.

To gain an understanding of some of the practical considerations of the actor, I spoke also to a handful of industry professionals, including New York and Los Angeles talent agents. This volume includes interviews with Juliet Taylor, the preeminent New York casting director of the films of Mike Nichols, Woody Allen, and Stephen Frears, and with Henry House, who manages and coaches the careers of many rising Hollywood stars.

Finally, while my focus has been traditional acting in traditional media, I wanted to include some of the modern hybrid forms such as performance art and radical, alternative theater. Scott Macaulay, director of the Kitchen Center for Video, Music, and Dance and now an award-winning film producer, contrasted acting and performance for me in an insightful and provocative way. Spalding Gray, a classically trained actor who manages to combine successful careers as a self-obsessed monologist and as a traditional actor for hire, to me exemplifies the modern hybrid performer.

Although people were chosen as representatives, each individual was unique, indeed often straddling several areas. For example, while Robert Falls was initially selected as a representative of regional theater in America, he has subsequently become an increasingly noted director of acclaimed New York theater productions such as Nicky Silver's *The Food Chain*. This trend, perhaps parallel in Hollywood to "hyphenating" (i.e., a movie star becomes a writer-director-actor-producer), illustrates how many of the boundaries of traditional career paths are blurring, if not vanishing entirely.

While interview content obviously varies from individual to individual, particularly given that subjects often worked in radically different parts of the entertainment industry, I nonetheless endeavored to ask a core set of questions in each interview. These questions—probably the eternal inquiries about the nature of acting—were essentially "How does the actor transform himself or herself into a character?" followed by "How can he or she best train to do this?" and "How does the trained actor then pursue a successful career?" To this end, I asked interview subjects about their own training, what they observed about the training of actors they worked with, and what aspects of acting talent and training were apparent during the audition process. I asked directors about their rehearsal process and how they facilitated the actor's transformation into a character. I asked industry professionals all of the above along with asking them to define the unique challenges the actor faces in the marketplace today. I attempted to balance inquiries about achieving the highest standards of artistic expression in one's work with questions about the banal, harsh practical realities of struggling just to get any acting job, under any conditions. And I asked everyone about the changing role of theater and film in today's world and its implications for the modern actor's career path. In short, I strove to discover what it means to be an actor today.

Thus the same core sets of questions appear in each of the interviews, along with questions tailored to address an individual's specific expertise or position in the acting arena. Of course, the give and take of any interview's dialogue also determined the flow of the conversation and the material covered. Nonetheless, the themes of discussion generally stayed focused on these areas of inquiry.

What are the conclusions one can reach from the answers I received? Certain topics elicited nearly universal agreement. Almost every interview subject insisted on the need for specific training to act effectively onstage. Other questions met a greater diversity of opinion: several individuals confidently told me they could instantly and unfailingly spot talent at an audition, while other experts told me they were never really certain they had not inadvertently missed someone great among the masses.

For me, the diversity of opinion herein is both stimulating and enlightening. Not having been trained by any one master teacher myself, it seemed to me self-evident at the outset that more than one method can refine acting talent. Although many professionals now, and even more in the past, would vehemently disagree with me, I can conclude from my conversations that many methods do indeed work and that the individual's response to the teacher and way of working is all-important. Simply put, different methods work for different people. I can also happily report that while the lack of serious, mainstream New York theater is often lamented, exciting and innovative work is being presented to eager audiences Off and Off-Off Broadway and in thriving regional theaters across the country. None can deny its problems, but American theater is not dead. More accurately, it is being reborn, albeit many blocks (sometimes even states) away from the Great White Way.

The initial confusion I felt was long ago clarified. In its place an even greater curiosity grew, not just about the craft and career of acting, but about the nature of the actor's creative process itself. As with any artistic endeavor, this is an inquiry without an end, with its deepest satisfactions inherent in unanswerable questions. Its rewards have been many. Indeed, the journey of writing this book has enormously enriched my understanding and respect for the demands and difficulties of the actor's art, the great challenges of this profession, and the unique joys produced by the transcendent moments an inspired actor creates.

# *Acknowledgments*

●————————————————————————————●

First and foremost, sincere thanks to the many individuals whose interviews are included in this book. All the experts I met with were more than gracious in sharing their time, their experience, and their insights. Without them this book would not exist.

Second, my most heartfelt thanks are offered to Leslie Mitchner at Rutgers for her editorial guidance and her great belief in this project. Her enormous faith has made this book possible.

I would also like to acknowledge literary agents Beth Vesel and Madeleine Morel for their prior contributions toward this book's publication. My many assistants who worked on this project at various stages of development merit praise, as well: Allison Hopper, Michael Hummer, Lisa Grundy, Karl Herlinger, and particularly Sarah Kate Levy for her tireless footnote research. In addition, generous contributions from the Actors' Fund and the PEN Writers Fund provided greatly appreciated financial support during the editorial process.

I would like to thank my parents, Edward F. and Helen Vilga, along with Carol Vilga and Genevieve Vilga. In the long journey toward publication, when called upon, each of these people offered vital encouragement, guidance, and faith.

Finally, and most important, I want to thank Nela Wagman for her artistic insights, her editorial input, and her love.

# Acting Now

# *Stella Adler*

*Stella Adler is considered by many to have been, along with Lee Strasberg, the leading American teacher of Method acting.*

*Born into a celebrated acting family who were stars of the Yiddish theater at the turn of the century, Adler made her stage debut at four and subsequently appeared in nearly two hundred plays during the course of her career. She was a member of the Group Theatre founded by Harold Clurman (later to become the second of her three husbands), Lee Strasberg, and Cheryl Crawford. Adler had a volatile falling out with Lee Strasberg over their differing interpretations of Stanislavsky's Method, the first systematized training for the actor to develop the internal resources for a performance. Strasberg based his work on Stanislavsky's early emphasis on developing an actor's emotional memory through controlled recall of his or her conscious past. After traveling to Paris to study with Stanislavsky herself, Adler found that he had revised his theories to place new emphasis on the actor creating through his or her own imagination and being truthful to the imaginary circumstances of the play. This became the basis of her own work as an actress and teacher.*

*Adler taught professionally for many years, including being an adjunct professor of acting at Yale and for many years the head of the undergraduate drama department at New York University. She founded the Stella Adler Conservatory of Acting in 1949, where she inspired acclaimed actors such as Marlon Brando, Warren Beatty, and Robert De Niro. In 1988, Bantam Books published her book,* Stella Adler on Acting *with a foreword by Marlon Brando. An inspiring and dynamic, as well as a demanding, often harsh teacher, through her life and work Adler deeply affected a generation of actors. Indeed, former students report the charismatic teaching she offered instructed them as much about living an inspired, passionate life as it did about the technique of acting. Stella Adler died in 1992 at the age of ninety-one.*

●———————————————————————●

**Vilga:**   What do you feel is the basic urge that makes someone decide to become an actor?

**Adler:**   I think a lot of people have something in their character which is an artistic challenge. Sometimes the artistic challenge is very strong and begins to urge the person to do something about it. Sometimes it's the piano, very often it's in acting. The acting urge is very strong because it's very close to movement and dancing and expressing oneself through joy in many things.

A lot of people feel that impulse toward acting is acting and that therefore they can act. They see an image and think that they can just do it. That image only stimulates that instinct that you have in you. Something draws you toward the movement, toward the words, toward expressing yourself. That's when what you call "the talent" begins to stir.

**Vilga:**   Is talent something that you can pinpoint in someone?

**Adler:**   I don't think so. I think that you can pinpoint the imitation of the talent, the cliché of the talent. It's so in the society to imitate, to do what somebody else does. We are tempted to say, "Oh, I want to act like Joan Crawford." When the image is available, we see it on the street, you see it on the screen, then people begin to feel they already have it. When they begin to feel they have it, they get restless and try, and so almost everybody has a little bit of the urge to try to act.

**Vilga:**   But that's not really talent?

**Adler:**   Real talent one can't tell about immediately. You have to wait until the occasion makes the person dance like Nureyev. It is not based on spontaneity. Real talent is based on craft and the solidity of a base. Real talent develops inside by growth of that talent, by working at it, thinking about it, doing it, and studying it more and more. The real talent begins to need the work. The means to it are easier now because there is a craft developing. The craft was created somewhat by Stanislavsky, somewhat developed through actors who were on the stage for a long time performing for many audiences. Images began to stimulate in the actor a desire to emulate it, to try and do it. Influence is a tremendous thing in acting.

**Vilga:**   Do you believe that, given enough training, almost anyone could become an actor?

**Adler:**   No. Craft itself is like playing the piano. It's made of wood. Everybody can produce a tone on a wooden piano. In order to make the wood really sound you have to have the talent that you put into the wood, behind the wood, from the inside. The piano must sound from the inside, not from the wood.

**Vilga:**   Do you ever feel there are actors who are able to create that without craft?

**Adler:**   No. I think that influence has a great effect in talent. I think you feel surrounded by it in a society where talent is revered. It can awaken the talent in other people. If you can't really do Shakespeare, if you can't really do Molière, if you can't really get to that point, if it is not revealed on the high level, then it dies out. The talent has to be stimulated and grow, and grow from the image around you of talent.

**Vilga:**   Do you feel that that climate exists in the theater today?

**Adler:**   No. I feel it doesn't exist.

**Vilga:**   Is there a particular reason or set of reasons?

**Adler:**   I think of it as a set of reasons. I think the motion picture has given the average person the sense that they can do it. Mostly they can only do a part of it, but not the whole of it. That needs more talent and more training and more discipline. The average person has an image of talent such that they think that you can just do it.

**Vilga:**   With that climate, what should the actor seek out?

**Adler:**   The school that started literally fifty years ago with the influence of Stanislavsky began to stimulate in different countries a sense in actors that their talent can expand, can grow, and can meet certain heights. In different countries like France or Germany, they can do *King Lear*, they can do the big plays. Whereas it is very limited in America. The audiences don't see enough of it, and the actor doesn't dare enough to do it, so you don't see the acting one must see.

*Vilga:*   Should students then go to Europe to see what is happening?

*Adler:*   No. The actors in all the European theaters apprenticed through being in the chorus, being around actors who are rehearsing, and being stimulated by watching the director and the rehearsal. They grew slowly from carrying the spear to being influenced by the rehearsal period and began to get more and more stimulated. Suddenly they could say, "My talent is growing." The actor doesn't have it when he has his spear, but it can grow from his spear into *The Merchant of Venice.*

*Vilga:*   In your book you speak about theater and not specifically about film. I know that except for a few films, your background is in theater. Do you have less respect for the acting in films, or is it that your personal preference is for the theater?

*Adler:*   It depends on the film, depends on the director and the theme and the way it is executed. I find that American themes usually have a very dull background. You see a street, it's a street. Whereas you see a European street, you begin to identify with the aesthetic of the architecture, or of the town, or of the picture where it is playing.

*Vilga:*   In terms of the acting within a film, do you feel that a separate kind of training is needed, or do you feel that if trained for the theater one can do film?

*Adler:*   It depends if you can act. I think that if you can act, you can act anywhere. You can act on the street, in church. It's a very fluent craft. It can use any platform.

*Vilga:*   Do you feel that film is part of the reason that theater is in this depressed state?

*Adler:*   It's another medium. I think the screen demands other things. It's not as collaborative as the theater. The theater collaborates very much with the author, and therefore the author and the actor are together in interpretation. In film, the author takes a lesser stand, a lesser position. Therefore the action is larger, the excitement and the progress is larger. The words are less important. Whereas in the theater, language is much more important.

*Vilga:*   Would the director be more important to the film?

*Adler:*   I think the director has another job in film. He has to illuminate it and light it and make the background interesting. He uses a great many things which you don't need in the theater. You can stand on the stage and do the best play by just speaking. You don't have to have a lot of scenery. Whereas in film, the decoration is more important. You have a chance to go to the real streets and the natural lights. It's a much more difficult profession for the screen because you must use the variety offered, which is a change of set and a change of ambiance.

*Vilga:* In the theater production, how do you see the director's role in terms of the actor?

*Adler:* Mostly interpretation. If actors say something, the stage director needs fewer tricks. The actor is able to say something through whatever platform he has. If he has a drawing room or a kitchen, he can say it with one piece of kitchen or drawing room furniture. Whereas in the movies he has to have a lot to create that.

*Vilga:* In terms of shaping actors and their conception of art, how much should the director be relied on?

*Adler:* I think that the actor is more independent in the theater. He needs the director more in film. He uses him less in the theater. The film director doesn't use the language that you use in the theater. He uses sets and places which are interesting, but he doesn't use language.

*Vilga:* In your book you speak many times about how the truth must pass through the actor's imagination but at the same time the actor is reaching out to the playwright's ideas. Are these different processes, or is one simultaneously reaching for the playwright but interpreting oneself?

*Adler:* You can't reach to the playwright's imagination. He creates his own imagination, which creates the play. The actor has to use his own imagination. You can't use the writer's.

*Vilga:* But is the actor's job to try to understand the writer's ideas? Is that the actor's primary focus, through his or her own imagination?

*Adler:* The ideas are not imaginative. They exist in the text and in the relationship of the characters. Whereas the imagination is there unknown and more or less felt by the audience—but you can't enter an actor's imagination.

*Vilga:* Do you feel your previous work with emotional memory was help-ful when you began to work with Stanislavsky and the imagination? Or do you feel that it was not necessary to have done that, that you could have begun with the imagination?

*Adler:* I think you have to begin with the imagination. If not, the charac-ter does not exist and the imagination has to create the part. The man on the stage has to create a complete inner life which comes from his imagination and has to draw on the author, but he can't substitute for the author. He can't say what the author says. He can enlarge what the author says, he can expand what the idea is.

**Vilga:** In your book you speak about the difference between truth in life and truth in the theater. Is the truth of the theater a greater truth or simpler truth, or is it the same thing as truth in life?

**Adler:** The truth in life can be an individual truth. Whereas the truth in the theater is public, throughout the world. The family life, for instance, is understood in all theater. If it's true for a wife to be happy or unhappy, that's true all over the world. The author is putting an idea on paper which demands a larger canvas; it demands that this is happening all over Russia and Spain and everywhere else, and it is that much larger. We understand European plays because we understand their ideas since we have them ourselves. Theatrical truth is a truth that everyone can share.

**Vilga:** Many of the things that you have spoken about, such as conveying the large ideas of the playwright, apply best to significant or great plays. How would an actor approach lesser work, for example, a television show? Is it the same kind of thing? Should an actor always be striving for the idea even in lesser material?

**Adler:** I think the actor works with the material so that it is bigger than the author writes it down. He has to enlarge it. He cannot play on the level of the author if the author is on a lesser level than he is. The idea can be small, but the actor cannot approach it that way.

**Vilga:** Is that easily done?

**Adler:** Yes.

**Vilga:** How would an actor approach something like that? If actors know something more than the playwright, then do they have to bring some more of themselves to that role? Or do they just create something that is not there?

**Adler:** If he plays a shoemaker, he will find him in the working class, and he will find in his community and his way of life things of the working class, its trouble, its difficulties, its advantages. The characters must be large. They are larger as types than the author can state. For example, there was really no working-class theater of any great stature before the Irish theater. The Irish started with the working class and produced the best working-class plays. Then they spread all over, including to Russia. You didn't have working-class plays in Russia until that time. Then that class began to be featured in the theater because they related to so many people. Let's say this shoemaker, he belongs to the working class. Now the working class is so large that he borrows from the working class all the things that the working class donates to civilization: a way of life, a way of cooking, a way of living, a way of having children, a way of dying.

**Vilga:** I wanted to ask you about the difficulty of the high standards that you maintain actors should set for themselves as artists versus some of the enormous difficulties of the profession. Is there any advice you have for the actor in terms of that?

**Adler:** The talent can be somewhere out there, somewhere out of time, in some small platform, and suddenly the talent will reveal itself. Then people will say, "There is a talent in Philadelphia. You must go and see him." So it begins to spread that somebody has a special talent somewhere. It begins to reveal itself after all. In other words, there are many Marlon Brandos, Robert De Niros, and Al Pacinos—they just don't have the chance to be in the movies.

**Vilga:** You say in your book that the actor should just focus on the work and ignore the audience and they will love him or her. At other times it seems as though the actor is more directly engaged with the audience or aware of the audience. How should the actor approach or not approach the audience?

**Adler:** It's difficult to move the audience. I think if you leave them alone they will come to you. If you don't leave them alone, they are aware that you are making an effort. I think it's best to know the existence of the audience, but not in any way try to please them emotionally or reach out to them or cater to them. That's fatal.

**Vilga:** In a film, where you do not have an audience, how would an actor approach that?

**Adler:** When acting in film the imagination creates an atmosphere. For instance, the girl is in the ballroom, so she works from the actual ballroom. She gets emotion from the place that she is in. The audience is not going to applaud at the end of the scene, but she is very much involved with where she is. If she is sitting alone in the bar, she is very aware that she is alone in the bar, and that gives her enough to work with. She doesn't need the audience to give her more. I think that's the difference for acting on the screen. The theater actor needs the noise, the ensemble, the soul of the audience. I think the motion picture actor has learned to cut it down. The motion picture actor doesn't need the soul of the audience, where the stage actor does. Give a stage actor a cold audience, they can't work.

**Vilga:** Can they warm the audience up?

**Adler:** Yes. Naturally. They bring to the stage that thing which is more challenging, more full of personality, full of individuality, and that interests the audience. If you are an ordinary man walking in the street, you don't interest an audience. Now, that same man walking on the street, if he is on the stage, he can interest the audience by his skill of creating the character, understanding the author, and having what psychologists call "high personality."

***Vilga:*** There is also the phenomenon of charisma. Is that something that an actor must possess? Is that innate in the actor?

***Adler:*** It's something that you are born with. The audience is very alert to the difference in personality between one actor and the other. The audience would rather see an interesting girl dancing than a good dancer.

***Vilga:*** Can that get in the way of a part, or is it just something that happens with an audience?

***Adler:*** The audience makes a choice always of whom they prefer. Always.

***Vilga:*** Do you think it's generally the entire audience? Are the audience's responses collective or individual?

***Adler:*** It's interesting if an audience is divided in their choice. If you have an audience that favors one actor, you get what you call the "clique." They will root for one actor and they will not root for the other one. If both actors are of equal merit, the audience's choice is often where the author wants to put it. He wants you to like Othello, he's not going to let you like Iago. The author pushes the audience toward what he wants.

***Vilga:*** What do you feel is the actor's greatest responsibility toward himself or herself as an artist?

***Adler:*** He has really no interest, no real deep interest, in things that don't arrest his attention in the theater. He is alert to what Picasso said: he knows everything that is in the room. The actor knows everything that he is surrounded with. He is aware of where he is and he is aware of the quality of where he is. He is aware when the sun comes down. He is aware. He watches and he sees. He sees more than anybody. He is trained to see.

***Vilga:*** Is there anything that I haven't asked you that you wish I had? Anything that you want to add?

***Adler:*** I think that we have underestimated the platform. Once we used the platform in a purely theatrical way. Whereas in the modern theater, the theater of realism, we have given the platform a tremendous truth and life. That has stimulated actors to be better actors and to respond more to where they are.

If you were in a bar onstage twenty years ago, you were in a make-believe bar. Whereas today, you create the bar in the actor, along with all the attention to costumes and props, so it's a creative merger between all the people who are working in the bar to make that bar interesting and authentic. That place has taken on a greater proportion of truth and interest for the audience.

*Vilga:* And the acting itself? Has that improved as well?

*Adler:* Yes, the actor has become more conscious and is made more conscious of the responsibility to the place. He is more stimulated by it, he is more talented when he knows where he is. Stanislavsky said, "Every stone knows where it is." You have to know where you are in order to behave in a certain way. I think it's very good image to say, "Where are you?" and act with that sense of stimulation your answer gives you. You will get better actors from that.

*Vilga:* Is there anything else you would like to add?

*Adler:* I think maybe we ought to talk about lack of size of the theater.

*Vilga:* What would you like to say about it?

*Adler:* That the author always wants to say something. Suppose he wants to say something about the death of a salesman. He doesn't want to say it through one actor, he wants to say something about a larger life that exists. The salesman has created a way of life in America, so the salesman is a universal aspect of the playwright. If he is not played by a large actor, he becomes small. We lack actors of dimension, size, and I would say nobility of spirit, the responsibility of spirit.

*Vilga:* Why is that?

*Adler:* America is a money country, yet we don't understand the value of an actor who wants more money. The producer would rather have a cheaper actor. He values things in terms of money. He doesn't understand that the play depends on the actor and not on the money. So the management, or the people who run the theater, don't know enough about casting to decide the play.

*Vilga:* Are those actors not available, or is it that the casting people are not choosing the right ones?

*Adler:* Actors of that size are not available anymore. Some of them have been shrunken by the values of the motion picture or of Broadway. They have not lived up to their potential in growth as actors.

*Vilga:* In regard to the size as an actor or as a person: are they inseparable?

*Adler:* The size of the character has to exist in the actor. He can't borrow it. He can't imitate it. He has to have in him the size that is needed in order to play Hamlet. He can't just know Hamlet, you have to be Hamlet. You can't put a man from the street who knows the lines onstage—the audience knows the lines! The actor has to have the aristocracy of mind, soul, spirit, and background in order to express a certain kind of play properly.

**Vilga:** It seems that actors have to work on themselves in order to be able to bring that to the stage.

**Adler:** That's talent. To work on the character means that you have enough size in you to be expanded so that you can play the character of the queen. You have to have enough variety to be able to reach into yourself so that you can bury yourself into different parts and not just play yourself.

**Vilga:** When you see actors who basically play themselves, is that acting, or is that something very different?

**Adler:** If they are basically themselves and that's what they play and they are understood because of this characterization, they are bad actors. The play must be served by having the different characters created through the variety of actors who play the different characters.

**Vilga:** What one piece of advice would you give to the young actor?
*(Adler pauses and thinks for a full minute. She makes a sweeping gesture that takes in the room and her home).*

**Adler:** Look. Observe the world around you.

**Vilga:** Very straightforward. Thank you.

**Adler:** You're welcome.

# Harold Baldridge

*Harold Baldridge has been the director of the Neighborhood Playhouse School of the Theatre in New York City since 1981. The Neighborhood Playhouse was founded by Sanford Meisner. Having graduated from the Playhouse in 1960, Baldridge became an acting instructor, production supervisor, and stage director there from 1961 until 1972. He has directed regionally, including being the artistic director of Theatre Calgary in Canada from 1971 to 1978. He has also taught acting at the Banff Centre for the Arts since 1972.*

**Vilga:** What makes the training at the Neighborhood Playhouse unique?

**Baldridge:** Every senior instructor that teaches here has studied with Sandy Meisner and has been trained to teach by him. Even though Sandy's not teaching at the school full-time anymore, it's still pretty much coming from the trunk of the tree. The fascinating thing about Sandy's work—and I think all of us who teach it feel the same way—is that Sandy himself adjusted it over the decades to each particular group of students. For example, the famous repetition exercise, which is being taught by everybody—and incidentally a hell of a lot of people who probably shouldn't be teaching it—was introduced here in the sixties.[1] When I was a student here thirty-five years ago, we didn't do repetitions. We did something else that achieved a similar purpose. As an aside, Sandy was sitting in the chair you're sitting in some time ago and he said to me, "I don't know . . . maybe I'll throw out repetition." I said, "You can't—that's your most famous exercise." (*Laughs*)

Sandy Meisner's mind has always been like that. He was always looking at the current decade and wondering what the kids needed and adjusting his work accordingly. His great interest was simply to teach better and find new, improved things that work for young actors-in-training.

We try to keep that spirit of discovery alive in the school. Richard Pinter, who's the director of the acting program now, and I both feel that as an acting teacher you're constantly investigating what works with students and what doesn't work for them in terms of exercises and step-by-step techniques. Nonetheless, even with ongoing refinement, it is basically the same stuff that always works. We always take students right back to the beginning, no matter how much experience they have. No matter how many times they've been onstage or in front of a camera, or whether they have any experience at all, the first year is only about you and your instrument.

The other thing that makes the Neighborhood Playhouse unique is the tradition we have of a "fusion of the arts" in training. We don't just emphasize acting class. We feel strongly about fusing the art of acting with that of dance, of voice and speech, and music. The training focuses in all these areas.

**Vilga:** What is the range of students here?

**Baldridge:** I spend some of my time interviewing eighteen- and nineteen-year-olds and telling them to study liberal arts for a couple years before they come and get as specialized as we are. Students shouldn't become too narrowly specialized too early. For the ten or twelve years I was out there working in the business as a professional director, I got tired of working with uneducated actors. What's happened over the last ten or fifteen years is we have all these universities that are suddenly offering professional training programs, so we have these fascinating hybrids arriving here.

They'll have a BFA degree, and they'll have studied six weeks of Strasberg, six weeks of Meisner, and six weeks of Stella Adler, but perhaps they've never read a Shakespeare play![2] That I blame the university for. It used to be you went to university, got your liberal arts education, then you specialized at a school like the Neighborhood Playhouse or the American Academy. Now the drama departments, many for very good reasons, have become more specialized, especially with the BFA and MFA programs. What we're finding is that kids arrive with weaker and weaker educational backgrounds. Six years ago I introduced a new class that I teach myself, called "Script and Style," in which we sit around and read plays. We read *Hedda Gabler* and *The Importance of Being Earnest* and *Cyrano de Bergerac* just to give them a little background in what their theatrical heritage is. They respond enthusiastically to the work even though they may not have ever been exposed to it before.

**Vilga:** How effective is sampling different training?

**Baldridge:** I think it ends up just confusing students. Thirty-five years ago I studied here for two years, and then I studied with Strasberg for a little bit, and then I studied with Stella Adler, and then I studied with Harold Clurman.[3] I've been in all those pockets at one time or another. In retrospect I am always glad that I started here. I feel that Sandy's work provides the strongest basic foundation. If you get his technique under your belt, then the other things are almost like postgraduate training, because they're less step-by-step specific. Many other methods have good things about them, but sometimes I find kids that get thrown into too much too early, especially areas of emotional recall and sense memory work, which doesn't help them much when they're just beginning to study, in my opinion.

At the Neighborhood Playhouse we make the students start with repetition and other improvisational exercises, and then they do nothing but those exercises from September through the end of November. Then they get their first text. Even then, that text is but a vehicle to continue doing the same exercise. The text is just somebody else's words that happen to be coming out of your mouth, which you're not to interpret or to characterize in any sense of the word. Then they go back to the exercises until they get another scene, in which we add the next step, which might be emotional preparation and getting into the deeper use of your imagination. It will be that way the rest of the first year—step by step—adding the next rung on the ladder.

They never play another character here in the first year. It's always themselves on the line, investigating themselves. I mean, they may be doing a scene in which the character's name is Charlie, but it'll be them in Charlie's situation without them having to worry about "How do I become the character Charlie?" That we get to in the second year. We strongly feel that once you understand your instrument and what you can do and what you can't do, then character acting becomes not much more than adding to or subtracting from yourself. You remain the core of the creative unit. However, it's not just a matter of discovering and opening up yourself and expanding possibilities. It's also getting rid of stuff that doesn't belong.

*Vilga:*  Do you mean mannerisms?

*Baldridge:*  I'm talking more about things that are tied in with the ego. For example, we might accept the kid that comes out of high school who has been the star in all the high school plays and thinks he can play anything. Suddenly he gets here and he discovers that he has limitations, which is a very good thing. I think that the good pro knows what he can do and what he can't do. In life, we may all lie to ourselves in convenient areas, but an actor can't afford to do that. If he's going to go out there in the marketplace and try to sell himself, he's going to be completely exposed. Getting rid of the bullshit, to put it bluntly, is a lot of what this training is about. Eliminating misconceptions about one's self-image—maybe that's a gentler way of putting it—and misconceptions about the way other people see you.

Another part of it has to do with the general education process in our country. In the Western world so much of our time in our formative years is spent trying to give other people what we think they want that sometimes we lose track of who we are. Everything we do is based on seeking approval, so we end up playing roles and developing veneers that please other people. Often when you're twenty-one or twenty-two, you end up not having much knowledge of who you are at all. An actor has to crack through that stuff and get rid of this facade that doesn't really belong to him.

*Vilga:*  How is that done? How do you bring someone to those realizations?

*Baldridge:*  It's through the nature of the exercises. Really the basic core of all Sandy's beginning work is to get your attention outside of yourself in a highly concentrated way. If you don't have any time left to think about yourself, your head doesn't have time to edit or direct your response. When you're freed up from conditioned responses, something may emerge that's really you. You finish the exercise and say, "Oh my God, I didn't know I could do that."

Many of these students are little social beings when they arrive here. They're fully formed in that sense, but there are lids on areas that are very hard to get off. Getting your attention off yourself leaves that true self free to emerge. Here's my own example. I came here after four years of college in Canada. I had this vision of myself as a serious young actor—Hamlet, of course, and all the major serious roles. I still remember to this day a class that I had up here on the third floor of this building where I made everybody laugh. Now, I had never allowed myself to think I could do this. Suddenly a whole new horizon burst forth: I could be funny, I could make people laugh. The narrowness of my previous self-concept melted away.

Breaking through those kinds of social presumptions is what a lot of the work is about. Getting to the truth of oneself. "Truth"— that mad, crazy word that doesn't mean anything but that's so central to everything we do.

To me the actors that are really interesting—Robert Duvall, Robert De Niro, and artists like that—are interesting because no matter how complicated the character is they're playing, it's always rooted in who they are. Therefore it rings true when you watch it. You say, "I believe that," as opposed to the actor who just applies it on the outside. You couldn't care less about the human beings those other actors create. They don't touch you because they are not really in touch with themselves as actors.

*Vilga:* After the first year, are all students invited back for the second year?

*Baldridge:* I interview between 150 and 200 a year, and I accept between 70 and 80 for the first year. Then after working with them for eight months, the entire staff in a very grueling meeting sits down and we discuss everybody. We invite between 25 to 35 back for a second year for a grand total of 110 students. How many we ask back for the second year determines how many we admit into the first year. This year we have 88 in the first year and 22 in the second year. It varies from year to year.

The second year is much more individual, so we need that class to be smaller. We only have so much room. However, there's a lot of people who come here for but a year and do go on to very respectable careers in the theater. You should look down in the lobby before you leave and see David Mamet's picture down there. David wrote across it, "Not to worry. I wasn't asked back for the second year either." (*Laughs.*)

So the first year here is the primary year. The first year's about uncovering the current you, and the second year's about the stuff you pile on top of that, taking yourself in even further directions. The second year is more technical in that you're dealing with character, with bigger emotional problems, with different styles, and with Shakespeare. We have a fencing class in the second year, a jazz movement class, Alexander technique, and a musical theater class.[4] After Christmas in the second year, we say, "Okay, now you've spent a year and a half working in classrooms, tearing yourself apart. Now let's try to put all the pieces back together again with what you've learned and what you've brought in terms of performing experience before you came here. Let's see if we can make it work for an audience."

We spend the last four or five months of school working on performance technique. We do something in February that usually comes out of their singing classes and out of their movement classes: we present a musical revue evening, which gives everyone a chance to get up onstage and do something for friends and parents. It's a very in-house thing. Then at the very end of school, the last two weeks in May, we put them in a group of plays or scenes, giving them a chance to really build a performance out of what they've learned here. We invite some agents, producers, and casting directors, in the vague hope that it might open a door across town when they go out from here into the marketplace.

***Vilga:***  Have you ever thought of adding a third year to the program?

***Baldridge:***  We talked about it. It would be lovely to have. It's partly a problem of space here in this building and, of course, stretching the finances of students and parents. It would also be nice if they had a performance year here where they could show more finished work. Either that or I'd like to send them directly out into a repertory company. There's just so few good opportunities for young actors. Thirty-five years ago, when I graduated, at least they were doing plays in New York that still had casts of fifteen people. Your chance of getting the butler's role and saying "Dinner is served" was at least there, but it's not anymore. Casts consist of two to four actors at the most, unless it's a musical. There are, however, many terrific hole-in-the-wall, Off-Off-Off Broadway productions where often the acting is much better than what you see for seventy dollars a night on Broadway.

***Vilga:***  Do you audition people for this school?

***Baldridge:***  No. They come in for a half-hour interview. I'm more interested in the personality of the potential student. We used to audition, but because we're not in the business of casting and putting on plays, it's almost a useless exercise. If I'm casting a play, then I'm going to audition you because I'm looking at a part and I'm looking at you in relation to that part. When you're interviewing to come to the Neighborhood Playhouse, I'm looking at a potential actor-in-training for eight months—maybe two years—of work. Most students have some experience either from college or community theater when they come here. They've obviously had enough interest to apply. They're not just somebody who said one day, "I think maybe I want to be an actor," for no reason at all. A lot of serious thinking has gone into it, especially if they've moved to New York to pursue the career.

What I look for are students that are willing and open to try things. I have had a few nineteen-year-olds in here who have already made all their life decisions. Nobody's going to change their minds, so unfortunately they're middle-aged at the age of nineteen. I say to them, "Well, there's not much point in you studying. You might as well go out and try to get a job." So much of learning to act is risk taking, going into areas that you're not sure about. We don't put on a lot of plays or put them in front of the public much, because what we're asking them to do in our classrooms is walk that risky tightrope. We ask them to say, "I'm not sure this is going to work, but I'd like to try it." Sometimes they fall flat on their ass, but nobody here holds that against them. The problem with performance is that what you do *has* to work, because you have an audience. You have critics who might write bad notices or a producer who might fire you at the end of the week. Here, in our classrooms, you can fail abysmally and it's perfectly okay. I think an artist needs that freedom to fail until they find their path, especially during the early formative training years.

Students do go through bleak periods. I had a student in here just last Friday who said to me, "I don't know, I've been going to class for three weeks. And I just can't act. Nothing is happening! Maybe I should go into the insurance business." I said, "Hang in there. Just keep working on it." Now, I probably won't see that student again for maybe two weeks, when I'll bump into him in the hall. "How's it going?" I'll say, and he'll respond "Fine, I just had a great breakthrough." Learning to act has always been that way. You have a breakthrough and then there's a bleak plateau. There's nothing steady about it, nothing nice and upwardly curvy.

Another thing we don't allow is auditing of classes. We don't bring strangers into the space that we set up for the student and the teacher. Again, we feel as soon as we bring in a stranger we're saying, "Perform." We break the first-year group into three classes of about twenty-seven, twenty-eight people, and after about two months they get to be like brothers and sisters. Everybody has seen everybody at their worst and at their best. You know it's okay if you fail. You're amongst friends. You have a sympathetic teacher saying, "Oh well, that didn't work. Why don't you come back tomorrow and try it another way?" By giving them this supportive atmosphere, they develop very rapidly. Of course, the fact that it's a full-time school intensifies their progress. Nothing beats working on your craft daily.

If you don't solve something today, you know you're coming in tomorrow to try it again. Students come in at nine in the morning, and they're here until six at night. They get three hours of acting classes every day on an average. An hour to an hour and a half of voice and speech work every day. An hour and a half of movement classes four days out of the five. Two ballet classes and two modern dance technique classes. They get singing

technique three times a week. It works out to more than thirty hours a
week of classwork. The second year is more involved because of all the
different kinds of classes. They still get acting every day, and in March we
even investigate what they're going out into professionally, in the marketplace. We try to give them a little sense of what show business is like
before they face the realities of getting an acting job.

*Vilga:*   How do you do this?

*Baldridge:*   They prepare some auditions, they prepare some songs, and
they prepare some monologues. Then we usually get a few professional
people in just for them. Someone like Vinnie Liff. Vinnie is the casting
director for *Phantom* and *Miss Saigon* and all the major Broadway musicals. Vinnie came in and watched their auditions on a Monday and then
came back on a Wednesday and told them exactly what he thought of
them. That's very helpful to them. Vinnie didn't talk so much about what
they did on the stage. He talked more about how they introduced themselves as young professionals, how they presented their picture and résumé and the whole business part of it. That's what they're babies about
unless they happen to have been out in the marketplace before.

*Vilga:*   Is having one day of career counseling enough?

*Baldridge:*   You have to find your own roots. Your own way of doing it.
There is only so much you can teach about "show biz." The rest you learn
out there in the marketplace, I think. It was the same when I was a student
as it is now; so much of it's luck and being in the right place at the right
time. It's the business of making connections—"networking." And sometimes it's just luck: a student of mine here in the sixties was auditioning for
a summer stock program. She overheard the director say to the producer,
"Who are we going to get to direct those plays at the end of the season
when I go away?" The producer said, "I don't know," so she came back to
my class and said, "I know you like to direct. Why don't you contact these
people?" I contacted those people, and it resulted in ten years of work for
me. So much of one's career is that way. We try to help students a little bit
in that area without getting their heads stuck too much within the world
of show business, because that's not our focus here.

*Vilga:*   So students might have résumés, but you don't allow them to
audition?

*Baldridge:*   No, not while they're here. They shouldn't want to, really. If
you're tearing yourself apart in classes, you're not going to really want to
put it all back together and get in front of an audience. Not if you're
serious about learning your craft. By the time we have these mock audi-

tions in March it's the right time for them to begin thinking about getting out there in the marketplace. It's appropriate.

**Vilga:** What are the demographics of the school? Where do your students come from?

**Baldridge:** Interestingly enough, I would say that only about 5 percent of our students are from New York City. Our student body is largely from outside the city. Ninety-five percent of them come from all over North America, Canada, and the rest of the world! This year we have fourteen foreign students. Many of our students are not only adapting to a new school, they're also adapting to New York City. But that's another part of an artistic education. Somebody once told me: "If you want to be an artist, you've got to live either in New York or London or Rome or Paris, because you have to be in a place where you walk down the street and you know that nobody gives a damn whether you live or die. You know you have to do it on your own." (*Laughs*) There's probably a certain amount of truth in that. All the support systems are cut off. No mom and dad to lean on anymore. All the other people who liked you back home aren't there anymore. I think that strengthens the backbone of an artist. That's what allows them to go out into a crass marketplace later and try to sell themselves.

**Vilga:** What about the general criticism that acting courses take people apart emotionally but can't put them back together? Do you find that happening sometimes?

**Baldridge:** I think it's more a specific problem with certain teachers, and we've experienced a few here, where it becomes almost a neurotic part of their teaching behavior. Fortunately we don't have any teachers like that right now.

There is that danger of a teacher becoming "God." So many of them did. Sandy had a few problems of his own years back because of the exalted position you get in the student's eyes. I think it's better than it used to be. I think we went through that period in the sixties where it was the worst. When it was the whole Actors Studio Strasbergian actor, that whole commercial image of the mumbling actor, the noncommunicative James Dean and Marlon Brando.

**Vilga:** That wasn't really what Strasberg was teaching, though.

**Baldridge:** No, but things did get crazy over there at the Studio. One night I was in class with Lee, who would sit there in his chair and make statements. Someone asked, "What do you mean?" and there were gasps around the class. You felt like it was heresy if this guru were questioned or even asked to translate his remarks into English.

I think student actors are much more practical now. I have great faith in the current batch of kids of the last three or four years. We've moved away from the "Me-ism" of the eighties a little bit. They're less interested in making the almighty buck and more focused on doing good work and on trying Shakespeare or Chekhov or Ibsen. There's a healthier, more positive attitude, at least amongst the students that we're working with.

**Vilga:** Do you think actors in general are better trained today?

**Baldridge:** Yes, I think so, probably because of all these people like Meisner that have hammered away at different ways of making acting training work. Certain movies and even television now aim higher. There are very good creative, inventive actors playing roles on television that change and are not just handing out the same tired thing, week after week.

**Vilga:** If you're taking away some of the structure that society puts on the individual in the training here, would it make sense to get them younger, or is it better to have them more well-rounded?

**Baldridge:** I don't think you can train an actor until he's past his adolescence. I think you as an individual have to know who you are first. You have to have lived a little and experienced life a bit. All sorts of life questions are so important to have already asked yourself before you start seriously studying as an actor. You can't deal with those kinds of complicated life questions without getting yourself confused as you work on your acting. The art of acting is, in that sense, the Cinderella of the arts. I think you can start a ballet student at age eight or nine but not an actor. Prior to about eighteen, it's better to be creative and take dance classes and speech classes. You shouldn't start messing around with actors' psyches before their psyches are really formed.

Yet in some ways, the impulses of a child are very useful. Indeed, a lot of the work is about getting yourself back to that state of creative, childlike wonder, so that you can investigate yourself moment to moment and investigate the actor you're working with. But a child doesn't have enough experience or mental organization to really put the technique to work. We do have a school on Saturdays here for kids between age eight and seventeen, and we teach them dancing, speech, creative dramatics and other imagination stuff, but we stay away from digging into oneself deeply. It's hard enough when you're older.

**Vilga:** What do you think of all the people who bill themselves as Meisner teachers?

**Baldridge:** And just hang out their shingle advertising "Meisner technique?" Sandy and I have talked about that a lot. I always said, "Sandy, be like Martha Graham, who copyrighted her work." Sandy should have probably done that long ago, because there's a lot of people now who are saying they teach Meisner technique and Sandy's never heard of them. None of us has ever heard of them. They may have studied with somebody who's studied with somebody who's studied with somebody who's studied with Sandy back who knows when.

There's a group of teachers that have gone through this school under Sandy's training or trained through his private classes who always come out a whole, responsible Meisner teacher. Then there are people who out and out lie. There is one in California right now and one in Florida who say they studied at the Neighborhood Playhouse with Sandy and none of us have ever heard of them.

***Vilga:*** Is there anything you can do about that?

***Baldridge:*** If they do use the name of the school, then I step in and pass it on to our lawyer, who writes them a nifty little letter telling them to stop unless they can prove to us when they were here and who they studied with.

There are some people teaching who studied with people who haven't even met Sandy, much less studied with him, and who may only have read the book.[5] Sandy never wrote that book as a how-to book. It's an overview written by Dennis Longwell. Dennis observed the Meisner process for two years with a yellow pad and a tape recorder. The author wrote his observations, and then he took them to Mr. Meisner. Meisner checked it over, and then together they changed some things. It's basically a description of what happened in the series of classes over a course of two years. It has its value, and it certainly is exciting and gives you an insight into the kind of work we do, yet it certainly isn't to be taken Step One, Step Two, Step Three, Step Four. It is not the Meisner technique. It's *Meisner on Acting—* exactly what the title says it is.

***Vilga:*** Sandy has said, "It takes twenty years to become an actor," and yet obviously the program here could not be twenty years.

***Baldridge:*** What I believe he means is two or three or four years of training in one way or another and then fifteen years out there doing it. Then maybe you can look back and say, "I know something about this." At least that's the way I've always understood what he meant by that statement. Acting's a practical craft; you have to get up there and do it to find out what the hell it's about.

I say to every applicant that comes in this door that it's like plumbing. If you want to be a plumber, you apprentice yourself to a master plumber and you watch him put those pipes together and then you try it. The first four or five times you do it, the water squirts in your eye. Eventually by doing it, you get to be good at it. Acting is like that. You can read every book written on acting; it doesn't make you one bit better of an actor. It gives you a lot of information and a lot of resources, yet you have to get up there and take the first step, physically and practically. We're dealing with a practical craft here.

Getting rid of the garbage is what it boils down to; that's what training is about. Michelangelo said, "The statue of David was inside that block of marble. All I had to do was get rid of the garbage." It's getting rid of that garbage that's the hard part for any artist.

**Vilga:**   Once students begin to pursue a professional career, do you recommend they continue in classes or workshops?

**Baldridge:**   Yes. I think some of them even go off to study Kabuki or Grotowski or whatever.[6] If they've got this basic technique, more involved and even esoteric interpretation work certainly doesn't hurt. We only have time for so much here at the school. The American actor certainly needs to improve his skills at Shakespeare and heightened language. I don't think there's anything wrong with that. An actor is never finished training.

The other thing I advise actors when they come to me and say, "What can I do now that I'm graduating? What study would help?" I tell them, "Read great novels," because literature is largely about family relationships, and what an actor deals with all his life in drama is relationships. Brothers and sisters, mothers and fathers, uncles and aunts. A deep understanding of those relationships is what actors need outside of getting lots of pure technical information through classes and performing. And, of course, you keep working technically. If you're a serious actor, you have to keep working on your voice and body. You have to keep working on manners and learning period styles for all of your artistic life.

**Vilga:**   Is there a difference between training for film and theater?

**Baldridge:**   I think the basic technique can be adjusted to film fairly quickly, although you can't avoid a few struggles. It reminds me of a film I did in which I had one of those sound buttons in my ear. I was doing a scene with a girl driving the car with the director screaming in our ears, "Don't talk so carefully. Your diction sounds like you're on the stage!" Meanwhile I was trying to act truthfully with the girl and maneuver the car!

We remain a theater school since we're training people as actors for the theater. Our students, I think, because of the honesty of Sandy's work and because of the honesty that's involved in acting a role for film, seem to come out very well in that medium. I think it's why they do a lot of commercials well, too. If I give you our brochure, you'll certainly see a good percentage of film and TV success stories.

I was talking to a casting director a couple years ago and he said that they started to look for Neighborhood Playhouse graduates when they were doing replacements for Neil Simon's *Brighton Beach Memoirs* and *Biloxi Blues* because they knew they'd be talking to honest human beings. He said he knew our students would have the talent but also that they had even probably read the newspaper that day! That they were interesting people and not glitzy, show business clones. That's probably the nicest compliment anybody can give our school: we're turning out real people in what is sometimes an impossible, phony world.

**Vilga:** If you had one piece of advice to give to the young actor who just came to you and said, "I want to act," what would that be?

**Baldridge:** "Don't," probably. Given the current economy and the state of the theater and what's out there employment-wise, if a student can find another thing to do with their life, they should. Parents certainly worry about students studying acting, for all the reasons I've mentioned. On the other hand, training here is not just learning about acting. It's also learning about yourself.

There was a student who graduated from here fifteen years ago who's a good friend of mine and is now a vice president of a stock and bond company on Wall Street. For whatever reason, he didn't end up in the theater, so he's probably a millionaire by now. Every time he sees me he says, "I never regretted going to the Neighborhood Playhouse, because I know it's made me a better human being. It's also made me a better businessman, because I know how to read the other guy like an actor." Training like this can be a valuable part of anyone's education.

I also had a doctor here from Boston who was thirty-nine years old. He was a specialist in urology, and he'd been practicing about six years when he came in to interview for admission as a student. I said, "You're crazy. You don't want to study acting. You've got a lucrative career already." He was married and he was quite settled in his life. He replied, "No, I've got to do it. I've been wondering all my life whether I could act or not, and now I just have to do it." He was so insistent I finally, against my better judgment, let him come. Well, he was a wonderful student, he had a wonderful year, and it was such a bonus for all of us to have a real doctor in the class. Afterwards, he decided, "I don't want to be an actor, but I had to do this. I had to explore this for myself." Now he's back in medicine, but he's a different person. He went back, divorced his wife, moved to another facility. It really did change his life. He was an unusual student, but he fit right in and the other younger students liked him, and so it was an entirely positive experience having him here.

I know a lot of unhappy people who sit there at age fifty saying, "I wish I would have tried this." It's expensive living in New York. It's expensive and difficult to go to a place like this. But it may be worth it thirty years down the road rather than sitting there wondering the rest of your life: "Should I not have done that when I had the chance?" I've found it's almost always better to take the risk and see what you can learn rather than wonder what you might have missed. That's what life is all about anyway: the risk. And the resulting discovery, which can be joyous!

# *Tanya Berezin*

Photo: Edward Vilga

*Tanya Berezin was born March 25, 1941. She attended Boston University from 1959 to 1963. In 1969 she was one of the cofounders of the Circle Repertory Company in New York City. She was the artistic director of Circle from 1986 to 1994.*

*As an actress Ms. Berezin has appeared in television programs such as* St. Elsewhere *and* Law and Order, *films such as* Awakenings, *and plays such as* Angels Fall *and* The Mound Builders, *for which she won a 1975 Obie Award. She is the resident acting coach for ABC-TV daytime dramas and coaches private clients as well.*

**Vilga:**   When did you feel the initial impulse to act?

*Berezin:* When I saw Betty Hutton in *Incendiary Blonde* when I was six. (*Laughs.*) There and then I said, "I want to do that."

*Vilga:* Do you think that's true of most actors, or does it vary actor to actor?

*Berezin:* I think it's different with everybody. I keep thinking of Judd Hirsch, who was an engineer.[1] I don't remember exactly how old he was when he started studying, but it just looked like something interesting to him, so he went to an acting class. Judd is one of the best natural actors I've ever known. It's not that he wasn't trained, because he was, but here's an incredible, natural actor who didn't know that he was to be an actor until he was a fully grown human being. He was at least thirty when he started. So I think there are all different sorts of reasons. Some of the reasons may be neurotic. No matter how much love we get, we don't feel like we have enough, and we need more. Certainly that's a little neurotic, but if good acting which makes people happy or makes people feel things comes out of neurosis, that's great.

What makes people become actors? Some people become actors because of what other people think actors are. If they're very good-looking and enough people say, "You're so good-looking, you should be in the movies," they might decide to try it. For them it's an ego thing, not an emotional exhibitionism necessarily, but a feeling that they're special in some way, and they want to display that specialness. Sometimes that is wonderful—there's no getting around that—but sometimes it can be completely self-indulgent and not absolutely wonderful. A lot of people become actors because of wonderful performances they've seen other actors do. They see great work and say, "I want to do that" or "Wouldn't it be fun to do that?" and are brave enough to try.

*Vilga:* Did you train as an actress?

*Berezin:* As I said, I wanted to be an actress since I was a little girl. I studied when I was a kid at a settlement house in Philadelphia, and I loved every minute of it. After high school I wanted to come to New York and study, but my parents just had a fit about it and said, "No, you have to go to college. If you want to be an actress, you still have to go to college." They were hoping that I would somehow get over it, but I didn't. I went to Boston University School for the Arts and studied there, and then I came to New York. I began to study in New York, and I did the usual thing of becoming a cocktail waitress and looking for work and meeting a lot of other young struggling actors.

At the same time, I also started going to La MaMa.[2] In fact, the first play I ever did in New York was at La MaMa. I saw some very exciting work there, especially since when we were trained, way back in the dark ages of the very early sixties, new plays never entered the college curriculum. We were only exposed to the classics or plays from the fifties. During that time, I got a summer stock job where I met Rob Thirkield, who I eventually married. He introduced me to his friends Lanford Wilson and Marshall Mason and a bunch of other young writers and artists.[3] I realized then that those actors who I admired most—the ones who I wanted to grow up to be like—were people who had created roles, not the people who had done the fourth Broadway production of a work. It felt like suddenly there were astonishing opportunities to do great new work for the first time.

We began Circle Rep in 1969, and it all evolved very organically. It was not created from a set plan; one thing just led to another. All through my career, I acted mainly with Circle Rep, but I got to work for some wonderful regional theaters outside of New York as well. Then when Marshall Mason resigned as artistic director at Circle Rep, the people on the board said it was very important—and they were right—to have an interim artistic director during Marshall's last year to plan the first season after he was gone and so forth. I said, "Well, I'll be very happy to do that, because it'll be very interesting for me. However, you must understand that I will only be interim director for the short term. I will only do it until someone else is hired, so don't even think of asking me to continue."

Yet I found that I really enjoyed it. It came at a forty-something time in my life when one begins to get a little bored with oneself as an essentially solo entity. The opportunity to make things happen and to be involved with the whole play was very exciting to me. I had a lot of support from the board and from the members of the staff with the things that I don't know about or didn't understand, such as fund-raising. More and more it turned out that I loved this new position. The idea of staying with it first came from members of the company who suggested that I be a candidate, and I've stayed with the artistic director position for eight years.[4]

**Vilga:** Can you define what's unique about Circle Rep?

**Berezin:** When Marshall began the company, the idea was to have an artist-driven theater, and also to create a performing ensemble that did new work. It's rather obvious that all of the great theater companies had great playwrights attached to them, and all the great playwrights of the past came out of great theater companies. Shakespeare, Molière, and Chekhov all did. The point was to bring together artists and have them working together all the time, and to have the thrust of the theater come from the needs of the artists, rather than from business demands. From our earliest years, we served writers so well that they were intensely attracted to us. When the new scripts started coming, it just seemed sensible to be devoted to young playwrights. You just can't have all these good scripts roaming around not being done. Over time we began to do more and more original scripts rather than producing revivals or classics.

Another uniqueness of Circle Rep is that we don't only produce plays on our main stage. There are over a hundred members of our company, over two hundred members of our lab—altogether, almost four hundred people—for whom Circle Rep is home. People come and go. They come here and work in the lab, they work in television, they work on Broadway, they work everywhere. There is an independent artistic life that goes on here that drives the choices that are made. Keeping that life vital and moving is exciting. One of the ways we do that now is by always looking for young people, always finding new artists, young or not, who excite us, who might stimulate the company in some way.

**Vilga:** What do you think about the state of the theater in general? Why do you think it's depressed?

**Berezin:** Only because of money. The state of the theater financially is terrifying. I think theaters are going under left and right because of the general condition of the economy. Ever since the turn of the century, we've had to compete with other forms of dramatic expression, whether it's movies or the nickelodeon or television or VCRs or whatever. Our audience seems to be becoming more and more limited, which is scary. It's something that people across the country talk about all the time. Where is the audience of the future? How do we encourage them now and bring them in? That's extremely important. It's very sad to me, because it makes it really tough on us. We're scrambling all the time, but the people who are really hurt by it are the newer emerging artists that have no venues of their own.

People get discouraged so early; writers go to television and film. I don't think that they ruin their work, and I believe they'll still grow as writers, but their development as playwrights is stunted by writing for other mediums too early.

**Vilga:** Why is that? Because the mediums are more limited?

**Berezin:** If a writer's a good writer, they will always grow as an artist. Yet each form of writing is a craft as well as an art. The craft of playwriting has to be developed with constant contact and growth in the theater. You need to learn the form well so you can break it in interesting ways. If you're writing a little bit for television and a little bit for film and a little bit for the theater, you're not going to master any of those forms. I hate losing people to television so they can make a living, something which people can't do in the theater. It's a real miracle when someone does make a living in the theater.

*Vilga:*   Can anything be done about that, or is that just the way it is?

*Berezin:*   I really don't know. I think it's audience development. If you have people who want the theater, they'll come and they'll buy tickets. Then artists will be able to raise families and work in the theater. What's happening right now is that theaters are trying to find a way to do that by becoming involved in film in one way or another so that we can serve our writers in both venues. I don't think there's an easy answer. I think it comes down eventually to really asking, "Do I want to work in the theater and at what price?" Each person must find their own way of doing it.

*Vilga:*   What have your experiences been in terms of working with actors with different kinds of training? Are there certain kinds of training that you feel are particularly valuable or a waste of time? Or does it vary actor to actor?

*Berezin:*   By the time we deal with actors, they have found their way of dealing with whatever training they've had or not. The old "whatever works" adage applies. I would never now look at who someone trained with and say, "Oh, they trained with so-and-so, therefore we don't want them." On the other hand, there have been various little two- or three-year pockets where a gaggle of people from one school will come out who were particularly terrific. A couple of years ago, it was North Carolina School of the Arts.

I myself trained in the Meisner technique with Jim Tuttle in the sixties. I had worked with a lot of other teachers before then, but I found it to be an absolute revelation. Through the experience of learning that technique I found a real faith in myself, in the joining of myself as a person and as an actor. As I grew as an actress, it was even more exciting. I found that if you really understand Meisner technique and really use it when you work, when you have opportunities to study other things, it can all come in and ride on that technique in a beautiful way.

For example, I remember a master class that we took one year, a hundred years ago, when we did *Hamlet* and *Mary Stuart* and we had a voice teacher here, Clyde Vincent, who's now lost to us. But Clyde brought in Chuck Jones, a master teacher who also taught us the Linklater technique.[5] All of these new, specific techniques I found could really be absorbed by the Meisner technique and would enrich it. On the other hand, I know actors who haven't been trained at all who are just thrilling. I also know other actors who've been trained in completely different ways, like Swoosie Kurtz, who came out of LAMDA.[6] Swoosie is fabulous, marvelous, and totally wonderful. She's as truthful as anybody I know, and she really understands and has a sense and a knowledge of theatricality that's just wonderful.

*Vilga:* Do you think that it's possible for actors to be really very good without training?

*Berezin:* It depends upon the actor, because I think some people become trained without formal training. There are some people who just know how to either become someone else or to absorb another person's experience or believe in another person's circumstances. They are just able to do that and make it real and truthful. An actor who is uneducated or uncultured but who has a raw talent is going to be limited. His or her horizons are too narrow. There are, on the other hand, actors who just learn—as there are writers who learn—just by being in the world. They simply absorb knowledge and use it in their work. You don't know where it came from, and yet they have a great sense of the theatrical, an amazing ability to concentrate, and a natural ability to believe. I certainly wouldn't advise anyone not to train, but every once in a while one of those people pops up and surprises you.

*Vilga:* Do you think that anyone with the right amount of training could become an actor?

*Berezin:* I think anybody can become an actor, but I don't think anybody can become a good actor. I believe that the purpose of all—you should excuse the expression—"art" is to throw light on the question, the problem, the dilemma of human existence. A good actor—and certainly a great actor, but even a good actor—becomes an actor because of their interest in human behavior: what makes people tick and live and thrive and what makes people not. A good actor, and certainly a great actor, is able to throw light on that in some sort of inexplicable way when living a character. Somebody who's not gifted can learn how to do it and learn how to be sort of believable and learn how to get a laugh and all of that, but it's never lifted, it never becomes transcendent.

*Vilga:* I know you don't really audition actors here, but can you tell generally in an audition if great, uplifting talent is present?

*Berezin:* Actually we do audition actors for roles in plays, and yes, you can tell when talent is there. Yet you sometimes can't tell when it's not there because of the audition circumstances. Somebody can come in and give a terrible audition and be a wonderful actor, and you won't ever know it because they don't audition well or perhaps that one thing either they've chosen to do or you've asked them to read for isn't right for them. You certainly can see talent often, but the real danger is dismissing someone great.

*Vilga:* How far does the problem of typing actors go? Do you think that a great actor can pretty much play anything?

**Berezin:**  I don't think there's anybody who can play everything well. Even the greats have not been great in everything that they've done. It's not so much type as it is your very own nature as a human being and its limits. We all have psychic limitations in terms of how well we can truly understand another human being. There's that, and then there are certain realistic, concrete things that serve a play. I'm so conscious of that because we do so many new plays. I think we do a lot of risky casting and a lot of off-center casting, and I would be even more open to it if we were doing plays for the fourth or fifth time. For the first performance of a play, you want the production to be done as richly and as specifically as possible so that the play communicates fully to the audience. If it's very important for somebody to be beautiful, or it's very important for somebody to be Italian, or if it's very important for somebody to have certain external, concrete things and an actor doesn't have them, it's a problem. I think that the perfect example is casting Robin Bartlett in Craig Lucas's *Reckless* as this wonderful, sweet, curious, little bit of lost woman. Robin had done all those Eve Arden things for so long, and been beautifully brilliant in that wonderful dry humor of hers, that it would have been a surprise for anyone to think about her doing *Reckless*.[7] Of course she was extraordinary in it, because there's nothing that says that a strong, smart woman can't be lost. That's what was so beautiful about her performance in *Reckless:* she didn't make the character an ignorant innocent. She was a smart innocent. Now, that's exciting.

**Vilga:**  If you could, would you change your own training? Would you go back and do it differently?

**Berezin:**  If I could do it all over again, I would do it all just a little bit earlier. Training too early doesn't help, because you're not a person yet and so it doesn't land. One of the things I never did that I would like to have done after I studied with Jim Tuttle and learned the Meisner technique is to have spent some time at the Royal Academy or at LAMDA to learn those wonderful theatrical techniques.[8] It took me twenty years to learn them by stealing them from other people.

   One of the great learning experiences for me as an actor was to understudy Swoosie Kurtz in *Fifth of July*. I had to do her performance—which I could never do—but I had to learn her blocking and her behavior and all of that. Eventually I learned where it was coming from. I could internalize it, and I finally understood, "Oh, that's where it comes from!"

**Vilga:**  Do you mean techniques of voice and movement?

**Berezin:**  No, I mean ways of communicating to an audience. Swoosie is just incredibly theatrical. She knows her audience, she feels the audience in the palm of her hand. She can be incredibly serious and yet bring the house down with laughs. There are ways of doing that that she communicates so well with people. Until that time, I was rather audience shy. The times that I got to play *Fifth of July,* because it was such an outgoing character and was created by Swoosie in that particular production in such an outgoing way, I got to experience that for myself. It was an experience that I carried with me in my work after that.

*Vilga:* You said that you didn't think people should start training too young. Is there an age or a time when you think they should begin?

*Berezin:* It's hard to tell, because everything you do feeds you in one way or another. For me, what training should be is learning a way of working, something you need to take away with you that you can use every time you approach a script. I think that people who are college age are a little too young to really absorb that and understand how it's working on them. I think when they're about twenty-three or twenty-four they become a little bit more defined both to themselves and the world. A technique is between you and work; it's not for anybody else. So you have to understand yourself a little bit. I would say anywhere between twenty-three and twenty-eight would be fine.

*Vilga:* And young actors, should they try to act?

*Berezin:* They should act in plays, have fun, and get a good education. They should go to college and go through the whole training program, even though they'll probably come out still not knowing what to do when they get a job. I think that actors without knowledge of the world are lost. They don't understand what good writing's all about, because they tend to see a character through a very narrow vision.

*Vilga:* Do you think that the standards of acting have gotten better, or are they the same as they've always been?

*Berezin:* Oh, they've gotten a lot better. There are always going to be tacky stars that people like because of their persona or because they're more beautiful than anybody who ever walked the earth. I think that the actors who are working now are very good, and I think that the audiences in all three media expect a lot from them in terms of believability and excitement and so forth. It's encouraging that some of our major stars are major actors. Meryl Streep is a fabulous actress, and she's a box office star, or at least was a minute and a half ago and probably will be in another minute and a half. That certainly hasn't always been true. Kevin Kline or William Hurt are other actors who keep growing and acting everywhere. These are all actors to be reckoned with, and they're all box office presences.

*Vilga:* Do you ever see certain training as a waste of time?

***Berezin:*** Worse than training which is a waste of time is training which is downright dangerous. There are people who mess around with young people's heads and create cults around themselves. That is much worse than a waste of time. I don't think any training which is not harmful is a waste of time. Every experience that you have makes you a richer person. It's hard to be more specific because it's all very individual. For example, I never profited much from theater games and never saw much use for them. For some people, theater games are quite helpful. It might give certain people a feeling of freedom, and they might remember how well that freedom felt and would want to experience it again. The only thing to really avoid are the bad, destructive teachers out there.

***Vilga:*** Is there a way of knowing if a teacher's bad or not?

***Berezin:*** I think that if you have a feeling inside of yourself that it's wrong, it probably is. The dangerous thing is that often young people become convinced that the teacher knows better than they do just because he's the teacher. I wish I could spell out what signals to watch for, but I can't.

***Vilga:*** Do you think that star quality or charisma is important to an actor?

***Berezin:*** Absolutely.

***Vilga:*** Is it definable?

***Berezin:*** I don't know if you want to put this in the book, and I'm stealing this because I can't remember who said it—it may have been John Bishop—but a star is somebody that you either want to be or someone you want to fuck. It's always one or the other because star quality has to do with the audience being fully engaged by someone. When an audience is intrigued by the actor, they're intrigued by the character and the connection to the character. Often when people don't have a good time in the theater or in the movies, what they say is, "I didn't care about that person." I don't know anybody who couldn't care about Katharine Hepburn. In the worst script in the world, they will still care about her. Often her own personality is strong enough for you to translate that into caring about her character. It's not anything any of us can create; we either have it or we don't. It's a very effective, wonderful, magical thing, and it's true in any field. There are stars in sports, and they're not always the best players or the ones with the best stats. Stars have a charisma. They make you want to be connected to them in some way. In theater, the whole idea is for the audience to identify with the drama's characters, and people tend to want to identify with someone that they admire in some inexplicable way.

*Vilga:* When actors are working, what should their awareness of the audience be? Is it latent, or is the actor always conscious of the audience being present?

*Berezin:* I think that "latent" is a good word. The actors are certainly aware an audience is present. Everything that they're doing has to do with the action onstage, but certainly they feel the audience. For example, when you're landing a joke, you certainly know that you're landing the joke for the audience. The audience is always there, but they're there under everything almost like a subconscious self in a way. When you're onstage, what you're doing is your conscious action while your behavior and the audience relationship are subconscious.

*Vilga:* Is the actor working toward feeling that in an imaginary circumstance, or is it a rehashing of personal memories?

*Berezin:* I think it's different for every actor. For me, I've always thought that the best way to act a play is to start with the imaginary circumstances and let the action of the play affect you moment by moment by moment. I think things like emotional memory can set things off when the inspiration isn't working and when you're not on the train. If you can begin *Glass Menagerie* coming home from the school and finding out that your daughter has just been lying to you and proceed through the whole play using all Tennessee Williams's circumstances, you're fine. Everything you need is contained in the actions of the text.

*Vilga:* Is it unnaturally draining to be feeling those things every night on the stage?

*Berezin:* It's exhilarating and draining. It's the best kind of tired. It's the kind of tired you are after you work in the garden for eight hours; it's tiring, but it's life-giving. You always come out physically and maybe psychically a little drained, but also rekindled in some way. Except every once in a while, there's a play that doesn't give you that. The circumstances of the play don't allow your particular character to complete. If the character doesn't complete, or if you've had a performance that night where you didn't complete, it can be truly draining to leave the stage unresolved.

*Vilga:* Can you describe the state where actors do lose themselves in the character onstage?

*Berezin:* I've known some actors who really get in and, on some level, do lose themselves in the character. Part of their technique might be to go out shopping at Saks Fifth Avenue and be that character shopping all day long. For some of them it's great, but it just makes no sense to me whatsoever. For me, it's placing myself in the circumstances of the character. One does get lost in what is happening to you onstage, because action is happening. You are doing things and things are happening to you, and they definitely feel like they are really happening.

I remember a very funny story. When we were doing Schiller's *Mary Stuart* I was playing Queen Elizabeth, and Stephanie Gordon, a very good friend, was playing Mary Stuart. I really got into the power of Queen Elizabeth. I really got swept up into the idea that I could say anything and it would be done. There's such a contest between Elizabeth and Mary Stuart, and there's a scene—which did not happen historically, but in Schiller's imagination—a scene where they confront each other. Afterwards, this person from Mary's court says, "I have always believed that Elizabeth won the fight in the court," but the character from Mary's court says, "You were brilliant, you were wonderful, you proved that you were the queen." Twice during the run, the actor who played it said, "You are wonderful, you are wonderful, you proved that SHE was the queen." I would stand backstage and feel such triumph, because I proved it. I proved it! It wasn't like being Elizabeth, but it was that idea that I as a character had won!

*Vilga:* What are the particular challenges with new plays?

*Berezin:* Primarily, the fact that the play has never been done before and nobody has ever played this part before means that you are truly discovering the character as you are rehearsing. You don't have anything else to go on but your knowledge of yourself, your understanding of the character, and your understanding of humanity. You can't do it the way Maureen Stapleton first did it on Broadway.[9] You have to find the way you're going to do it. It's a wonderful feeling when you're starting from zero and asking, "Where is my character coming from, where is she going, what does she want, and what does she turn out to be?"

*Vilga:* Can you speak about the differences between stage and film acting?

*Berezin:* I don't think that they're worlds apart in terms of training, but I think the experience of them is quite different. What I try to do when I'm working in a film is to do the kind of work I do in a first rehearsal for a scene. It's a question of filling yourself with all of the circumstances you know, all of your associations, every sort of imaginative idea that you have, then going on the set and doing nothing but being alive. There's certain marks you have to hit, but mainly you just let it pour out and let the camera get whatever it gets, which is very much what the first rehearsal of a scene is like. The director helps you make choices, but it's really about properly preparing what's going to pour out of you.

*Vilga:* What acting has most affected you?

**Berezin:**  I remember when I was younger, every time I watched Anna Magnani work, I just was completely astonished.[10] Both working with Bill Hurt and watching him work is a joy. We were in *Mary Stuart* together. He played my secretary who I made sign the death warrant. Working with Bill for me was the ideal, because when we were onstage together, you felt like you really didn't know what was going to happen next. It's not that either of us didn't do what we were supposed to be doing; we never forgot the blocking or the lines. It's just that you were so in the moment that you had no idea what the next moment was going to be until you got there. That's the ideal, it's what one constantly strives for, but somehow, doing it with him, it was easy. I see a lot of that in his work, even when I'm not right next to him. There are many wonderful people who I've never met whose work I adore: Anthony Hopkins, Vanessa Redgrave, Meryl Streep.

It's a question of when the audience feels like they're in very good hands, but there's an element of danger in the air. It's the idea that you really don't know what's going to happen with this person from one moment to the next. When that happens and you're watching the actors and you don't know what's going to happen to them, you really are experiencing the play fully. You're not just getting the idea of it, you're actually experiencing it.

**Vilga:**  What's the most interesting or meaningful thing about what you're doing for you as an actress or as a director or both?

**Berezin:**  The most meaningful thing for me is knowing when a play has really been experienced by an audience, when the acting and the theme of the play have all come together and have had an impact that's more than theatrical. Having a hit is great, but when you're in the audience and you see the audience feel it, it's just the best. In the end everything we do is about communication.

**Vilga:**  One of the questions I've asked everyone is if you had one piece of advice to give to the young actor, what would that be?

**Berezin:**  Can I say two?

**Vilga:**  Certainly.

**Berezin:**  I'd like to make clear that it's very important to know, when you're studying, whether what you're learning is something you can take and use in the future. For example, there are scene study classes where you can study with people who might call themselves acting teachers but who are really very good directors. They can make the scene work really well in class. Later when you finally get a part and you're sitting alone with the script, have those people taught you what to do with a text or how to develop a role? Do you know how to prepare at home so that you can have a good rehearsal? That's really what the actor's job is: to do your homework so you can come to rehearsal with life in you to offer to the other actors and the writer and the director. That's the first piece of advice I would give the young actor: make sure you are learning techniques that become tools you can use on your own in the future.

Secondly, I think that you've got to concentrate on becoming as fine an artist as you can become. Let your agent or manager or whoever worry about your career. We're living in career-obsessed times. There's no getting around the realities of the business, but I think it's very frightening for an actor starting out to focus excessively on the career before they've learned the craft. We can't deny that careerism will raise its ugly head, and we will have to deal with it when it does, but to be focused on it can stunt an artist's growth.

I remember one student saying to me, "Someone told me that I should figure out what I should sell and just be that in the marketplace." To hear this from a twenty-one-year-old is really disconcerting, because how can they possibly know who they really are? How can anyone else know either? Alan Schneider told me when I was in college to get out of the business.[11] He thought I was misplaced. He told me that I should go sell insurance. So what does anybody know about anybody else?

**Vilga:**  What should a young actor do to build a career, then?

**Berezin:**  You need to focus on your work. Let the career things come and go and change and grow. You can take little hints from other people, but to focus on the career will prevent you from being able to do your real work.

Another thing I learned from Alan Schneider was that if anything can prevent you from becoming an actor, you should let it, because the profession is absolute madness. You have to be a person who can't be stopped. If you're going to do it, you've got to be 100 percent committed. If that's true for you, then you should absolutely go for it. I know it's been a wonderful, rich life for me. I've raised two children, I have wonderful friends, and I have no regrets. A life in the theater has rewarded me enormously, but if you don't have the commitment for it, it can be brutal.

# *André Bishop*

Photo: James Hamilton

*André Bishop was born November 9, 1948, in New York City. He graduated from Harvard University in 1970.*

*Bishop has worked with the New York Shakespeare Festival and the American Place Theatre. He began as the literary manager of Playwrights Horizons in New York City in 1975 and became its artistic director in 1981. Bishop left Playwrights Horizon in 1992 to become the artistic director of Lincoln Center Theater.*

*Bishop has been an instructor at New York University and Hunter College, has served on the board of overseers for Harvard University's Loeb Drama Center, and has been a member of the National Endowment for the Arts theater panel. He has won the Margo Jones Award, a special Drama*

*Desk Award, the Lucille Lortel Award, and numerous Tony Awards since he came to Lincoln Center.*

*As artistic director of Playwrights Horizons, among the world premieres he produced were* Sunday in the Park with George, Driving Miss Daisy, The Heidi Chronicles, Assassins, *and* The Substance of Fire.

●──────────────────────────────────────●

**Vilga:** How did you come to work with actors?

**Bishop:** Actually, oddly enough, I came to doing whatever the hell it is I do via acting, which is probably the story of most people. I always wanted to be an actor, like everyone I suppose. That's all I did in college. I came to New York and was going to go to the Neighborhood Playhouse. I didn't continue there because I just didn't want to go to school anymore. I decided I wanted to have a regular job in the theater, so I worked for the New York Shakespeare Festival in the Delacorte box office. Then I worked in publishing. When I decided to study acting again I studied privately with Meisner disciples, first with one superb teacher and then with Wynn Handman, who's also a superb teacher. The two classes were linked. One was the basics of Meisner technique, while Wynn's was really scene work.

I learned from Wynn not just about acting or a technique but about plays. Since he runs the American Place Theatre and they do American plays, he used a lot of scenes from rather "newish" American plays for his students. He loved Sam Shepard, and of course he had produced Shepard's early plays. When Wynn criticized a scene he would also teach the class about history and language. He paid attention to language and letting the language take you.

I learned intellectually almost as much as I learned from a technique point of view. I did get a few parts, and I did work a little bit on radio, but I was lost for five or six years in my twenties, creatively lost. I gradually started working at Playwrights Horizons when it was a small theater, doing odd jobs and becoming the literary manager. That led me to where I am today.

Now I think I have a very good nose for what's of the theater and what's of the stage and what's performable. Perhaps all that comes from a combination of instinct and my actor training.

**Vilga:** How did these experiences shape your vision as an artistic director?

**Bishop:** The plays that I like tend to be highly performable, highly presentational. They tend to be plays that demand a kind of bravura acting as opposed to a kind of more naturalistic acting. That's the kind of actor I was, and I suspect that has affected the kind of producer I am. I think if I hadn't had an instinct for acting and I hadn't trained for a couple of years, I might be very different. Perhaps better in the sense of being more analytical about plays and texts, but I'm an analytical enough person as it is. For me, there's a direct link between my acting experience and my work now as an artistic director.

*Vilga:* Would you change your training if you could do it again?

*Bishop:* No. I don't think I would. I might have studied a little bit longer in the basics. I think that I rushed through a year and a half of basic training. Part of it was that I was sick for a couple of months in the mid-1970s. I had something wrong with my leg, and I was sort of out of focus for about two months. I felt that I got interrupted at a key time. Other than that, no. I think that the Neighborhood Playhouse and the Meisner technique combined—being in the moment, give and take, honestly listening, honestly responding, with a great emphasis on text and character and figuring out what is in a scene, and being truthful as an actor, not just as a character but to the author's intentions—all of that is vital, and I don't believe it is present in all acting training. So I feel very lucky. I wouldn't have gone anywhere else.

*Vilga:* Do you think other training is less effective?

*Bishop:* I hesitate to say. I mean, everyone I know who has a good career as an actor thinks that their training and their teachers were the best. I think it's what works for you. I always had an intellectual interest in plays and in text. I was an English major, not a drama major, because they didn't have a drama major at Harvard. Therefore, I suppose, the kind of training I had as an actor reflected that interest. Perhaps if I studied, I don't know where—the Actors Studio, say—I might have found out that maybe that training wouldn't have been right for me.

*Vilga:* Can you sense what an actor's training is when you see him or her audition?

*Bishop:* I used to, meaning about ten years ago. In the past ten years, it's gotten harder. I think as a producer you used to know that certain schools had certain kinds of technique that you could identify. In the best days of Juilliard, the early days of Juilliard, they had a very solid technique, sometimes to a fault. They could get through anything, any style. They could get up onstage under the worst possible conditions and deliver something. That was what a Juilliard actor was.

Again, I'm going back ten years, which was when I was focusing on it the most. Yale actors, again in the late seventies, had a pretty good technique with a probably greater sense of daring. If you asked them to get onstage and hump a chair, they'd hump a chair. That's what Yale actors were like. Maybe now I know less about it because this new profession called the casting director has grown up. In the early days here we did all our own casting. I also believe these schools change and evolve.

Beyond identifying training in auditions, I'd also like to say that I think that a lot of actors simply don't know how to audition well now. My memory is that maybe they did a little bit better before.

***Vilga:*** What's wrong with the way actors audition now?

***Bishop:*** When you go out into lobbies during auditions, you see actors auditioning for parts who never read anyone else's lines. They just sit there silently mouthing, translating the part they're going to read for into their own stuff, filtering it through themselves and turning it out.

Audition circumstances really are horrible. There are actors who need four weeks to explore and then they'll be wonderful. There are other actors who come in and give you what they're going to give you opening night. But how can you always know that unless you know them?

I think that actors sometimes go in and give auditions that seem to have nothing to do with the character or the character in the scene or the character in the play. I don't know what it is exactly, maybe it's just unfamiliarity with the play. Auditions that are just wrongheaded as opposed to good or bad. Plus we now have some unfortunate new audition practices in the theater. The director would once say, "That was good, think of it this way, try it again." Maybe it's because of TV and movies, where young directors don't work with actors the way the older ones do. A lot of young directors sit there, and if the actor doesn't come in and immediately deliver, they're dismissed. I hate that.

***Vilga:*** In an audition?

***Bishop:*** Yes, in an audition setting. It really makes me mad when I see these young directors who are talented but inexperienced who just want to see it out there presented for them, who don't know how to work with actors.

A lot of this conversation is tied in to the abilities of the director, or lack of abilities of the director, because they have their blind spots also. One who's good with actors can't stage; one who stages never talks to the actors. You see this a lot. Sometimes you see these auditions that go awry, and maybe if the director had steered the actor on the right track, that actor would have been wonderful. One sees that in acting classes all the time. An actor makes an adjustment, and suddenly a key unlocks a door. Not working with actors leads one in the theater to a certain kind of typecasting, which I think a lot of actors resent because it's dreary. They always seem to be forced to play the same part with the same bunch of mannerisms, and that's unfortunate.

*Vilga:*   How much of that is unavoidable because you're cast by what you look like?

*Bishop:*   I guess some of it is an unavoidable evil. I also know that good actors are more versatile than perhaps we who sit on the other side of the desk think. Years ago, there was an actress who took over in Wendy Wasserstein's play *Isn't It Romantic*. In the play there are two mothers, both very different. The Jewish mother and the Wasp mother. One's warm and funny, the other's cold and aggressive. We got a wonderful actress who was midwestern and, I thought, not right for the Jewish mother. We cast her as the Wasp mother, and she played that part for several months. Then when the Jewish mother was leaving she begged for an audition. I said, "No, you're crazy, what are you talking about, you can't, you're joking"—I said it nicely, of course. I tried to avoid telling this woman who I thought was deeply talented that it was just not worth her having an audition. She just didn't seem right at all. Anyway, finally really because we couldn't get anyone else, we gave her an audition, which was embarrassing in itself because the woman had been in the play for six months in another role. She got dressed differently, changed her voice, came onstage, and she auditioned. She was really quite good, and we called her back. She did it again, and we gave her the part. She was probably the best of all of the women who played that mother. Not really right for the part and not really quote "Jewish" unquote, but in a way she had something, an understanding of the inner life of the woman, that none of the other more overtly castable women had had. It was simply that she came in as a different person than she had come in when she was playing this other different role that she had to play. That was a big lesson to me. Now, maybe you can't do that when you open a play, maybe you can only do that when a play's been running. You can take chances because there's a precedent in the role for the actor to follow, even though they make it their own.

*Vilga:*   Can you tell talent at an audition?

*Bishop:*   Yes. You see talent in an actor who comes in and reads for a part and understands the scene and the play and whose acting of the part seems effortless. It can often be completely different than what you thought, but there's a quality of not-acting. Yet for me, because I just hate realistic behavior being confused as acting, there's always a technique underneath. They know where the laughs are, they know not to upstage themselves, they can be heard in the last row when they're auditioning, and they just are the person. It may be not what you thought the character was, but it just seems effortless, kind of buoyant.

I think there is also great room for actors getting better. You never know who's going to surprise you in five years or what suddenly will happen to an actor's abilities. It may be that they suddenly work a lot, they lose their nervousness, they've studied more, or they just come into their own when they are older.

So many good actors, alas, have gone to L.A. Again ten, fifteen years ago, people went to L.A. to visit or to work, but then they came back to New York. Now, as you're probably discovering, they all move there whether they have a job or not. If you looked at the cast of Playwrights Horizons shows in the past ten years, I'd say 60 percent of those actors have moved to L.A. and are mostly unavailable to us to be in plays.

***Vilga:*** Because they're doing films?

***Bishop:*** Yes, or they've just relocated there. It's hard getting them back to New York. People say, "Oh, there are always new people, there are always young people," and that's true, but you can't just do plays with twenty-year-olds.

There is a terrible drain to Los Angeles. I don't mean there aren't actors who live there who don't want to come back and do plays, because there are. What has happened in New York is that there's a whole category—and I can't mention names because that would be rude—of what I would call B actors, good but not great, or if you were lucky a wonderful understudy, who have been given parts because they stay in New York. There are more opportunities for that level of actor; they're needed more if they haven't gone to L.A. Frankly the New York competition is less stiff now.

Some of those actors I have seen over the past few years have really grown and have surprised me in ways I would never have thought they could. They've simply worked and worked and worked. Now they've maybe left the B category and they're floating blissfully toward the A category because they've had opportunities that wouldn't have existed for them ten or fifteen years ago. That's great when you see that. They become A actors. That's the only good thing about the talent drain to L.A.

***Vilga:*** Is there a way to counteract the fact that the American theater is depressed?

***Bishop:*** I don't think the theater is so depressed. I think people just get easily depressed in it and they think it's depressed. I mean, yes, we're going through tough economic times. That's been true of the nonprofit theater since the day I began working in it. I think there's no question that there's been a big drain from New York. When plants don't have light, they defoliate, they lose their leaves. There's no point dealing with the Broadway theater as the American theater anymore, because it isn't. Or even New York theater as American theater.

Look at the theaters all over the country that did not exist twenty-five years ago, that do new plays and classics and old plays and European plays and that are attended rather massively. Sometimes now in these new American cities, there are two, three, four, five theaters where ten years ago there was one. Someone's going to those theaters every night.

I think probably there are more people going to the theater and more employment opportunities than ever before in the history of the theater—just not in New York City. If you look at the roster of theaters in TCG there are three or four hundred of them, so that tells me there still is room for the theater.[1] I just think in places like New York everything gets exaggerated. Everyone lives in some state of crisis or another. It's all great or all terrible. The press feeds off that. I think the theater in some ways is very healthy, but maybe we in New York don't know what's going on in Kansas City so much.

**Vilga:** Do you think that training is necessary for every actor?

**Bishop:** I think they all need vocal training. I don't know a whole lot of actors who are born with a voice that really can project itself and that obviously is still important on the stage.

I think it's very important for actors to have a basic, decent education if they can afford one or their parents can afford one. There are those glorious few instinctive actors who never got through high school who had great careers in the American theater or on film. They exist. But the actors that I know who have handled their careers the most interestingly and the most intelligently have all been those actors who have gone to college and had a basic undergraduate liberal arts education. Who know about books and know how to add and know what happened in the War of 1812. Those actors, it seems to me, know how to cope with the world of the actor and the heartbreak of that world better. I don't know why, maybe because they have more intellectual pursuits, but I've noticed this a lot.

I think training is terrific, and I think all actors should study. Among other things, you make all your future friends in acting school, and in a way you make your future contacts there.

**Vilga:** Do you think different training is required for film and theater?

**Bishop:** I know less about that. I'm told there is a need for different training, but certainly all the great film actors—with some exceptions—come from the stage. Certainly in the old days they came from the stage.

Beyond training, I think part of it is so visual. A lot of it is how an actor photographs. I think there are these amazing actors who look like nothing much in person—and I would assume the same is true onstage—whose features somehow seem extraordinary when photographed and lit well. I don't know why that is. Faces that seem fascinating up close onscreen but aren't really in life or on the stage. I don't understand it, but I know that it's real, and I know that's why a lot of actors become successful in movies and others don't. It's just how their features take to the camera. Obviously you need to know where to stand and all that, and hopefully you have a good lighting person, but really it has nothing to do with the camera. It's just something inherent in the actor's features.

From my knowledge of it, what I've heard from my friends, you "do less" on the screen. I think it's easier for actors from the stage to work on the screen than it is for screen actors to work in the theater. I don't know if Spencer Tracy would have been especially interesting in a play. He might have been someone who seemed fascinating only under the camera's lens. That's why so many of the great stage actors haven't really had careers in movies.

In England it's different because there was very little British film industry. Before the war they had no actors except their stage actors. There really weren't English movie stars. Olivier and Gielgud and Richardson did early movies, but I don't think any of them were that good in movies, even Olivier. Certainly John Gielgud has a very big film career now in his very old age, and obviously Olivier learned how to act on film, but I always find his performances somewhat over the top in movies.

In America, for many years, there was always a division; there were movie actors and stage actors. The great stage actors of the old, old days—the Lunts, Katharine Cornell—really didn't make movies. It wasn't because they weren't good actors. It was because they didn't want to. It was considered low class in a way. It somehow wasn't considered serious. That's, of course, all changed now. Maybe those stage actors would have been too much for the camera.

**Vilga:** Is an innate charisma important to the actor, or does that come with the role?

**Bishop:** Both, I think. You know, people are always talking about star quality. I don't honestly know what all that is. I know it's probably a combination of physical and vocal attributes that collide gracefully with a role somehow. In the old days, of course, on the stage, a lot of plays were simply vehicles for the attributes of a certain star. That's the way movies and TV are today. In other words, plays were tailored for their stars.

Now, to go back to an earlier question of yours, one of the bad things—maybe because of TV—is that a lot of actors when they audition for plays or when they're in plays tussle a lot with the author and the director because they want the part to come to them, not them to go to the part. Somehow they get all mixed up and they think they know more about the character than the author. You hear these things, they're clichés but they're true. The author says something and the actor says, "Oh, I don't want to say that line, my character wouldn't say that."

Sometimes actors are right, because they are inside the mind of the character. A lot of smart authors pay attention, but actors can also just be completely nuts. The author usually thinks, "What do you mean? I wrote this character. You may think that the character may not say something, but I do." Sometimes I see that the actor simply wants to bend the character to them as opposed to bringing themselves to the character. That's a bit of a problem from time to time.

*Vilga:*   What effect do you see television having on actors?

*Bishop:*   I think TV pays the bills. That doesn't mean I don't think there's some very good TV. A lot of actors actually prefer acting on TV, and a lot of writers prefer writing for TV, because they say it's a little like being in the theater. They meet every week. It's very intense. They become a family for a short space of time. They do it all in a week, and they churn it out for thirty weeks or whatever, and then they have vacations. A lot of my friends say they prefer it because it has a communal sense. I also think that exists in film to some degree.

I think that there are a lot of wonderful TV actors who aren't totally great onstage. They can't be heard, they upstage themselves, and they don't know what to do with their hands, etc. I also think that audiences are used to hearing things more loudly and seeing things in close-up, so that's a problem, too. In the old days, before even me, there were no microphones even in musicals. You sat in the second balcony and you had to strain to hear. Part of it was because you paid so little you thought, "I will make more of an effort because I'm sitting in the second balcony." You adjusted. Your ears sort of figured it out. If you didn't always hear well, that was part of it. Now audiences won't stand that because they're used to turning up the volume. They're used to being in control of the performance. It's harder to do that in the theater.

*Vilga:*   And they're paying more money.

*Bishop:*   Yes, and they're paying more money. They don't want to sit far away and not see. I don't know if it's better or worse, it's just different.

*Vilga:*   With training, do you think that almost anyone can become an actor?

*Bishop:*   Yes, but if someone has no talent, then it's sort of a useless exercise.

*Vilga:*   Can you define talent?

*Bishop:*   Meisner always says, "Acting is behaving truthfully under imaginary circumstances." It's "as if." I think that's simplistic, but nonetheless that is what acting is.

I keep going back to that "corklike buoyancy" which is a phrase of the critic Kenneth Tynan's when he was describing someone—I don't remember who. Actors are somehow bobbing like corks above the waves. It just seems as if they've skipped between the page, they've successfully gone from the shadows to the spotlight, and you're not aware of the link between the two. There are other actors who seem to be doing the right things and saying the right things, but it's somewhat indicated. It seems from the outside in, somehow. It doesn't seem real. And believe me, I just do not hold reality up as a barometer of anything.

*Vilga:* You mentioned that you like bravura more than reality. What specifically do you mean by that?

*Bishop:* There's a breed of American actor, male and female, that I really like. Who knows why one really likes things—I think it's all very Freudian—but the kind of actor I like is the kind of actor I was, which is somewhere between leading man or woman in type and character man or woman in type. Those actors I find to be the bravest and the most bravura. I can't describe it precisely, maybe because they have feet in both camps. They're sort of leading man or woman and they're sort of character actors all at once, so of course there are not always all that many roles for them. For certain kinds of writers or writing, for plays of Shaw or modern writers, this kind of actor is a wonderful thing. They're not afraid to go out on a limb like a character actor does with voices and beards and walks, but they're also restrained because they have a sense of being a leading man or woman. They're character men and women, but there's a sexuality to them.

I think that what makes a leading man or woman is a sexual presence, and what a character man or woman lacks is sexual presence. I don't mean sexy. I can't define it exactly, except I think maybe that's what star quality is: a sexual presence of some kind.

These kinds of American actors that I just adore are like character men or women who have this sexual presence onstage. Some of them, alas, some of the men that I loved so much are dead, like Peter Evans, David Rounds. Take Ron Rifkin, who was in *The Substance of Fire*.[2] Look at him. (*Bishop shows me a photo of Ron Rifkin on the wall.*) He doesn't look like some pathetic old character actor. He's a character actor and he's a leading man. Quirky but a leading man. In a way, Meryl Streep is that. She's not really a leading lady. She's quirky. That's the way she always was onstage. I could name a bunch. To me they are the most interesting actors this country has to offer.

*Vilga:* Do you think this type of actor is uniquely American?

*Bishop:* I don't know enough about other cultures to know. I think English actors are very different from American actors. I think they tend to be more versatile because they simply are cast in a more versatile way.

There's less typecasting in England. There are companies there. They audition very little in England still. Often plays are cast by offers. It's a smaller world, a smaller community. Everyone knows everyone else.

**Vilga:** What do you think is the most difficult part of the actor's job?

**Bishop:** I don't know. I know a lot of actors complain about long runs as being difficult. They just get bored. Other actors love that.

I know what I would think is the most difficult thing, because this relates to the difficulties I had, is nerves. Performance anxiety. I would love being in the spotlight, but getting from the shadows to the spotlight is my undoing. The getting up there, the nerves before the actual performance, is in my view, especially if it's early on in the life of the play, the hardest thing. The play is being rewritten, and you're not quite sure which version you're performing. You don't feel totally prepared yet, or you don't feel well directed, and you've got to get up there and face the people. That to me—facing the people if one is uncertain—seems the most difficult thing of all.

You go down to the dressing room at half hour—7:30 if the curtain is at 8:00—especially early in the run. In most of the actors, in the early days of a run, you can really see terror. You see them not quite there. They're somewhere between there in the dressing room talking to you and where they're going to be. They're already making that trip to getting onstage when the curtain or the lights go up. In the early days of a play, you see these terrified, insecure creatures. How will they be received? How will the play be received? Then they get out there, and most of them, the good ones, deliver. You think, when you're sitting safely in the audience, "Having just been down into hell, how can they get up there and do this? How do they do it?" Well, it's this unbelievable combination of talent and technique and egomania.

People say all actors do is talk about themselves. Well, that's true. I don't see how you could possibly have that job and not be that way. That's what ultimately gets you out on the stage in front of people: an overweening ego. Wanting to be liked and praised, hopefully, and looked at. If you didn't have that, to me it would be just a terror.

**Vilga:** Is there a common personality type for actors, then?

**Bishop:** No. I think most actors are very different, one from the other, as people. There is one bottom line: they are of necessity focused on themselves. They are their favorite topic, which doesn't mean they're not intelligent or giving or generous. You can be an egomaniac and a saint. I'm sure Mother Teresa is as egomaniacal as anyone. You have to be to get through life. I definitely think the one common denominator that all actors have is being self-focused. They have to be with their body, asking how they feel each day. Their voice, how is it? Will they get sick? Singers are the same way, and dancers, too. How can you not be? I never mind that because that's what gets them out there.

**Vilga:** Are there ever incapacitating cases of stage fright?

**Bishop:** I've never seen that. I've seen performances often early on where they're nervous and you can see that. What is good about that and awful about that is when actors are nervous, they are very focused. A good actor in the early performances is very focused on what he or she is doing. Later on in the run, when they're at ease, they can be overly at ease. But if you're in a comedy and you're working too hard or you're too concentrated or too focused, you can't get laughs in the same way. For comedy or for musicals especially, routine is what frees you; repetition is what makes it spontaneous. It seems odd that that should be the case, but it is. It's a little bizarre. In my view, for comedies or musicals you can't have too many previews, because in the right hands it will only get better.

**Vilga:** What about the whole issue of reviews? Are they damaging to the actor?

**Bishop:** If they're bad, yes. But reviews aren't the most damaging thing, because some actors don't read them, or they say they don't, or some of them don't care. Some of them feel bad for a day. Reviews don't change performances.

What is bad is when before reviews their friends start coming and giving them notes. That can be often very damaging. Their friends tend to be actors who may or may not like the play. They go backstage and it's "Wonderful! Marvelous!" but they go out for a drink and the actor says, "Tell me what you really thought." The friend will often say things— sometimes helpful, sometimes not. The friend doesn't know, and the actor often doesn't even know, where in the process the director, if he or she is good, is leading him. They're just judging what they see.

I've seen actors come back after going out with their friends and deliver something quite different only to find that their friends were wrong. That can be quite damaging. Not only just in terms of giving them notes, which may or may not be the right notes, but also giving their opinions of the play itself. Then the actor can begin losing confidence in the play. Sometimes the most successful plays we've done were nearly derailed in previews from unintelligent advice from friends. That's worse than reviews in my view.

**Vilga:** Is there any way of reconciling the actor's standards as an artist with the practical demands of the career?

*Bishop:*  I don't see why not. I think what's demeaning for actors is to harness their talent and their training to grade Z material, the awful TV things, the awful movies. There are those good actors who do crap who can never move on because they get used to the money. Actors who should be playing Hamlet, who could be playing Hamlet—well, could have been playing Hamlet—but you see them on TV in these ridiculous fifth-rate sitcoms. That is really a waste. That's, I think, the awful thing, when you talk about the practicalities of a career. The standard of excellence is much lower than in the theater, and it's terrible. Eventually an actor becomes cynical. They know they're doing crap, but they'll excuse it. Then they don't care anymore. Then it's too late for them to play Hamlet.

I think a smart actor tries to balance the two and has a sense of what they're doing for money that isn't good, and what they're doing for money that is good, and what they're doing for free that is good, and what they're doing for free that isn't. There are a lot of crappy showcases in New York where you don't get paid and it's terrible, all at the same time.

But to see these glories of the New York stage fifteen years ago or twenty years ago, when I got out of college, who are now in Hollywood appearing in these ludicrous shows. The ones that were less talented, you think they should be there. The rest, you think, "Oh my God." They can't act on the stage anymore after a while, or they say they can't afford to. They say, "Do you know what it's costing me to do this play?" You always hear that. They get used to having managers and agents and a fancy lifestyle. It's terrible.

*Vilga:*  A lot of actors seem stuck at a lower level where they just want to get a job. Is that just the way it is?

*Bishop:*  I think that's the way it is. I think that's always been the way it is. When the theater was the principal employer of actors, you just wanted a job.

There's this wonderful old-fashioned play that was done in the fifties called *Career.*[3] It's a famous play, it's probably not a good play, but you should read it. It's about a young actor who just wants to act. He and his wife are very poor, and they've moved to New York. They live in this cold-water flat after they've had a happy life before on the farm. Now his marriage is all screwed up. They've moved to New York because he wants to make it in New York in the theater in the fifties, when the theater was still "it." It would be like going to Hollywood today, I suppose. He's tormented, he's abusive to his wife when she comes home from working, and they have a kid. The wife just doesn't understand the actor's dreams. She's not in the theater, she just wants to be his wife. At the end of one scene, which is the best scene in the play, in fact the only really good scene in the play, he comes home depressed. She's trying, but she can't do anything good enough for him, and the kid is crying, and finally at the very end of the scene they're screaming at each other and she says, "What do you want? What do you want?" And he just says two words: "A job." The lights go down, and that's the end of the scene.

It's very evocative. I think that this has always been true. When an actor isn't working he's studying, but what does he do all day long? Take lessons? Comb his hair? Go to the gym? Go out on auditions? In that scene in *Career*, it wasn't "I want to be this, I want to be that," or some great fifteen-minute speech. Just two words. "What do you want?" "A job."

**Vilga:**  If you had one piece of advice to give to the young actor, what would you tell him or her?

**Bishop:**  I don't know anymore, I'm afraid. Fifteen years ago, I would have just based my reply on the theater, homilies and advice about the theater. Now you can't do that. You're a fool if you do. I don't really have any advice. The clichés are maybe true. Yes, get good training. Yes, be persistent. Yes, learn to accept rejection. Yes, find the art in yourself, not yourself in the art. But I have no idea. I really don't know.

I think a lot of it has to do with my ambivalent feelings about movies and television, which are art forms I love. I love to watch them, but I have mixed feelings about what they're doing to the theater, or certainly the New York theater. They've helped, certainly, in the sense that they've been able to give our actors money so that they can afford to appear in plays. That's like a backhanded compliment. They've given our writers and directors employment, but frankly most of them leave and they never come back to the theater.

**Vilga:**  What do you think the best part of the actor's job is?

**Bishop:**  Actors just love to act. They love to get up on a stage or in front of a camera and be someone else using different parts of themselves. Acting is fun; it's hard work, but it's also fun. It's "Let's put on a show." It's dress-up. Or it should be. I imagine to be in a good play and to be good in a good play and to have the audience loving it—and that doesn't always happen—that must be wonderful.

# Robert Brustein

*Photo: Richard M. Feldman*

*Robert Brustein was born on April 21, 1927, in New York City. He received a BA from Amherst College in 1948 and an MA in 1950 and a Ph.D. in 1957 from Columbia University. Brustein has taught at Cornell University, Vassar College, Columbia University, Yale University, and Harvard University.*

*He founded the Yale Repertory Theatre in 1966 and was its artistic director until 1979. In 1980 he founded the American Repertory Theatre Company in Cambridge, Massachusetts, and is currently its artistic director.*

*Brustein, a noted author, has been a drama critic for the* New Republic *and the* London Observer *and a contributor to the* New York Times. *His books include* The Theatre of Revolt: Studies in the Modern Drama, Seasons of Discontent: Dramatic Opinions, The Third Theatre, Revolution as Theatre: Notes on the New Radical Style, The Culture Watch, Critical Moments, Making Scenes, Who Needs Theatre?, Reimagining American Theatre, *and his latest,* Dumbocracy in America.

*Brustein's awards include the George Jean Nathan Award for dramatic criticism, the George Polk Memorial Award for outstanding criticism, the Eliot Norton Award for outstanding achievement in American theater given by the New England Theatre Council, the Tiffany Award given by the International Society of Performing Arts Administrators, and the American Academy of Arts and Letters Award for distinguished contribution to the arts. He has been awarded fellowships from the Guggenheim, Fulbright, and Ford foundations.*

*His directing credits include productions of* Don Juan, The Seagull, Ghosts, Six Characters in Search of an Author, The Changeling, Tonight We Improvise, Right You Are, *and* The Father.

*He is the author of three plays—*Demons, Celebrities Anonymous, *and* Nobody Dies on Saturday—*a musical,* Schlemiel the First, *and eight adaptations.*

● ———————————————————————————— ●

**Vilga:**   How did you begin working with actors?

**Brustein:**   My own training began when I was four or five years old and I had a lisp. I was unable to pronounce the letter *L,* so my parents sent me to something that was then called an elocution school to correct my *L*'s. With training on phrases like "the lazy lion leaped over the lair" or something like that. (*Laughs*) What they didn't know was that it was also a drama school or drama training program. While I was there, I was in a lot of plays and got bitten by the theater bug. I did a lot of acting in camp, in high school, and then in college. I went to the Yale Drama School for a year, where I studied acting and directing, but I left there in disgust and founded, with six other students from the school, a theater called Studio Seven at the Provincetown Playhouse, in New York. From there, I helped to found a group called Group 20, which played first in Connecticut and then moved to Wellesley, where it was known as Theater on the Green. It was one of the earliest postwar classical repertory companies. From that point on, I would go to Wellesley every summer while continuing in my education, eventually getting my doctorate.

There was even one year when I decided to be an actor and give up teaching. I made the rounds in New York for a year, but I didn't altogether give up teaching, because I was still conducting a seminar at what was then the old Columbia Drama School. I did some Equity showcases and appeared in some *Matinee Theaters* and *U.S. Steel Hours* on television. Essentially, that was my training, mostly by doing.

**Vilga:**   What was it about the Yale Drama School that caused you to leave it?

**Brustein:**   I don't want to hurt feelings, but the acting teacher then was both the acting teacher and the voice teacher for the entire school. This meant that she had classes with all three years of the acting students as well as the directing students, in both of these highly specialized areas. I remember that the approach to acting had a lot to do with sense memory and a lot to do with identifying yourself as an object: a chandelier or a writing table or something like that. It seemed extremely silly to me in my young and rather rebellious days. It just didn't seem logical or sensible to me as acting training. I bolted and reacted against what I thought were rather hidebound and old-fashioned and conventional techniques of the entire school. Stanislavsky was not being taught or even acknowledged that he existed. Clifford Odets had to be done surreptitiously, as it were, as underground theater.[1] The best experience I had was in one of those productions, which we rehearsed all year and eventually produced underground.

The only other exciting thing, outside of some of the students themselves, was something known as the takeoff, in which the students had the opportunity to vent their spleen and anger over the quality of the work that was being done on the main stage in satiric cabaret-type skits. It was ferocious satire, quite often very imaginative and funny. Men always played the women's parts, which became a real Aristophanic romp. I loved to watch it.

**Vilga:**   How is the training at ART different from other programs?

**Brustein:**   The training at ART is a manifestation of an evolution out of the training we created at the Yale Drama School. I was dean there for thirteen years. I came back some eighteen years after I left as a student and completely revamped the existing program. What I did was increase enormously the number of contact classes that acting students had in voice and movement, dancing, fencing, and particularly acting.

We had a kind of trial by error and evolution at the drama school, in which we eventually found out what worked. It took me about ten years to discover it. I discovered what didn't work, and that was the traditional master teacher approach. We had tried this with a great variety of very gifted master teachers. People like Bobby Lewis, Stella Adler, Bob Benedetti.[2] You name the teacher, we had the teacher. It never seemed to work. We could never find a way to integrate the intense kind of master teacher relationship with the work that the Yale acting students did with the repertory theater. It occurred to me about eight or ten years down the road that the master teacher was really the Yale Repertory Theatre. It is the theater that can teach students better than any single person. The single individuals, no matter how gifted, were usually stuck in a particular technique, whether it was to work on scenes or to discuss intentions, objectives, and actions. They looked at a scene and then sent the student back to redo the scene. They would look at it again and critique the same. As a result, the students never got training in how to develop an entire role. They never got an overall sense of what the arc of the play was. They never understood how their character connected with other characters in the play. Not only that, even though all of these teachers spoke about creating a total actor, almost all of them were single-mindedly interested in American realism. They never really advanced into verse drama, into postmodernism, or into experimental theater even though they all, as I say, professed an interest in it.

I understood through my readings that the reason for the evolution of the master teacher had to do with the deterioration of the theater. When the Group Theatre disappeared after its nine or ten years of life, all of those actors like Lee Strasberg and Sandy Meisner and Stella were dispersed into the culture.[3] Since they had no theater, they began to hold classes. The class became the be-all, it became the focus of attention, so that the class, in fact, became the idealistic alternative to the existing commercial theater.

Take a student, for example, who had to make a living by doing a television miniseries, or commercials, or even a rotten part in a bad Broadway play. They could go to one of these classes and work on Chekhov or Odets or Arthur Miller. This type of serious work they did with Bobby or Stella or Sandy. They could see what they were able to do artistically in some more hallowed and idealistic atmosphere than the atmosphere of the commercial theater. The fact is that when we started the Yale Repertory, we started what I think is still an idealistic theater, a theater that did the kind of serious work that good actors must always do. As a result, the classroom did not have to have that kind of sacrosanct, alternative quality.

**Vilga:** What's the purpose to the classroom, then, if the theater itself is the teacher?

**Brustein:** Indeed, what we determined to do is first of all look at our theater and ask, "What is it that we do?" followed by, "How can we shape a training that will support what we do?" After examining it carefully, we saw that essentially we do three things.

We do something we call poetic realism, by which I mean Anton Chekhov, Ibsen, and Strindberg's more naturalistic plays. Not naturalism but poetic realism, realism that has a depth to it that you can explore. So we decided that the first year of the training would be Stanislavsky oriented. Stanislavsky was always the basic building block of our training. Voice and movement classes would be supportive of a realistic training. There would be investigation of objectives and intentions. Actions. Sense memory. And we would have a faculty-directed project at the end of that year, probably a Chekhov play like *The Seagull* or *Three Sisters* in which we would have a student take a part that he or she normally would not take. Students would also have obligations in regard to the repertory theater—they would carry spears or do walk-ons—but we'd endeavor to stretch the student as an artist. That would be the culmination of the work in poetic realism.

We also recognized that another aspect of the repertory theater was very verse oriented, particularly Shakespeare and the Jacobeans, but also the Greeks. As a result, the second year would be devoted to verse speaking and scansion, learning how to find an action and, at the same time, understand and scan the verse properly. Movement would thus be more oriented toward the kind of formal movement that you would use in classical drama. Voice would concentrate on breaking down the verse. We'd have singing, and this singing would be related to songs of the period. We would culminate with a verse project, *The Revenger's Tragedy* or *Measure for Measure* or a similar blank verse play. In that year, the actors would also have obligations with the Yale Repertory Theatre. They would have smaller roles, and they would be doing understudy parts, and they'd get a chance to play the understudy at a matinee.

The third and final thing we decided we did as a theater was something I can only refer to as postmodernism. It included all the kind of radical new plays that we were involved in doing, plus Brecht and Beckett and Shepard and Mamet. The third year would be devoted to a highly experimental kind of training, which would extend the actor beyond naturalism, to a kind of supernaturalism. We had such instructors as Andrei Serban and Lee Breuer coming up like that, to take them through the class and to take them through some project. Serban did a Shepard play, *Mad Dog Blues,* on the local beach in New Haven or North Haven. Lee Breuer did a production which eventually evolved into the famous and infamous *Lulu* that we did here at the American Repertory Theatre in 1982 or 1983.[4]

Those third-year students would also be a cabaret company and do cabaret work. We extended the so-called takeoffs into six satiric cabarets. They would study the music of Brecht and Weill and other contemporaries of that kind, like Sondheim. They would do featured roles, larger roles with the Rep—as, for example, Meryl Streep did in her whole third year, where she played a lot of leads. Meryl sometimes forgets that she got her professional start at Yale Repertory Theatre. She often refers to Joe Papp as the one who gave her her start. Really, he wasn't. It was the Yale Rep.

*Vilga:* How did this program influence what's taught here at the ART?

*Brustein:* I brought this philosophy of training with me here when we started the institute. Here, the relationship with the Rep is even stronger than it was at Yale, and it's a two-year program, cut down from three years. We don't offer a degree here. I never wanted to do that at Yale, because I think the degree distracts the student from the proper focus on becoming a professional actor. If you think you can always go and teach somewhere, then you're not really taking the plunge. It's not really jumping into the water.

Now we have a two-year program, which we've compacted and contracted from the development that I spoke about at Yale. The American Repertory Theatre, in effect, is the old Yale Repertory Theatre under a different name. It has the same aesthetic.

*Vilga:* How do the classes function here in terms of the repertory company?

*Brustein:* Classes are only part of the training. To really learn to act, you have to do it with a professional company. There's a big difference between doing it with your peers and doing it with professional actors. The difference is obvious. You aim higher. You have to keep up. If you're running with a professional track star, you're going to run faster than you do with athletes from your college.

Acting students need to work both with their peers and with professionals. An old friend of mine, Fredric March, was a very great actor.[5] You probably know of him from film work, but when he got onstage he was possibly our finest American actor. He did the original James Tyrone in what is still the best production of [Eugene O'Neill's] *Long Day's Journey*, namely the first production under the direction of José Quintero, the one that had Jason Robards playing Jamie. He had never taken a day of training. It's true that there are genius actors, purely instinctive actors that get where they're going without training. In March's case, however, it wasn't just that he was a very gifted actor. In fact, he was a pretty rotten actor when he first started out. He had trailed around with a company throughout the country barnstorming. He watched from the wings. He understudied. It was the continual connection with the company, which was the traditional European way of learning. When he got his chance, he was ready.

We've tried to combine that here with what we acknowledge to be the very important aspect of classes as well. It's not only classes. It's not only professional experience. It's a combination of the two that the actor needs.

*Vilga:* Is there any acknowledgment of the mechanics of professional careers when one is here?

**Brustein:**   Career Day, you mean? At least it's called Career Day at Yale. Frankly, I'm of two minds about that. I love most of my students, and I'm very concerned about their professional futures. We talk about those futures constantly. In fact, we have a class, in addition to the training, called "The Repertory Ideal," which meets once a week with the entire institute, where we talk about the options in American theater these days. Of course, options for actors now include film, television, commercials, and commercial theater, but our students know that we stand for "the repertory ideal," a very powerful and eloquent ideal, which is also self-sacrificing, I suppose. It's almost a monastic ideal, this concept of a permanent repertory theater company. Not just a bunch of actors gathered for a single show, but actors that work with each other over a period of years and develop together like a good ball team. That's what we tell them is the highest expression of their art.

At the same time, given the kind of culture we live in, how many companies can realistically exist? Not many. Ours is limited by funds. We can only maintain a certain number of companies. America imposes limitations on us through its essential philistine lack of public support for the arts. So to answer your question, yes, we do have Career Day, but I'm against it. At the end of the year, we even have something else that stabs me a little, the so-called showcase. The actors, under the supervision of one of their instructors, create a showcase, which they bring down to New York and show to agents and directors. A lot of them get jobs out of it.

I think that our obligation in any training program essentially should be to create as fine an actor as possible, someone who is capable of doing anything. Of course, if they've gone through a program like this, they can do anything, from Greek tragedy to American musical comedy. Therefore, these actors are employable, usable, and highly desirable.

**Vilga:**   Do you feel that the training in this sort of theater allows them to do things like film? Does that require a separate training or just an adjustment?

**Brustein:**   Not at all. The last thing you should be training actors for is film or television. If you're a good actor, you'll learn that technique in ten minutes (to my regret and chagrin). You do get proud of the success of your students and former colleagues. Yet it's ironic that almost all the major TV series and movie stars came out of serious theater, meaning theaters like ours and schools like ours.

They were never trained for that. Sigourney Weaver was never trained to be a movie actor. She was trained for the stage. Meryl was never trained to be a movie actress. Henry Winkler was not trained to be a television star, nor was Ken Howard. Nor was Max Wright. Nor Christopher Walken. These people are essentially stage actors, which means they're real actors. They weren't discovered in Schwab's drugstore. They were well trained, and if you're trained, you can do anything.

*Vilga:* Given a decent actor, can you satisfactorily complete the training in two years here?

*Brustein:* I think that if the training is intensive, two or three years is enough. Remember, the ART Institute doesn't take recent college graduates but people who have been in the field for a while and who have had some professional experience. These people are not beginners, meaning people who maybe just had a couple of courses in college. It's called the Institute for *Advanced* Theatre Training at Harvard, and we mean that.

*Vilga:* Do you feel that acting is a unique ability that certain people have and certain people don't?

*Brustein:* Yes. I have rarely seen people who have made themselves into actors. There are two common errors. One is thinking that if you don't have the talent, you can become an actor through a lot of training. That's an error. The other error is that if you have the talent, you don't need the training. The fact is, you need the training and the talent.

There is a terrible misconception, and I think it's generated a lot in college as well, that though you have to train to be a dancer, you have to train to be a violinist, a harpist, or a cellist, you don't have to train to be an actor. Somehow, your native talent is going to carry you through. This is true in very few cases. You really do need the training. You have to learn how to project, you have to learn how to move. You have to learn how to simulate poise and confidence and relaxation. This doesn't come naturally to the great majority.

*Vilga:* How does one tell that the talent is there?

*Brustein:* A good auditioner can spot talent based on a couple of audition pieces. We generally ask applicants for a classical piece and a modern piece. From that we can tell a lot about the actor. You can tell about his or her equipment. You can tell about how far the voice has been trained. You can tell about movement. You can tell about intelligence through the level of the interpretation. You can tell most of all about daring, because that's the kind of actor you're always looking for: the actor who will dare. The actor who will make a leap, where another actor won't.

*Vilga:* What are the methods taught here? Do they tend toward any particular system?

*Brustein:* It varies according to the instructor. The first-year acting training, which is the one you're referring to, is now being given, really, by a woman named Jane Nichols under the supervision of the directing teacher, Ron Daniels, who's very Stanislavsky oriented. And as a result they're getting intensive work in Stanislavsky. But it's not Method Stanislavsky. I mean, it's not Lee Strasberg's type of Stanislavsky. I don't know how to describe it, except that it's pure. Just the study of Stanislavsky's text.[6]

**Vilga:** What about criticisms of Method training and Method actors?

**Brustein:** I've made a lot of those criticisms myself. You see, I think the Method as it evolved under Lee Strasberg became essentially a breeding ground for movie stars. What Strasberg's version of the Method taught you to do was to play upon and market your personality. It encouraged you to find certain traits that would be commercial and salable and use them. He did not teach transforming as an actor, which is very important in our training. If you're going to be in a company, the audience is going to see you maybe five times in the course of a year, in five different projects. They don't want to see actor A up there being actor A from play to play to play. They'll get tired of you very soon. They want to see an actor display his capacity to transform into a variety of characters. *Building a Character* is a book of Stanislavsky's that the Actors Studio never got to. Certain Method actors don't build characters, they build personalities. The difference between personality and character is profound—we can go back to Ibsen to try to find out what that distinction means—but it's something every good actor understands.

**Vilga:** Most films are based on the fact that movie stars are appearing as themselves again and again and again.

**Brustein:** That's right. That's what sells. Unfortunately, eventually people get tired of you and you are a piece of old meat and you get thrown on the scrap heap unless you're a genuine actor. Hollywood's had transforming actors from time to time. Paul Muni was one. Charles Laughton was another. Meryl Streep is basically a character actor. I think she shows it too. Like all actors, she still is limited by her roles, but she's capable of a much wider variety of roles. She first came to public attention in a production of a play called *The Idiots Karamazov,* by two then-students, Christopher Durang and Albert Innaurato.[7] She played the ancient Translatrix, as she was called, Constance Garnett. She sat in a wheelchair, and she brandished a cane. She was magnificent. It may have been the best performance she ever did.

**Vilga:** What do you think about the future of the theater? Is it getting any better? Is it getting worse?

**Brustein:** The future? Look at my new book, which I hope you will, called *Reimagining American Theater.*[8] It takes these two positions: one is that the assumption that the American theater is dying or in some sort of decline is a mistake based on the fact that New York is in decline. Most of the attention has always been on New York, but the fact is that the theater has moved out of New York. It's now in a great variety of cities. I won't say it's healthy, but at least it's surviving in these cities. For the most part, theater is much more serious and significant across the country than it is in New York. It also tends to be much more daring than it is in New York. If you look at opera, the great operas don't premiere in New York anymore. They premiere in St. Louis and Chicago and Houston and Seattle and San Francisco or the Netherlands and Germany, where Philip Glass's operas are all being performed. New York premieres uninteresting new ones. If these benighted scribblers about the drama would ever get out of New York and take a look at what's happening elsewhere in the country, I don't think there would be these gloomy predictions about the death of theater. There's still the unfortunate assumption that New York *is* the theater even though it's just not anymore.

Secondly, there are problems with these other cities, which I don't want to in any way deny. There are country-wide problems with the culture, with the economy. There are problems of timidity. Problems with fraud. Problems with the government, especially all this latest obscenity nonsense. Nevertheless, the theater is being reimagined. There are some extraordinary playwrights out there and some extraordinary directors. I've seen a lot of actors now coming back to the theater who a few years ago I never thought would ever return to the stage.

*Vilga:* Why do you think that is?

*Brustein:* I don't know. I think every actor who is a genuine actor recognizes that famous Stanislavsky prescription that he or she must love the art in themselves, rather than themselves in the art. Once again, it's a distinction between character and personality. You don't love the personality you've created. You love the character you've created. Doing that is a God-given talent, which you nurse and nurture and nourish. It doesn't belong to you. It's yours to be a caretaker of. The way you exercise that talent is on the stage; you don't get to do that in a movie very often. If a real actor wants to come back and air their talent, take it for a walk like they would a classy, thoroughbred dog, then they've got to go back to the theater.

*Vilga:* Do you see major film stars coming back to the stage more often?

*Brustein:* I think people who started on the stage who then made reputations as stars in films will come back to the stage as actors. The word "star" is anathema to genuine artists. It's part of what is killing the theater. The scribblers try to make these instant stars, and producers benefit financially from these instant stars, and studios market these instant stars. This all helps destroy what we think of as acting.

**Vilga:** Do you think that acting training itself has changed significantly in the past ten or twenty years? Do you think it's gotten better?

**Brustein:** There's different kinds of training. There's Juilliard. There's NYU. Yale has undergone three major changes in the last thirteen years. There's the ACT. There's the North Carolina School of the Arts, which is now under new directorship by Gerald Freedman. A new artistic director comes in and changes the whole nature of things. So it's hard to generalize about such a various and versatile situation.

**Vilga:** Do you think actors are better trained now than they used to be?

**Brustein:** Yes, they're better trained than they were when I was a kid.

**Vilga:** Because of these programs?

**Brustein:** Yes, there are a lot of programs, and I think a growing recognition that actors do need training in one way or the other. As I've said, training can be in the form of experience or it can be classes or a combination, but there's got to be some form of training.

**Vilga:** Is there more respect for the actor today?

**Brustein:** No, no more than there ever was. I think in a puritan culture, the actor is still not recognized. I saw a sign in a bar the other day, it's an old sign, but it still applies: "We don't accept children, drunks, or actors." Did you know that in some places actors are still not allowed to be buried? Are there any actors in Westminster Abbey? Maybe there are now. Mostly poets, however. Actors are not endorsed or respected by our society. In this country, if you're an actor, it's hard to get a credit card or a telephone.

**Vilga:** Then if you become successful, it's just the opposite extreme, where you become a quote-unquote "star" and utterly untouchable.

**Brustein:** Yes. It's interesting, though. If you're looking for people who are generous, there's no more generous human being than the actor. With rare exceptions, like Burt Reynolds or Paul Newman, they're not generous with their money but with their talent. I was just watching a special on Groucho Marx last night. When you're poor as a young person, you always feel that you're going to be poor in your old age, and you just don't give anything away. What you give away is your time. You do a benefit on a Monday night, when you're not working, but not cash. You can count the ones that do on the fingers of one hand.

**Vilga:** If you had one piece of advice to give to the young actor, what would it be?

**Brustein:** Find out which actor you most respect—which is different from whose career you want to emulate because he or she's a star—but find the actor you most respect for their talent, and do your best to find out how that talent evolved, and then try to follow that yourself. That's probably the shorthand way to grow as an artist.

The second bit of advice I would give, of course, is to act as much as possible. Get on the stage. Get up on the bicycle and ride it. Fall down, get up again, and ride it again. That's the only way to learn.

The third piece of advice I would give is stick to the stage. That's where the satisfactions are. They're not financial satisfactions to any great degree, and they're not fame satisfactions. I know that this culture holds out money and fame as the only goods worth having. Yet there are other more important goods like self-satisfaction and the capacity to make art with like-minded people. That you can only do on the stage.

# *Ellen Burstyn*

*Ellen Burstyn spent her early years as a model and actress, appearing regularly on* The Jackie Gleason Show *and other television programs. Burstyn debuted on Broadway in 1957 in* Fair Game. *Other theater credits include the 1982 Broadway production of* 84 Charing Cross Road *and the Off-Broadway production of* Park Your Car in Harvard Yard *in which she starred with Burgess Meredith. Burstyn starred in the one-woman play* Shirley Valentine *on Broadway in 1989, and in 1992 she appeared in* Shimada. *Her starring role in* Same Time, Next Year *in 1975 brought her a Tony Award as Best Actress, as well as the Drama Desk and Outer Critics Circle Awards. In 1978, Burstyn created the role in the film version, for which she was awarded a Golden Glode and received an Academy Award nomination.*

*Burstyn won the Oscar for Best Actress in 1974, as well as a Golden Globe and the British Academy Award, for* Alice Doesn't Live Here Anymore. *She has been nominated for Oscars in three other film roles:* The Last Picture Show *(1971),* The Exorcist *(1973), and* Resurrection *(1980). Other film credits include* The King of Marvin Gardens *(1972),* Harry and Tonto *(1974),* Twice in a Lifetime *(1986),* Dying Young *(1990),* The Cemetery Club *(1993),* When a Man Loves a Woman *(1994),* How to Make an American Quilt *(1995),* The Baby-Sitters Club *(1995), and* The Spitfire Grill *(1996).*

*On television, Burstyn received an Emmy nomination for her title role in* The People vs. Jean Harris *and another in 1989 for her starring role in* Pack of Lies. *She has also starred in over a dozen other television movies.*

*Burstyn was the first woman to be elected president of Actors Equity Association (1982–1985) and served for six years as the artistic director of the Actors Studio, where she had studied with the late Lee Strasberg.*

● ─────────────────────────────────────── ●

**Vilga:**   When did you first identify your desire to become an actress?

**Burstyn:**   One of my earliest memories is the awareness of performing. My brother and I would put on shows in the garage and charge a penny admission. My mother gave me dancing lessons when I was three or four and then piano lessons and so forth. Mathematics didn't come easily, but putting on the class play did. Whenever we did plays or musicals or anything to do with performance, I was always the writer, the director, the producer, the leading actor, or a combination of all of those. Even though I was performing really early, I didn't know necessarily that I wanted to be an actress. I didn't make up my mind that this was what I was going to put all my energy toward until I was twenty-four—which is late, I think, because most people make that decision earlier.

There were so many other things that interested me as career possibilities. For example, I was an art major in high school in Detroit, a school that had the best art department of any high school in the country. When it became clear to me that I wasn't one of the best in the school, I decided against that career. Then I considered being a lawyer, so I spent a lot of time in the Detroit Public Library's law department, reading law books until I decided against that, too. I also like animals, so I thought about being a veterinarian. When I left home and set out on my own, I was dancing and modeling, and it's a kind of easy step from modeling to acting.

I started doing commercials and appeared on *The Jackie Gleason Show* as a regular when I was twenty-three. Then one day I decided, "Okay, I'm on TV now, and I'm going to do a Broadway play this fall." I went around to everybody saying, "I'm going to do a Broadway play this fall. How do you get an audition for a Broadway show?" Somebody actually got me an audition, and I got the part, so I began my career with a lead on Broadway.[1]

**Vilga:** That's really amazing.

**Burstyn:** It's amazing, but I don't recommend it. It was not the way to start an acting career, because I had no technique. As long as I could just do what came naturally and there were no problems, I could shine. But the moment that the trouble hit the fan, which of course it always does, I just started shriveling. I really had no way to sustain a performance. I managed, but it's like learning how to swim by being in deep waters. It's a do-or-die situation.

**Vilga:** Was the role very close to your own personality and experiences?

**Burstyn:** Yes, it was—she was a model from the Midwest—but it's not necessarily easy to play someone that's close to your own experience. Sometimes it's easier to play something that's far from who you are, because in the panic of trying to figure out how to play somebody that's not you, you start asking questions that stimulate your imagination, and then you're actively involved in the creative process. Whereas if the part is close to you, you often don't know what creative work you need to do. Actors sometimes think, "It's me, so I can just say the lines and it will be great." In doing that, you're not being very creative; you really are only just saying the lines.

When you're actively involved in the creative process, it's like being an inventor, because you're creating something entirely new. As an artist you need a way to get into the creative process, some method that works for you. Once you're in, then the artistic impulses start coming, and if you are relaxed enough you can act on those impulses and respond to them and relay or translate them into a recognizable message. If you don't engage the artistic process, then nothing's going to happen.

**Vilga:** Was it during your Broadway debut that you realized you wanted to get more serious training?

**Burstyn:** The play was successful, and I ran a whole season under these awkward circumstances. Afterward, I decided that I should learn how to really do this acting thing, so I went to Stella Adler. I didn't take the whole course, which I probably should have, because I was already working. I just took a scene study course. I continued working as an actor while trying to study. I moved to California, where I studied with Jeff Corey, but by that time I was working regularly in television shows, doing guest shots and other things.[2] Then I got a movie, *Goodbye Charlie*, directed by Vincent Minnelli and starring Walter Matthau and Tony Curtis.

Minnelli's way of directing was to do the scene for me and then have me imitate him. Naturally I felt really misplaced. I felt really false. I was wearing an old wig of Shirley MacLaine's, and my face had been painted on by Debbie Reynolds's brother, who was a makeup man. I was just sitting there in Shirley MacLaine's wig, wearing a gown by Edith Head, with Debbie's brother doing my makeup, waiting for my chance to imitate Vincent Minnelli.

I remember thinking, "So this is it. This is the big time. Twentieth Century Fox." The next step was for me to play Debbie's part. But this voice went off in my head saying that I didn't want to succeed this way. This wasn't what I wanted as an artist. I made up my mind then and there to leave California as soon as I finished that film and go back to New York and start studying with Lee Strasberg. That was about twenty-seven years ago. So I went back to New York City and got a job in a soap opera called *The Doctors.* I used to go to Lee's class and be assigned my acting exercise and then practice it on the set of the soap.

For years I continued to study with Lee, while also taking Peggy Feury's class, because in Lee's class at that time you didn't get to work often.[3] Maybe you got to work once every six weeks, and I wanted to work more than that. Then I moved back and forth between New York and California. I also studied with Bruce Dern, who was teaching in 1970.[4] As you can see, most of my teachers have come from the Method stream.

**Vilga:** What were your first experiences working with Lee Strasberg like? Was it radically different from what you'd been doing before or been exposed to professionally?

**Burstyn:** I'm sure you've discovered by now that Stanislavsky did not invent the system but simply reported what actors had been doing for centuries. A lot of things were familiar to me because they were things that had come to me while I was working. Behind you is this show poster of Angela Lansbury in *Pretty Belle.*[5] "Pretty belle" is a good description of what I had developed at that point. When I went to Lee, I had a "pretty belle" facade. I was cute, I was pretty, and I fit everybody's darling type of a presentational ingenue. Lee just ripped it right off me; he just didn't accept it.

**Vilga:** Were you prepared for that?

**Burstyn:** No, I cried for two weeks after the first time I worked for him. Day and night for two weeks I cried. Not because he hurt me—he wasn't cruel—he just didn't accept my mask. He was asking me to work without it, and I had no idea who was under the mask. If I wasn't this construction, I didn't know who I was. It felt like an enormous risk to reveal myself that way.

*Vilga:*  It seems rather cruel to remove someone's persona so drastically.

*Burstyn:*  It was the only possible way for me to get to the next level of work. It was absolutely necessary because, for me, that's really what the work is about. Everybody has a mask in life. Everybody is acting. The actor is the person who learns how to stop acting and knows how to lift the mask and reveal the reality behind the persona. That's what I learned from Lee, and I think that's the quality in my work that people respond to. I always tried to find at least one moment in every film I did or in a play where there was that moment of unmasking, where I felt completely exposed.

*Vilga:*  As a person or as a character?

*Burstyn:*  At that level, when you really work deeply, there is such a blend of those two things that you don't separate them. The point is to find how your truth is the character's truth. I don't know that you can get to the character's truth without getting down into your own deep waters. You have to explore the poignant fact that on some level there is no difference between you and the character. Essentially you must get to your own raw material and make the character out of it.

*Vilga:*  How are you able to sustain something like that? Do those moments you're describing where you feel so fused as artist and character happen frequently?

*Burstyn:*  Hopefully you build a piece of work in which you know all the steps toward achieving this. Onstage when those certain moments occur, you always get to them by going through certain steps. If you repeat those steps, I've found, rather than having it then become stale, simply going over those same facts every night and doing the same inner work actually deepens them.

I think that roles only get stale if you just keep on skirting the surface of them; if you just allow them to touch you the way they do but not doing anything to connect deeply with them. It's that connection between you and the character that makes it sing. When I'm in a long run my experience has been that when I get the clearest about the process, those transcendent moments become very reliable. I haven't really had the experience of having them not work for me. That's why Lee's work is so valuable. It's entirely reliable. Working that way is very hard, but it's consistent. If you pick a really good sense memory that stimulates you toward a particular effect, then whenever you do the work with the sense memory you will always get the same effect.[6]

*Vilga:*  Did you find that exercises like the sense memory work came naturally for you, or were they difficult?

**Burstyn:** Some of them seemed quite easy, while others were harder. That's very individual, and you can't say what you're going to respond to. It's like music—people respond to all different kinds. I'm not saying the work tells you that "Here are the rules, now simply follow them and you'll be an actress." It's just not like that. It's really about finding the ways to stimulate whatever talent you have. Some people don't have any talent to speak of, and some people have a lot of talent but no technique. They haven't found the right ways to stimulate their talent.

**Vilga:** Is the Strasberg work for everyone? Are there people for whom the sense memory exercises don't work?

**Burstyn:** I don't know anybody who does sense memory where it doesn't work at all. I know a lot of people who don't know how to do sense memory but they think they do. They take a stab at it and then say it doesn't work, because they're not really getting into it.

**Vilga:** Do you think that there is a certain amount of time one needs to really explore sense memories?

**Burstyn:** From the time of really getting into Lee's work to the point where I was really manifesting in my employment took me seven years. Lee said he felt that was pretty typical, which is pretty amazing.

**Vilga:** What did you think about working with Stella Adler?

**Burstyn:** She was remarkable. If I had taken that whole course, it probably would have been a better experience. Taking just one scene study class with her, it wasn't all that it could have been. For me personally, I would consider Strasberg the acting teacher of the century.

He had a theater mind, and he was a philosopher. What you learned from Lee was not just a part of acting; he really sent down a depth charge through your entire being. Working with him really introduced you to your own depths. He was also a great theater historian.

**Vilga:** Do you have anything to say about the criticisms that people level against Strasberg of dabbling too far into actors' psyches or crossing the line between acting training and therapy?

**Burstyn:** I never experienced that personally at all, and furthermore, I never saw it happen, and I studied with Lee for many, many years. I think people who criticize him for dabbling in people's psyches think that acting is a false face you can put on, that it's merely pretending, and you're supposed to keep all acting at the level of pretending. Lee was just about something else, something deeper and more real.

Yes, the psyche is involved in any creative act, but I never saw him abuse this. As a matter of fact, I saw him go out of his way to keep the dialogue between himself and the person who was working in class always focused on acting. Now, it's true that all the time we use our relationships to our mother, our father, our dog, and that comes up, and he advocated using it because that's what made it personal. Yet when an actor started taking things into areas that were needful of therapy, I always saw him pull the conversation back to acting.

*Vilga:* Did he ever push people too far?

*Burstyn:* I never saw it. He sometimes pushed people to discover emotionally where they didn't want to go, and then he could get very demanding. Yet I was always so grateful for every word he ever said to me, because it was the best penetration of my defenses, defenses which I wanted penetrated. If somebody wanted to protect their cover story, then they were definitely in the wrong class.

*Vilga:* I attended Stella Adler's last master class, and I was really amazed at her ability to point to the fatal flaw in a scene. When something was not quite right, she would just be able to uncover with razor-sharp accuracy what was not truthful about the work.

*Burstyn:* Yes. You do develop that technique after looking at enough scenes. It's easy to see, too, when an actor is largely connected to the material, to spot when he's disconnected. If you go to those moments of disconnection, you'll find out why the disconnection happens.

*Vilga:* Are you teaching now?

*Burstyn:* I've taught at the Studio for years, and I still do occasionally, but I'm doing my own classes nearby, on Eighth Avenue. I'm just doing a month class whenever I have a free month. I put together a class and put an ad in the paper and get a group together and do a class to work on whatever I'm doing. I work with Jean Huston. She's a psychiatrist and a philosopher and teacher. I do a synthesis of a lot of different work—Lee's, for example—and I keep the class examining acting as a spiritual inquiry. I try to help the actors get to their depth, just as I was saying about Lee. It may have always been that way, but I notice it a lot now that so many actors are really only interested in getting a job. They only study so they can take classes for tips about giving good auditions and that kind of job-oriented thing.

For me, acting is almost a spiritual discipline. First of all, the visualizations and meditations resemble spiritual techniques, which stem from what acting originally was; the original actors were priests and priestesses in the temples. For the real actor, I think it's a spiritual calling. I don't see it being talked about much anymore, but I think many good actors experience their art that way.

What the actor studies is the human being. Think of all the different facets and sciences that surround understanding what it is to be human. That's why the study of acting is so fascinating and why it takes so long to learn it. An actor examines the question of identity and the task of isolating the various personas in an individual. There are a lot of different people in each of us. Identity always seems to me to be an integration of a gang. We all move our consciousness around inside of us into all these different composite people that we are. The actor must learn how to move that consciousness out farther than other people.

**Vilga:**   How else do you work?

**Burstyn:**   I'm very interested in mind-body connections with artists. There's a writer who is also a musician who wrote about what goes on in the mind of the jazz pianist when he's improvising.[7] It's his theory that the mind of the jazz pianist is in the hands, not the brain. He believes that the mind is located throughout the body, as well as the brain. Certainly I've experienced that. For instance, I have a friend who is a concert pianist, and he said to me one time after he had learned a piece, "I've got it in my hands right now." That's where the memory was for him: in his hands. I noticed that when I'm learning a script, if I just sit down and try and memorize it off the page, it doesn't go in very well. The moment we get up and do the moves and the blocking, all the lines go in because I feel them in my body.

There's mind everywhere, and you can feel that when you're acting. It's one reason exercises for sense memory work, because you activate mind throughout your body. That's kinesthesia. If you are a kinesthetic kind of person like I am, I get things and I understand things more with my body than I do with my intellectual capacity.

One time I had the experience of doing a play with an actor who froze, who went completely and totally blank and couldn't remember a line. I had to do the whole play playing both parts. I would say, "I suppose you want to tell me about . . . " and then I'd answer him. As the play progressed with him not saying one word, me saying all the lines, he still made all the physical moves we'd staged. He went to the piano when he was supposed to, and when I said his name he stood up on cue. He forgot all his lines, but he retained all of the blocking. There were two different kinds of minds at work there; two different brains, or maybe halves of the same brain. Whatever it was, one thing went and the other thing was still active. He was in an absolute trance.

**Vilga:**   Did he recover?

**Burstyn:**   It was a very heavy play in terms of lines, and he had memorized them all in around two weeks. We opened, and it was about his third performance when he froze. Afterwards he just said, "Oh my God. This has never happened to me before. I don't know how this could have happened." Rightfully, he came back after he got really rested, and then at the beginning of the next week he was fine. He never had the problem again.

*Vilga:* Have you found that the training required for film and stage is different?

*Burstyn:* The basic work is the same inner work. Of course, in film you act a lot more with your own close-ups through your face. On the stage, you have to act with your whole body. But the character building that you're doing of emotional states and the kind of revelation that you're working for is the same.

*Vilga:* What about various training for things like commercials and cold readings?

*Burstyn:* Well, I guess some people need them. It's certainly not the most important thing. The most important thing is learning how to do the emotional work, and that takes real effort and real time. I wouldn't waste my time doing those other things, but of course some people might really need them.

*Vilga:* Many actors do seem much more concerned about getting jobs than about their artistic growth.

*Burstyn:* Yes, and I think that's the problem. They should find where the priorities are. Their greatest concern should be in getting to the deep level of work. Jobs would follow after that, rather than trying to go out and get jobs first.

*Vilga:* Do you have any recommendations about how one would select a teacher?

*Burstyn:* When I started studying there was Stella Adler, there was Lee Strasberg, there was Bobby Lewis, and there was Sandy Meisner. There were a lot of great teachers around, but we're not in the same situation today.

It might be wise to ask other actors if they are inspired and excited by their teachers, then sit in on those classes and observe them firsthand. Of course, you can't always tell everything by observing. When I first went to the Studio I thought that they were all nuts. I thought I was in the loony bin. I remember as I sat in on a class I thought, "These people are completely off the wall." Lee made me promise when I signed up—they made everybody promise—to stick with it for six months before dropping out. He said, "It'll take you that long to get it," and he was right. Actually it wasn't six months, it was about six weeks, but my first superficial impressions about the work were totally wrong.

*Vilga:* Is there anything else that I haven't asked you that springs to mind?

*Burstyn:* I think that it's that the art form itself that's suffering. For example, the scheduling that goes on with television shows is really destructive to the actor's growth. I've just been appalled that for the last two shows that I've done, no time was taken with the performers, and whatever gets done without a mike drifting into the shot gets printed. I think the level of acting in general isn't as deep as it has been, and we are being satisfied with less. Now when somebody does just a little something more, it looks awfully good and they get an award for it. I think there's a real danger of a kind of cheapening of standards.

*Vilga:* Do you think that actors aren't up to standard, or it is just the conditions they're working under?

*Burstyn:* Both. I think that we don't have the teachers that we had, and I think that the amount of money that's being allotted to film production doesn't allow for rehearsal or for care being taken. I think because of a lot of mercenary considerations sacrifices are made, and those are causing the art of acting to be dishonored. That's why it's so wonderful when you see something good in regional theaters where they've taken the time to go through the rehearsal process, and they have backing and support from their audience, so that they can risk a little more.

*Vilga:* What do you think about theater in New York?

*Burstyn:* I just had a really bad experience where we had a play that everybody connected with, believed in, and thought was a really high-quality work. We came into New York playing our previews for two and a half weeks with the audiences being wildly enthusiastic. We built a production that we were very proud of and felt very confident in, and the reviewers just cut us off at the knees. We only had three more performances after we opened, and every performance ended in a standing ovation. The audience was standing out in the street, and people were coming backstage in tears saying, "Why is the show closing? I haven't seen this kind of work in a long time." It's hard for me to understand what the reviewers have in mind when they kill a production like that with savage reviews.

*Vilga:* It often feels like they are reviewing criminals.

*Burstyn:* Exactly, except the press usually don't review criminals so harshly. They're supposed to protect their rights. They call them "alleged rapists."

***Vilga:*** Do you think reviewers have more power these days?

***Burstyn:*** Yes. Look at the time of Sarah Bernhardt.[8] When they mounted the play in her theater, word of mouth would spread. People heard that it was one of Bernhardt's better performances, and so the audience came. Now we don't have that situation; you have to be an instant success or you're doomed.

***Vilga:*** If you had one piece of advice to give to young actors, what would you tell them?

***Burstyn:*** To get into a good class and to study and to never stop studying. Even if you don't have immediate employment, you have to be working all the time on acting. You can't just expect to act when you're lucky enough to get hired. That would be like a concert pianist only playing the piano when he had booked a concert tour. I think that's really the most important thing; if you're an actor, you must constantly be working on your craft. You must never stop developing and perfecting your talents as an artist.

# *Robert Falls*

*Photo: Suzanne Plunkett*

*Robert Falls has been the artistic director of Chicago's Goodman Theatre since 1986, after serving in that capacity at Wisdom Bridge Theatre from 1977 to 1985. The recipient of numerous Joseph Jefferson Awards during his eighteen-year career as one of Chicago's preeminent theater artists, Falls accepted the 1992 Special Tony Award for Outstanding Regional Theatre on behalf of the Goodman. He received a 1995 Obie Award for his direction of Eric Bogosian's subUrbia at Lincoln Center Theater, and his production of Tennessee Williams's The Rose Tattoo at Circle in the Square was nominated for a 1995 Tony Award as Outstanding Revival of a Drama. Falls is a past board president of Theatre Communications Group, the national organization of nonprofit professional theaters in America.*

*Falls's directing credits at the Goodman also include a major revival of* Pal

Joey, *world premiere productions of Steve Tesich's* The Speed of Darkness *and* On the Open Road, *John Guare's* Landscape of the Body, The Tempest, Galileo, The Misanthrope *set in contemporary Hollywood, and Nicky Silver's* The Food Chain. *He has also directed the American premiere of David Hare and Howard Benton's* Pravda *at the Guthrie Theatre, John Olive's* Standing on My Knees *at the Manhattan Theatre Club, and the national tour of* Orchards, *an evening of Chekhov stories adapted for the stage by such well-known playwrights as David Mamet, Wendy Wasserstein, Spalding Gray, and John Guare.*

●——————————————————————————●

**Vilga:** How did you begin to work with actors?

**Falls:** I originally began as an actor. Certainly when I was in college at the University of Illinois that's what I was studying. In my senior year in college I met a man, a teacher named Edward Kaye-Martin, who became a real mentor of mine. He was certainly the most brilliant acting teacher I had ever seen working. I continued studying acting rather extensively with him in Chicago, and then I followed him to New York, where I studied privately with him. Early on I discovered that I was probably much better as a director than I was ever going to be as an actor.

My directing career began in the seventies, and ultimately I became the artistic director of two prominent theaters here in Chicago—one the Wisdom Bridge Theatre, where I actually did begin a training center for Chicago actors that has since split and become two different training centers, which are still operating here in Chicago. One's called the Actors Center, and the other's called the Training Center. They are probably the two principal acting workshops in Chicago. In 1986, I became artistic director at the Goodman Theatre. My career has been predominately as a director, but obviously I have a strong interest in the actor's art.

**Vilga:** What made you move from acting to directing?

**Falls:** I found that the muscles required for acting are very different than the muscles required for directing. They are two very different things. It became increasingly difficult for me to shift gears from acting to directing. Ultimately I just felt that directing was the area that I was going to have more success in.

**Vilga:** Could you elaborate on the specific muscles that the actor needs?

**Falls:** I think that the key to acting is letting go of the third eye of watching yourself. It's existing very spontaneously within the moment onstage and letting yourself respond emotionally within any given moment instinctively. Those things are obviously very different than the director's craft. The director must watch, analyze, be looking at and thinking about the effect that everything is having on an audience. I don't think that actors necessarily should be thinking about the effect they're going to be having on an audience when they're acting.

*Vilga:* Are they ignoring the audience or just latently aware of the audience?

*Falls:* No, I don't think it's ignoring the audience at all. I think that one has to allow the audience in. One doesn't close off and start acting away from an audience. It's allowing the audience's energy to be a part of the performance, but it's still concentrating and living within the moment with that particular actor onstage.

*Vilga:* Is this a Meisner-based approach?

*Falls:* Yes, very much so. My own study of acting was very much in a Sanford Meisner tradition.

*Vilga:* Is that what Mr. Kaye-Martin was doing?

*Falls:* Yes, it was. Over the years, he developed his own style, but first he had trained with Sandy and then worked a lot with John Cassavetes in some of his early workshops.[1] That was his background, and that was the background that was passed on to me, which I found very useful. Even so, as a director, I found that one lets go of one's attachment to any particular training, because you have to work with so many different actors.

*Vilga:* How do you work with actors of different backgrounds? Do you allow them to work individually?

*Falls:* Absolutely. It doesn't make any sense to homogenize the acting process. The thing that I've discovered over the years is that acting is rather mysterious in the fact that so many people can be so good at it and have completely different approaches to it. When you're working on a play, part of forming an ensemble is to harness the energy and the backgrounds of all those actors who are coming from many different approaches and make it work onstage as a whole.

*Vilga:* Have you found one approach tends to make better actors, or does it really vary individual to individual?

*Falls:* It's pretty much individual to individual, I must say. I think I'm fairly flexible, as a director must be, to swing with whatever you're getting, but I tend to be attracted to actors who can speak the same vocabulary I do. Fundamentally my job is not to teach anybody acting nor to pound a method into anybody. My job is to make a play work. That's very different than teaching acting.

I have my preferences. I love actors who speak the same language I do. I hate actors saying, "The character would do this, the character would do that." I have an instant empathy for actors who are able to improvise emotionally, because that's the way I was trained. On the other hand, in recent years I've fallen in love with older actors who have none of the Method or Meisner-based approaches. I'm enthralled by great actors with the strong sense of craft and lots of tricks up their sleeves who have been in play after play for forty years. They are consummate professionals who approach performing in a wonderful way which is totally refreshing. It's absolutely great when you see an actor who can just come in and do a wonderful piece of shtick with a hat or who makes a big entrance that mesmerizes the audience.

Basically, over the years, I let go of a certain rigidity where I thought actors had to have a certain way of working to be good. In a way, they each have to create their own way of working. The actor that you have trouble with is an actor that has no method to their madness and just flounces around. Most actors who are worth their salt know what works for them, and they developed a personal approach to acting along the way.

**Vilga:** Do they ever have trouble working with each other if they have different approaches?

**Falls:** Yes, sometimes.

**Vilga:** Is there any easy way of resolving that, or do they just work it out?

**Falls:** They have to work it out. When you're working in the rehearsal room, generally there's a fair amount of respect that everybody gives everybody else. For example, I directed a production of Eugene O'Neill's *The Iceman Cometh,* which is just a great play for actors. In the course of one scene, I remember, there was one three-character scene with three actors onstage. On the one hand you had an actor who's an old pro in his seventies, who really was concerned with the hat and his entrance and how you get the hat bit working. Then you had another actor who truly needed an emotional memory and had to work himself up to the place where his character was. Then you had a third actor that was more Meisner trained who needed to use what he was getting from the other actors. There are three actors in a scene all of whom are working in completely different ways. A certain amount of patience and respect was required. I don't think those three actors ever particularly enjoyed working with each other, but they all had an actor's respect for the way the other person got it, and they all respected the fact that the other person onstage was a wonderful actor who came at it from an entirely different way than they did. It can be tricky, though.

*Vilga:* Have you ever come across training that you think is simply a waste of time?

*Falls:* So much of it depends on the actor. For example, I have worked on Shakespearean productions with actors who have been trained in a strict method, and it simply hasn't really worked. Ultimately, when you're dealing with a Shakespearean text, you have to deal with the words first and foremost. For example, I am not particularly an Anglophile, and I'm not particularly technically oriented when it comes to Shakespeare. Yet when I have worked with some actors—more in workshops than anything else—who come from a heavy Method approach, I find it simply doesn't work to explore the emotional life underneath a Shakespearean text that intensely first. I think an American actor can do Shakespeare better than anyone, because they can add the emotional work, but first you have to just trust to put the words out there properly.

*Vilga:* When you began the Chicago Training Center, was it because there was a lack of something in Chicago?

*Falls:* Yes. I felt there wasn't really a place in Chicago in the seventies where professional actors could continue to perfect their craft. Chicago has always been dominated by Northwestern and the Goodman/DePaul School of Drama, which were very good schools for young people. Also, the predominant Chicago training ground for actors has been the Second City, which is marvelous and very unique.[2] I firmly believe that Second City improvisational training in Chicago, which developed in the fifties parallel to the Actors Studio, is one of the key training grounds for acting in this country. There's this huge group of people that came out of Second City. Look at people like Mike Nichols and Elaine May and the whole improvisational comedy of Bill Murray and Dan Aykroyd and John Belushi. It was almost diametrically opposed to what was going on in New York at the time. It was an acting training ground that was completely aware of the audience, and it was completely improvisation based. Second City is a fascinating thing that has always dominated the Chicago landscape.

*Vilga:* What about university programs for actors?

*Falls:* Universities tend to be little fiefdoms, little domains of academics. You meet remarkable actors who come out of university programs, but at the same time there are things lacking. Until I met Edward Kaye-Martin, I was in a traditional university background, and there was no technique, no approach to acting. It was a very shallow, hit-or-miss training. I find that when I meet a lot of young actors, they tend to be the same way; that there's just not much going on in those programs. At the same time, life is the best teacher of acting. Again, some of the best actors I've ever met have no traditional university background in acting.

*Vilga:* Are there actors who can do it without training?

*Falls:* Yes. There are people who have the imagination and the emotional life and simply make the leap. Performers who have been doing it long enough so that it's just a natural thing. Viola Spolin, the grande dame that inspired Second City, sought to restore the childlike sense of play in actors.[3] I've encountered many an actor who on their own has maintained that sense of play and almost childlike attitude toward theater, which makes them marvelous actors without a shred of training.

*Vilga:* Do you think that anyone can be trained to act?

*Falls:* I don't believe in that at all. I don't think anybody can be trained to act. You can become a much better actor with training, but you have to have talent and imagination in the first place. Despite some of what I'm saying, and despite the fact that over my years as a director I've met many good actors who haven't had it, I'm a great believer in training. Anybody can say they're an actor. Whether they're hirable and whether anybody wants them to be in plays is an entirely different story.

*Vilga:* In an audition is it easy to spot talent? Can you tell that someone is a good actor based on a few minutes' work?

*Falls:* Yes. You can tell pretty quickly if someone's an okay actor, but you're always looking for somebody special. You're always looking for someone who makes a leap. I'll hold auditions for a play and I'll see two, three hundred people for five roles. Generally the people I'm seeing are good actors. I wouldn't be seeing them if they weren't. I wouldn't waste the time looking at bad actors. You're looking for somebody who brings a particular life to a role. Out of those couple hundred people, you'll always see a handful who just seem extraordinarily interesting. That has less to do, I think, frankly, with their training than it does with some innate specialness that they have.

*Vilga:* Some star charisma?

*Falls:* Yes. An extra charisma. It can be an energy. It can be a sexuality. It could be a sense of humor. It could be just something which sets them apart from the group. I don't think it's something that was trained.

*Vilga:* Should actors be concerned with their type?

*Falls:* Absolutely. I think an actor has to know what type they are. It doesn't mean that they can't transcend that, but by and large most casting is typecasting. If you have a very short time to make an impression with a casting director or an agent or producer or director, they're going to be looking at you in terms of a particular type. You might as well know who you are and what you are. I think there's a certain amount of marketing yourself that you have to do.

*Vilga:*  How would somebody get to audition at the Goodman? Are they only sent through agents or casting directors?

*Falls:*  No. We do a wide variety of casting. I have a casting director here at the theater. It's a small but vibrant community. In the course of the year, we will see basically anybody that wants to audition for the Goodman in open calls. I tend to only see people for particular plays, and the casting director generally weeds through them toward the interesting people she thinks I would like to see. We see people from agent recommendations or people that we know. We actively follow the theater scene here.

*Vilga:*  My sense is that the regional theaters are prospering more than the theater in New York. Is that true?

*Falls:*  Well, I'm not sure about all regional theaters, but it's very exciting here in Chicago.

*Vilga:*  Why is that, especially versus it being a difficult time in New York?

*Falls:*  Chicago is a unique community. There's just been an extraordinary amount of actors of great stature and talent who've come out of Chicago in the past ten years. There's an openness and a freshness and a vibrancy to Chicago which is unique. There's a lot of reasons for it, but we at the Goodman Theatre, as well as numerous other theaters, know who we are and we know what we do. There's a certain clarity to it. New York, for example, is extremely complicated right now. A lot of it is economically based, and that means it's often harder for young actors to break through.

I don't think it's possible to say any longer that the finest actors live in New York. Actually I think the finest actors generally live in Los Angeles. They've migrated there. I'm getting ready to cast a new play, and it's probably going to go to New York, but I'm not even bothering with having a casting call in New York. I'm going straight to Los Angeles first.

*Vilga:*  Are these actors in Los Angeles for film and TV?

*Falls:*  Yes. Only for film and television, which doesn't mean that they're any less gifted actors. It just simply means that the economics are such that actors can't afford to live in New York City anymore, and so an actor has to move to Los Angeles. It doesn't mean they wouldn't leave to do a wonderful role in a play, but they just have to base themselves in L.A. for economic reasons.

*Vilga:* Do you think that there is a significant difference between film and theater acting technique? Or do you think if an actor is well trained he or she can do either?

*Falls:* I actually do think that if an actor's well trained they can do either. On the other hand, I think they're very different things. It doesn't always mean that an actor who's extraordinarily successful in one medium's going to be successful in that other medium.

*Vilga:* How are they different?

*Falls:* The biggest single difference to me is that stage actors who are trained have a far better chance of working on film and television than actors who have only experienced film and television do in working in the theater. There are actors in film and television who are marvelous on film and television. What they're living for is the creation of that one perfect moment that is captured on film. All their energy and focusing go into that. In addition, they have the help of an editor and a cameraman and a lighting crew and the director and sometimes the composer all employed to preserve one perfect moment of performance on film.

To do it onstage, you have to be able to essentially do it by yourself. You must repeat it night after night while keeping it spontaneously fresh and alive. Now, that requires training. This doesn't mean that your average theater actor could be a great film star, but your average well-trained theater actor can certainly do film and television and go back and forth between the two. Whereas an actor who's only done film and television, the odds of them being able to carry off a play are very slim.

*Vilga:* You had mentioned earlier about how the Goodman does what it does and knows what it is. Can you elaborate on the specific character of your theater?

*Falls:* When I say that, I mean it's a nonprofit theater and what we basically are here for is for the art of the stage. What we do is we present to an audience a dialogue of new plays and classic works. We're constantly alternating between very interesting director-oriented productions of classical plays—like Shakespeare, Chekhov, Ibsen—and new plays.

*Vilga:* How many plays a year do you do?

*Falls:* We do about nine. Sometimes ten. Sometimes less. There is a very clear, defined personality to the work that we do. If you see it, you know it. It's different than what's in the commercial marketplace, which is just so hit or miss.

*Vilga:* What about the difficulties of actors trying to find work? Do you think that basically it's always been this way?

*Falls:* I think it's always been that way. It's a difficult life, but Chicago tends to provide fairly good opportunities for actors. It's still not as rich and generous as one will find in Los Angeles when one enters into that marketplace. Even so, one can find in Chicago the ability to do films, television, and commercial work and industrial work and voiceovers. Actors can support a life onstage. At the same time, money has always been low for actors. It's a low-paying profession except at the very top. When you break down the professional unions like Actors' Equity or SAG [Screen Actors Guild], you're looking at a few people on top with thousands at the very bottom. It's the same thing that Robert Anderson said about playwrights, and it's been often quoted: "It's a profession where you can make a killing but you can't make a living."

*Vilga:* When you direct a play, is there a traditional approach that you take in terms of preparing for it? Or does it vary work to work?

*Falls:* It varies work to work, but generally I like to spend a lot of time at a table, discussing the play with the company. It's also a way for me to get to know the actors, to get to know the way they think and the way they work.

*Vilga:* And then would you begin a rehearsal process after that point?

*Falls:* That is part of the rehearsal process. That launches you into getting on your feet and working the material. So yes, I have some similar things that I do, but a lot of it, too, is just to get to know the actor. I think as a director you have to instinctively psych out where that actor is coming from, what their background is, how they were trained or how they were not trained, and then go about creating a cohesive ensemble out of that.

*Vilga:* Do you ask them questions, or is this just something you have to sense?

*Falls:* You sense it, and quite often it becomes very clear. Often training is on their résumés, but it's clear to see from looking at their work what kind of actor they are.

*Vilga:* Is a good actor a piece of clay that can play anything?

*Falls:* I don't believe that any actor is a piece of clay or that they can play anything. I certainly am not interested in molding a piece of clay. What you're looking for is an actor who comes in with as much stuff as they can bring. That's very interesting as a director. The less work I have to do as a director, the better off I am.

There are directors who will maybe say, "Oh no, I prefer that piece of clay or that blank page," but that's generally an egomaniac who says that. The focus isn't on me, the director, here. The focus is on them. You're looking for an actor who brings as much experience, maturity, and train-ing, whether it is practical, on-the-job, or gained in a training experience.

***Vilga:*** Do you see common mistakes actors make at auditions?

***Falls:*** It's hard to make a generalization. Again, I look for actors who are themselves. Generally the work that I'm doing is not asking them to put on some wild character. Generally I'm looking for actors who bring an enor-mous personality and presence into the room with them and then are able to be simple, let it go and just be truthful.

***Vilga:*** Is there any acting that's particularly affected you or changed the way you thought about acting or directing?

***Falls:*** I can tell you one performance that totally changed my way of thinking about acting. Lots of performances have knocked me out, but I can vividly remember the actress Shirley Knight.[4] Shirley Knight was appearing in a play many years ago in Chicago by John Guare called *Landscape of the Body.* It was one of the finest productions I've ever seen and also one of the greatest performances I've ever seen.

Shirley Knight was playing a woman who was accused of decapitating her son in a brutal murder. She was being interrogated by F. Murray Abraham, another wonderful actor.[5] I remember the scene vividly. F. Mur-ray Abraham was bearing down on her, screaming at her, "I know you did it! I know you did it! Why don't you confess?" She just sat there without moving a muscle, just tears rolling down her face. It was so simple and it was so moving. She kept saying, "I don't know what you're talking about. Why are you saying these things to me? You can't say these things to me."

That was the scene, and it was just tremendously affecting. I went back the next night because I was so knocked out by that play. The next night, that scene began again. F. Murray Abraham started to bear down on her, screaming at her and saying these horrible things. Suddenly, she just stood up. She went from this total stillness, and she overturned the table, and she started yelling back at him. She played the scene in a completely different way than she had the night before.

Now, I was overwhelmed by this. As a director I had never realized the freedom that an actor had. Shirley Knight was completely truthful and completely honest on both nights. The scene took on a completely different life but had absolutely the same meaning. Both were true to the play and true to Shirley Knight and what she was feeling.

Now, I'm sure this was probably very upsetting to F. Murray Abraham, and this is not necessarily something that most directors or other actors would approve of, but it changed my thinking about the theater. It allowed me to look at a play in an entirely different way. I saw that, yes indeed, an actor can play a scene in a completely different way from night to night as long as they're being honest and truthful within it.

*Vilga:* Is that something you encourage performers to do? It sounds remarkable but also enormously difficult to sustain a production like that.

*Falls:* It is difficult. Sometimes I do, and sometimes I don't. If I sense the two actors onstage have the ability to do it, I will encourage it in certain plays. It's very tricky. I directed a production of *Hamlet* with Aidan Quinn. He was playing Hamlet to another wonderful actress here in Chicago who was playing Ophelia. The two of them got along fabulously; they had a great rapport. In the nunnery scene, the only way to keep that scene fresh from night to night was to let them emotionally improvise it. So every night that particular scene was rather different. Only in that particular scene did I let them do whatever they wanted to do with it. In the rest of the four-hour production of *Hamlet*, there were many moments that were rather rigid and the same. This one was fresh from night to night.

*Vilga:* What's the most interesting or meaningful thing to you about directing? What keeps you doing it?

*Falls:* The most meaningful thing for me is the ability to continually look at classical material as it takes on a new meaning in terms of the times that we live in. I can direct a production of *Hamlet* or a production of *Mother Courage and Her Children* by Brecht or Molière's *Misanthrope* and what's exciting is how contemporary these plays are for exactly the way we live right now. Finding those analogies when working with a cast and an audience is tremendously stimulating and rewarding.

*Vilga:* Do you think that people in the theater have a social responsibility as artists?

*Falls:* Absolutely. We have a responsibility to tell the truth. We're surrounded by such bullshit and liars in the government and in our media. Every aspect of our society is so filled with deception and dishonesty that I think that the actor and the director and the writer have the absolute responsibility to tell the truth. Anything else is morally corrupt. The pursuit of truth, of a true moment, or the pursuit of telling the truth of the way people live, the way they behave, the way they feel, is an extraordinarily valuable and courageous thing to do.

*Vilga:* How common are the moments when you really feel you've gotten to the truth?

*Falls:* It's rare. It's not an everyday thing. But when it happens, that's what the theater's all about.

*Vilga:*  Is there an example that springs to mind of when it has happened?

*Falls:*  It happens more often than you would think. I see it happen all the time, maybe not in the course of an entire play, but in the course of a scene, where there's just this absolute truth that's told.

*Vilga:*  Is it something that you can control, or does it just happens on its own?

*Falls:*  Most things in life are not particularly controllable. I think one of the great things about plays and working with actors is that you have an attempt to make some order out of chaos, as opposed to life, where you can't.

*Vilga:*  If you had one piece of advice to give to an aspiring young actor, what would you tell him or her?

*Falls:*  I would say: just live life. It may sound like bullshit, but that's my honest advice. Don't live only in the theater. Let life happen to you. I think that one has to try to work as hard as one can to open up as a human being before one can open up as an actor. I think actors just have to allow life in, and allow the pains and joy of life to register, and stay as vulnerable and as in touch with that as they can. I think it's a tough thing, because you are forced so often to harden and toughen up, especially difficult because acting is such a vulnerable profession. Really great actors are the ones that somehow have remained the most vulnerable or the most angry or what-ever was most organically true to themselves.

I'll give you two examples. First, Aidan Quinn. One of the reasons he's so remarkable is because he has remained very open. There's a vul-nerability to him that's not mushy or soft or anything like that. It's a sensitivity to life's experience that he's able to allow into his work, and it makes for a very exciting actor. On the other hand you see an actor like George C. Scott, who I think is one of the great actors of our time. What fuels him is an incredible anger, which is very exciting in an actor.

We all live a life where we are so afraid to feel things that we go to the theater to see actors feeling it. They're going to be our releases of all the hidden emotions and things that we have trouble with: fear, sex, sen-sitivity, anger. The actors that can really get there are the ones that we like a lot, because that opens up something in us that's hard to deal with in life.

*Vilga:*  How important is luck in the career of an actor?

*Falls:*  I think luck is fairly important in the career of anybody, but I don't even know if success is really about luck. It's more the ability to recognize an opportunity and to go with that. There are people who just know who they are and what they're all about and can promote that effectively.

**Vilga:** Then do you think that if an actor is well trained and talented, he or she can have a good career?

**Falls:** They may take a while to find their venue and find their right place, but yes, they do have a very good shot at doing work which satisfies them as artists. Ultimately, if they can do that and sustain a real and satisfying personal life, it allows for an extraordinary and unique journey.

# *Marilyn Fried*

Photo: Deborah Feingold

*As an acting coach, Marilyn Fried has worked with starring and supporting actors on more than two hundred films, many of them Academy Award winners. These include* Annie Hall, Interiors, Reds, Baby Boom, Manhattan Murder Mystery, Marvin's Room, Desperately Seeking Susan, The First Wives Club, The Little Drummer Girl, Robocop, Hester Street, The Good Mother, Hannah and Her Sisters, Goodfellas, Father of the Bride, Godfather I, II, *and* III, The Basketball Diaries, Jane Eyre, Bookworm, The Mirror Has Two Faces, Star Wars, The Empire Strikes Back, *and* Gorillas in the Mist. *Fried has also coached actors for both television and theater toward many Emmy- and Tony-winning performances. Fried has taught acting privately for more than fifteen years as well as at workshops with the New School for Social Research.*

*Vilga:* How did you come to work with actors?

*Fried:* I began as an actress myself. I studied with Peggy Feury, my first acting teacher, and then Lee Strasberg.[1] I worked with Lee for about seven years privately, then I auditioned for the Actors Studio and got in. I started working on Broadway shows in the wardrobe department and became friends with some of the chorus people in the shows. I began showing them the sensory exercise work that we did in the private classes with Lee. Everybody became so fascinated with it that during the matinees, instead of going out to eat, we would go down in the basement, and we would do the relaxation exercises and the sensory exercises. We all had a wonderful time. Ten people from the chorus would come downstairs and then we'd work. I wasn't taking any money for it until somebody said, "Why don't you really start teaching?" Somebody let me work in their apartment, and I began to teach professionally. Then I got a studio, and it began to grow from there.

*Vilga:* Why did you become a full-time teacher as opposed to pursuing acting?

*Fried:* I really liked the idea of giving back the work that I had gotten from Lee Strasberg. He was my mentor and, to me, a genius. An absolute genius. His guidance of the actor is what made him great, his guidance and his vision. It was about tuning an actor's instrument, so they have a technique and craft. That's the most important thing: an actor trains and trains and then goes out and does it. Lee used to talk about Vladimir Horowitz, who would practice a passage on the piano for hours and hours before he would actually go and play the concerto. It's the same type of thing with these exercises that Lee developed. This whole sensory work tunes the actor's instrument like a Stradivarius. Giving back that kind of work to actors is really what's most creative and exciting for me.

*Vilga:* What is the class you teach now like? Is it based on these exact same Strasberg exercises?

*Fried:* Absolutely. The foundation of the work is the sensory exercises and the relaxation. Then we take a break, and after that we do scenes. We do audition material. We do monologues. If no one's prepared we do something that's called the song-and-dance exercise—which has nothing to do with singing or dancing. It's all on behalf of tuning the instrument, which is very important.

*Vilga:* How long do people attend classes?

*Fried:* It's at least two or three years. Lee felt it took seven years before you were ready to use the technique professionally. I think it's somewhere in between. I think you can go to class for a while, then try and audition and see if you can successfully take the work out with you. At the very beginning when you first come into class and you're not really a professional actor, I think the training should be the absolute focus. Now, in the theater and in film and television, everybody is in a hurry to make it big. They don't have time for the training. They don't have time to build the foundation and to get the tools they need. Without the tools they may do a film or two, but they won't last. It's impossible, especially if you do theater. You simply need tools in order to work well over time as an actor.

**Vilga:** Is there a certain amount of time that you think is generally required to give an actor this foundation, or does it vary from person to person?

**Fried:** I think it varies from person to person. I think people can start studying and maybe two or three years later they're ready because the commitment to the work is strongly present. Basically it's the commitment to this kind of work; if you're committed 150 percent to the work, then you might progress quite rapidly, but then again each individual is different.

**Vilga:** Do people audition for your classes?

**Fried:** No. There's no need to audition. There are people who've been in class maybe three or four years, and then I'll let somebody in who has no training whatsoever. What's exciting about someone with no training is you have somebody who doesn't have any technique that's faulty. You say, "Let's start with the first exercise," and then they begin to tune their instrument properly. When you have somebody who has been trained deeply in another kind of work and they come to you and say, "I know there's something missing," you have to untrain them first. Once again you've got to say, "Let's start now from the beginning," but it's often much harder. It can be much more exciting when you have somebody who's never been trained. It's exciting because sometimes you see the growth almost immediately, because this work is based on commitment and layman's logic.

**Vilga:** Can you define layman's logic here?

**Fried:** Lee used to say, "Acting is layman's logic: doing things logically moment to moment to moment." That's the way an actor has to work. An actor has to work moment to moment to moment. A director is the one that says, "I need this (*snaps fingers*) and I want this now." The director is always asking for results. The actor can't work in result terms. He has to work moment to moment to moment. It's not about getting up and bounding out the door. It's realizing that before I get up, I open my eyes, and then I work moment to moment to get out of bed, to walk to the kitchen, to get the cup of coffee, then to get dressed, then to find the keys, all before I can walk out the door. An actor must work with that type of moment-to-moment awareness.

And it's about having the right tools at your disposal. Say a plumber comes into your apartment because you have a leak in the sink. You say to the plumber, "The bathroom sink's been leaking, and I can't stop it." He turns to you and he says, "Well, I can't fix it," and you say, "Why not?" and he says, "I don't have my tools." So you say, "What are you here for? If you don't have your tools, of course you can't fix the leak." It's the same thing with actors. If you don't have your tools, you're not going to be an actor. If you don't have your tools, you're not going to be a ballerina. If you don't have your tools, you're not going to be an athlete or a concert pianist or a painter. It's based on the commitment to the work and having developed the right tools for the job.

**Vilga:** Do you advise people in terms of other training besides the Method they might need as tools for their work?

**Fried:** Sure. For example, I think voice production is very important. They may want to take singing. They may want to take dance. They may want to take tai chi. All those things are valuable on behalf of tuning your instrument, but they're not what I teach.

**Vilga:** Do you think that any person in the class can become an actor if he or she does the work and is committed to it?

**Fried:** I totally believe that everyone has talent; it's what you do with the talent that counts. You talk about somebody like Pete Rose. Pete Rose was not a great athlete at all. He was somebody who was determined to be a great athlete. He worked at it. He committed himself. The love and the passion that he had for playing baseball is exactly what you need for acting. You need passion to be a ballerina. You need passion to be an athlete. You need passion to be in any of the arts. Unless you say, "I'll just do it no matter what," it's "Maybe I will . . . maybe I won't." That's not passion. You should be in another field.

You've got to have that kind of need. You've got to be hungry enough to say, "I can't live unless I have it. I can't live unless I do something creative, unless I act or paint or direct." You need that kind of passion in this business because it's so full of rejection. You wake up in the morning and you go out to your first audition and you're immediately rejected. Even if you get a callback, you'll be rejected if the chemistry's not right. Or "He's too tall" or "She's too short." Or "The blue eyes don't match the brown hair" or some other utterly superficial reason entirely unrelated to how talented you are. You really have to be centered within yourself, and you have to have that need and that hunger and that drive and that passion;

otherwise you fall by the wayside. You have to accept that this is a business based on rejection.

**Vilga:**  Can you define the need you spoke of more precisely?

**Fried:**  I think it varies person to person. It would be limiting to say that people who come from a certain social status don't have that hunger, but I do find that actors who come from humble means sometimes seem to have more of a drive or a need. Or if something happened to them as a child and they're psychologically cut off, they may want a form of expression, and the arts seem to be it for them, whether it's painting, acting, or music. I don't want to say that people who come from well-to-do families can't be great actors. That's too general a statement. But I do find that more often than not, it's people who are without means, financial or otherwise, people who are able to say, "I desperately want and need to express myself," who are usually more likely to succeed.

It's such a very tough career. I watch ice skaters like Nancy Kerrigan. Talk about people who are committed! From the age of four or five, they spend five and six hours on the ice, practicing every day. That is the kind of dedication and passion I think one needs to be a great artist. For me, we have today one of the greatest artists in Al Pacino. He's an artist with a total commitment to a craft and to a way of working. His mentor is also Lee Strasberg. Earlier we had Brando and we had Jimmy Dean. They had that passion, drive, and need. That's what I find lacking now. It's lacking when young actors say, "I got to get out there and make it fast," but without the tuning and the foundation. There's no patience. They don't seem to have enough patience to say, "Let me get a craft. Let me be prepared so when that great part comes along, I'll be able to do it right. I won't suddenly panic and say, 'Oh my God, what do I do now?'"

**Vilga:**  Is there an age at which you think it's too early to start training this way?

**Fried:**  I think when Lee was alive, he never took anybody younger than seventeen or eighteen in his classes. This was because of the nature of the work and the experience of life you need. I think he felt that at eighteen or nineteen you could handle this kind of work, and I think he was absolutely right. Yet you can also start training in your forties or fifties, by the way, and as long as you still have that passion, you'll work. Without the passion, no.

**Vilga:**  Do you think that this type of training is for everyone? Is there anyone who it's not right for?

**Fried:**  No. Some people find they don't want to put the time in, because it does take time to really do it. Or they may not want to open themselves up and deal with that kind of vulnerability. There could be other kinds of training that would suit them better.

*Vilga:* Do you think that the Method works equally well for theater or film or TV?

*Fried:* Absolutely. I think both mediums suit this kind of work. I think as long as the work is personal and you have a craft, as an actor you make the necessary choices and minor adjustments.

I just came back from working in California on a pilot for a sitcom, which is very difficult and totally different from the way that actors want to work. You can't just delve into a character and break down scenes under those conditions. You don't have time for that, so you truly must have a craft at your fingertips. It's a sitcom, with laugh lines, and it may not be what you think is great art, but there is a real science to it. If you don't have a technique or any tools, you can't do it. It may look easy, but it's not, especially if you're coming from work in the theater, which has continuity, a continuous throughline. This is a sitcom. This is about hitting your marks, being funny on cue, and learning your lines very fast. You really have to have the right tools to do this well.

*Vilga:* You do a lot of coaching of actors. What would a typical assignment be? Is it an executive calling you up and saying, "You need to coach this person for this role"?

*Fried:* Yes.

*Vilga:* What kind of preparation time would you have for that?

*Fried:* On this sitcom, for example, we had very little time. We arrived on a Sunday, and everybody was on their feet on Tuesday, I promise you. On Friday, we had two audiences, one at 4:30 and one at 7:30. I've never worked that way in my life. It certainly gears you up to just do it under that schedule. Even learning the lines: that's a craft unto itself under conditions like these. Again, I work to make sure the actor understands the premise and the plot, what the scenes are about, and what his character wants in a scene. You make those choices, and then suddenly you find yourself filming in front of an audience.

*Vilga:* And you work with the actors to fine-tune all this?

*Fried:* Absolutely. There's an interaction where responses and ideas are thrown back and forth. Obviously, you have to stay in the same ballpark as the director. You can't just go off and do whatever you please. First you must find out what the director wants from the actor. At the rehearsals, you listen carefully to the director so that you know you're in the same ballpark. You take those notes and then begin to work on the part. If there's no director and, say, there's an audition to be done, then the sky's the limit. Then we have all kinds of options to explore.

*Vilga:*  When you're coaching someone, let's say for a movie audition, would it be someone without a solid foundation of technique?

*Fried:*  Sometimes. Sometimes the person doesn't have any technique at all. Sometimes the person looks a certain way, and the producer says, "Gee, that gal is perfect. She's beautiful. I need her for this part, but I've got to convince the studio." Then they'll send her to me. You begin to try to give her some kind of tools to work with. I'll ask what she or he thinks that the audition scene is about. You try to begin to use their imagination and try to give them as much as you can in the little time that you have, because they have the audition coming up in a week.

*Vilga:*  How satisfying are the results for you from this kind of work?

*Fried:*  Very. Especially when you work on a film and the person you're coaching gets an Academy Award and you took part in that creative process, or you're working on a theater piece and the person you've worked with gets a Tony, all of which has happened a number of times. There have been a lot of actors I've coached who've gotten Academy Awards and Tonys and Emmys. Carol Kane, two Emmys for *Taxi*. Carol was one of these very gifted people, and we've worked together for years. Another wonderful actress, Diane Keaton, is someone that I have worked with over many years. They are both extraordinary actresses.

   I also think one of the most important things as a coach is to stay out of their way. To help create and help pull out that creativity, but stay out of the way. That's perhaps the most important thing.

*Vilga:*  Why is that important?

*Fried:*  It's important to open up the actor's imagination. It's important to delve in and let that person work. I found that in working on Scorsese's *Goodfellas* with Lorraine Bracco, who also got nominated for an Oscar. It's important to let the actor begin to create and use his own muscles to come up with it. You're there to go back and forth and interact and then go back to the script and ask questions like "What do you want in this particular scene? What's happening to the relationship here?" Then the actor's imagination begins to work. Once the imagination gets stimulated, it should come organically from the actor rather than being pulled from the coach.

*Vilga:*  Do you find that there are people you simply cannot help?

*Fried:*  No. I've never met anyone like that. As I say, everybody's talented. Everybody has an imagination. It has to be stimulated. It has to be used. I really believe we use about a quarter of ourselves in life. We really don't use our instrument as fully as possible. I think once you begin to stimulate another person, they get excited. Then suddenly they start taking off, and you take off with them, and you suddenly say, "Wow, isn't this great!" That's what's exciting.

*Vilga:* How do you incorporate the sensory work with the scene work?

*Fried:* We want to teach how to use the sensory work in the scene. That's very important. You cannot isolate sensory work. You've got to know that sensory work is a tool, and you've got to know how to use it. You try to show the actor that he can bring it into the scene work by making choices. If the scene calls for you to be drunk, there are certain tools that we have that the actor can choose to use. If the scene calls for an actor to be emotional and break down, there are certain tools that we have in the sensory work that you can call on. If he doesn't need that stimulus and he can go at it another way, or do it spontaneously, terrific. But if he needs it, then we have the tools that he can call on.

*Vilga:* Are there people who can just go to that place spontaneously?

*Fried:* Sure, there are some people who can, but then again, it dries up, and it's always better to have a reliable tool. If you're doing a long-running Broadway show, and it's a dramatic show, and it calls for you to cry every night on a certain cue, I think it's important to have a tool that you can count on. When a certain sensory choice dries up, if you have a craft, you can call on something else and get the same results.

*Vilga:* Have you found that with the right tools an actor can always just cry on cue?

*Fried:* Absolutely. If the director says on page 16 the person has to have an emotional breakdown in the scene, you start your work on page 14. You can begin working on that, so that by the time you get to page 16 as an actor, (*snaps fingers*) you can do it. Absolutely.

*Vilga:* What do you think about the general standard of acting in recent years? Do you think it's gone down or stayed the same?

*Fried:* I think the level of the work has gone down. Fewer really interesting new plays are done each year. In the time that I was growing up, we had Tennessee Williams and Arthur Miller—there's still Sam Shepard, who's a wonderful playwright—but all of those playwrights were writing for Broadway. Now it's too expensive. You can't do a dramatic Broadway show. It would cost you four million dollars. Neil Simon was going to do an Off-Broadway show, which is wonderful. Then maybe we can get the playwrights to say, "All right, let's do it Off-Broadway," and give actors a chance to really get their teeth into something. I love musicals, but

I think there's a place for us to have the theater that I miss and praise. That theater just doesn't seem to exist in New York. And as I said before, I think the level of the work has gone down because, I think, actors are too much in a rush to make it, whatever "making it" even means. Since they're in this rush, they're not trained properly, so you can't even get the kind of high standard of work great theater requires.

*Vilga:* Have you altered Lee Strasberg's work or modified it?

*Fried:* No, no, no. I'm not that imaginative. I only do Lee's work. All the relaxation, the sensory work, the scene work, the song-and-dance exercise. Again, all on behalf of tuning the instrument, making the actor's instrument a Stradivarius. That's what the work is about.

*Vilga:* Is there a point at which you tell students that they're ready and they should be out of the class?

*Fried:* No. It's up to each individual. Everyone knows when the time is right to leave. Organically they know. They start saying, "Let me see if I can take this work and go out in the real world and use it." I always tell them, "Go," because they know it's time. All of a sudden they get a callback and they go, "Holy Cow! All this training really works!" They may still come to class, but now they're beginning to use the work out in the real world. They're beginning to see that it's a tool they possess. And if they have their tools, they will get a callback, and then they'll get a second callback, and then maybe they'll get a job.

*Vilga:* What about the various criticisms of Strasberg and the work he did?

*Fried:* Lee was not an easy man. He demanded of you what was best for you. He wanted you to challenge yourself. A lot of people didn't like that. A lot of people said, "Well, this is fine." Lee would always say, "It's not fine. You can do better." Some people took offense at this. For me, I would not have tools, I would not be in the position that I'm in now, if it hadn't been for Lee Strasberg. It's as simple as that. Yes, he was demanding. Yes, he shouted. Yes, he did this and all of that stuff—but always on behalf of the actor. He was always trying to stretch the actor. He was always saying, "Do not accept mediocrity. Do not accept what is easy. You can go further. You must demand more of yourself. You must challenge yourself always."

*Vilga:* Do you think he ever went too far with pressing people emotionally?

*Fried:* No. Lee always said that if you had an emotional problem you should go to a therapist, go to a psychiatrist. There is a fine line which one as a teacher and a coach should never cross, but in my time with Lee I never saw him do that. If somebody had an emotional problem, he would always say, "Darling, I think you should see some professional. I am not the person. I'm not a psychiatrist." It was as simple as that.

**Vilga:** If someone needs to make a choice for a part and goes to something that's too painful, how do you avoid delving into dangerous territory?

**Fried:** You as a coach have to guide that. There's certain exercises that you could do to avoid that. As an artist, you should be able to have the tools to do the work. You're not working correctly if the choices you make overwhelm you.

**Vilga:** What do you think makes for a good teacher?

**Fried:** Guidance. Loving actors. Nurturing. Trying to be supportive and to guide them to what they can be.

**Vilga:** What's one of the things that surprised you most that you know now that you didn't know then?

**Fried:** I'm surprised when certain people that I have worked with have been full of doubt because they're not getting anywhere that we can see, until suddenly a light bulb goes on inside them. They begin to use the work properly, and it's like a duck taking to the water. It's breathtaking.

I remember sitting in Lee's class when I was there for, I would say, four and a half years. Going into the fifth year, it was like a light bulb went off in my head. I suddenly realized what he was talking about. So that's the surprise, when you see somebody that you're not quite sure about and suddenly things begin to happen. Their instrument begins to open up. They come to you and they say, "I felt it here, organically. It was different." Something in the voice is different, and the way they deal with themselves is different, and the way they carry themselves is different. There's a certain confidence that suddenly comes in. Those are the surprises, which are very exciting when you see them happen.

**Vilga:** What's the biggest frustration?

**Fried:** The biggest frustration is having people ask, "How long does this take?" You reply, "Remember: you have to be committed to the work." They say, "Okay, right, but how long before I'll be able to go out and be a star—six months . . . one year?" They think they should be able to run before they can crawl. That's very frustrating. Try to tell a young actor that they have to have patience, that they have to commit themselves to the work. They study for maybe a year, and then you find them studying with someone else, and if that's too slow they'll move on again. It's all because of their need to get out there and be successful without having the tools. That's very frustrating. You tell them, "Listen, you've got to train. You can't sit down and play a Beethoven sonata on the piano. Even though you want to, it's not going to happen. You've got to do the scales. You've got to practice at least three or four hours a day for years." "Years" are what people do not want to do now. That's the key here. It's like the sitcom, this mentality of "Let's do it and do it quick." That's the biggest frustration.

*Vilga:* How can you deal with the time when the work doesn't seem to be producing results?

*Fried:* You as the teacher and the coach need to know at this point in an actor's development what exercises will best stimulate him or her. If a certain exercise may not be working, you try another exercise to see if you can stimulate the actor another way. If they're stimulated in that exercise, then you might try a combination of the two. You as the teacher and the coach must have the vision to see where you're taking a student. You have to be able to use guidance to help the student develop their craft even when they feel frustrated with their progress.

*Vilga:* Can you avoid bad teachers as a student?

*Fried:* I don't know. Somebody called today and asked about studying with me. I asked if they had studied before, and they named somebody that I wasn't familiar with. I said, "Why didn't you continue with this person?" He said, "The teacher said he was not a big believer in technique." Well, this person had the awareness to notice there's something wrong, because he wanted to learn a technique in order to be an actor. He had the awareness to say, "Wait a minute, I think I better go somewhere else to get what I need." Whether young actors can always have that kind of awareness, I don't know. People can spend years with a bad teacher and not learn anything.

*Vilga:* Do you ever deal with practical parts of the actor's career, such as auditions and headshots?[2]

*Fried:* Yes, sometimes they'll bring in a headshot, and I'll look at it and say, "You know, I think you can do better." Or if somebody has an audition and gets a callback I say, "Wear exactly what you wore. Don't change anything."

*Vilga:* Why?

*Fried:* They called you back because they liked what they saw the first time. What you showed them was what they want to see again. Plus, it's always considered lucky, if you're the superstitious type. If you came in with one outfit, go back wearing that outfit exactly.

*Vilga:* Can you change your tie?

*Fried:* No, you can't even change your tie. Whatever you do, don't change the tie! Everything that you had on, just go back with that.

*Vilga:* Is there a common career mistake that you've seen actors making?

*Fried:* Again, it's the need to be successful immediately, even though I don't quite know what this means. Striving to be immediately successful is a mistake in the actor's thinking process. Yes, in terms of a career, when one gets to the stage of working with an agent or manager you have to make certain choices, like who to go with or not go with for representation and which scripts will further your career. These are individual choices, and they are always open for discussion, but to focus on career choices too early is a big mistake.

*Vilga:* If you had one piece of advice to give to the young actor, what would it be?

*Fried:* Develop your tools and craft and be patient. You must have a passion for this work. If you have no passion, you're in the wrong field. You really have to want it, because it's a business of total rejection.

*Vilga:* Is it fair to say that with a craft and a legitimate amount of luck you will succeed?

*Fried:* Yes. It's like anything else. If the scripts are right, if the auditions go well, if so-and-so is there to see you, if the director loves you, if the producer does—if all of those things happen. But you can't worry about that. You go in there and do the best audition that you know how, with the tools that you have, and then see what happens. Your main job as an actor is just to have the craft, the commitment, and the passion and let the rest of it take care of itself.

# *Spalding Gray*

Actor, performance artist, and writer Spalding Gray was born on June 5, 1941, in Providence, Rhode Island. He received his BA from Emerson College in 1965.

Gray made his stage debut at the Fryeburg Academy in 1965 for two performances of The Curious Savage. His Off-Broadway debut was as the King of May in Endicott and the Red Cross at the American Place Theatre in 1968. With Elizabeth LeCompte, Gray founded the Wooster Group in New York City in 1975.

Gray's principal stage roles include Hoss in The Tooth of Crime, Swiss Cheese in Mother Courage and Her Children, and the Bishop in The Balcony, all at the Performing Garage in New York City. Principal film appearances include the U.S. Consul in The Killing Fields, Earl Culver in

True Stories, *Peter Epstein in* Clara's Heart, *and Dr. Richard Milstein in* Beaches. *Gray has played himself in monologues such as* Sex and Death to the Age 14, India and After (America), Booze, Cars, and College Girls, Swimming to Cambodia *(stage and film),* The Terrors of Pleasure: The House, Monster in the Box *(stage and film),* Gray's Anatomy, *and* It's a Slippery Slope.

*Gray's awards include fellowships from the National Endowment for the Arts, the Rockefeller Foundation, and the Guggenheim Foundation, along with an Obie Award, an Edward Albee Foundation grant, and two Villager Awards.*

●————————————————————————————●

**Vilga:**   Let's begin by describing the work you do.

**Gray:**   Most recently I do a talk, actually, in colleges and other situations where I just get up with a microphone and then take questions. I've been trying to get it in shape. I also want to do a book, because it has been an odd route to get to where I am.

**Vilga:**   When did you realize you wanted to be a performer?

**Gray:**   I first realized I wanted to be an actor when I was in boarding school. By senior year I was in the senior play, and I was really not interested in anything else until that point. I was in the play, and that turned my head around. I was so sure that's what I wanted to do that I went to my guidance counselor and said I did not want to go to a liberal arts college, I wanted to go to a studio in New York to be an actor. He said, "What do you know about acting? You've been in one play. You've got to go to a liberal arts college." So I did. I went to Boston University and knew that I wanted to be in theater and tried to transfer into the BU fine arts program, but I didn't have enough background in theater, so I transferred to Emerson College in the second semester of 1961. That's where things worked for me. After my freshman year I was lucky enough to get cast in every play except for the musicals. Although my major was directing, I played small roles and big roles. I remember doing Alceste in *The Misanthrope.* I was doing a lot of scene work and acting and just doing it all the time. By the time I was a senior, in 1965, I was sure that I just wanted to go out and act in regional theaters, and never go to New York but be a professional actor playing the classics, in Chekhov and Shakespeare.

I was accepted at one of the best regional theaters in 1967 after I'd been doing some acting around in smaller theaters in New Hampshire and Northampton, Massachusetts, and Saratoga, New York. Of course that was 1967, and some theaters were starting to be affected by the 1960s consciousness and that more communal, group movement. I was reading more and more about such experiments in the papers and feeling that I was in the wrong place, doing these very traditional, not very experimental productions for conservative Texas audiences. So I was drawn to New York City, where I moved in 1967 and discovered a more alternative, experimental scene.

After living in New York City for six months I was cast in *Tom Paine*. *Tom Paine* was an ensemble piece directed by Tom O'Horgan.[1] Being in *Tom Paine* really spun my head around to begin to understand the theater not as departmentalized psychology or as a psychological approach to character, but instead it was more musical and dance oriented in the sense that your characters overlapped and were more essences or poetic aspects. I became interested in Brecht and Artaud, and I went that whole route, training with the Performance Group and then coforming the Wooster Group and performing nonnarratively, nonpsychologically in many of the pieces.[2]

Then in 1979, strangely enough, I evolved a narrative form of my own, a monologue form, which I think was always there in me. I was always a writer and this voracious reader in boarding school. I read all of Thomas Wolfe's novels and was very interested in autobiographic narrative. I didn't get back to it because there was no real autobiography for me until I lived long enough to have one. There wasn't a whole lot to work with. I then began to realize that that's where my sensibilities had always been, and they surfaced at the right time. Before that I was probably inhibited by a lot of the nonverbal Artaud fantasies and the workshops that I'd done with Open Theatre. I don't discount any of the training that I had, from traditional theater to Grotowski's plastiques.[3] They fit into freeing myself up physically and psychologically to do the form that I do now. I sit still, but I really move a lot in my chair. I am very physically connected to my breath and my body. I still do that kind of work, along with yoga and vocal work. So it started as a very traditional route, and to some extent has returned to one, in the sense that storytelling is the second oldest profession.

**Vilga:** In college and regional theater, were you following one specific method of training?

**Gray:** At Emerson College, I would say training was rather eclectic. Paul John Austin was the most instrumental kind of mentor/teacher there, and he had his own theater on Charles Street called the Image Theater.[4] He was a working director and had a company, and you could see what he taught in action. I'd say that he was very concerned with certain existential themes then, doing things like *No Exit* and reviving *Antigone* in the classic mode. I think that most of the scene work that we had in college was concerned with psychological motivation, asking, "What does the character feel and why?" We probably used an approach to character through some bastardization of Stanislavsky or versions of the Method we got from reading those books. The main influence, the book that I remember most as being very influential, was *To the Actor,* the Michael Chekhov book.[5] That was Paul Austin's main choice as a teaching text. There was voice work, but that was independent, like a separate class. It was not an integrated approach. You wouldn't do voice work together before putting on a play, and there was no idea of unity of cast and ensemble. It was sitting in a dressing room in a very traditional way, putting on makeup. It was so very old-fashioned, really. As I said, there was a great emphasis on Broadway musicals at Emerson College. That's where they would put a lot of their money, into doing the big musical.

*Vilga:* Sense memory work?

*Gray:* Yes, there was sense memory work. I don't remember it too well, though, but I think some teachers did work with that. You see, every teacher had their own method that they developed from working. One of the things involved in my work, which causes some people to say I am original or the apotheosis of Method actors, is that I am only working from myself. It's like I'm doing the pre-role work that you would do as a Method actor but stopping there. As I don't memorize a text, I'm having to say it fresh every night, because it hasn't been pre-written or memorized. I often refer to myself as an inverted Method actor.

*Vilga:* It's not pre-written or memorized?

*Gray:* No. All my monologues are evolved in front of audiences. When they are printed, they're transcriptions of two or three years' worth of evolution. To some extent, Method actors, because they memorize a text, have to use methods to make them pretend that it's fresh and that they don't really know it. I see that as the difference between bushwhacking up the mountain or having a path. In the text you have a path. Every night I'm bushwhacking a little differently and making a little different trail, so there are new little different trails going up the mountain each night.

*Vilga:* Do you think the quality of the performance varies because of that?

*Gray:* Yes, it does. Sometimes it's not as consistent, it needs tuning, and that's why I'm using a director now. I can get very sloppy with the attitudes and the moods and the intentions of a particular piece. You take it and break it down the way Michael Chekhov would—beats or sections of a text, and what you were feeling and what you hope the audience is feeling at a particular moment in order to make the text hold together as a whole. I find that I have to be careful with that, and that's why I use a director now. Eventually, once the monologue has a real shape to it, I finally begin to see that organic shape and then make specific choices of what should happen in certain places.

*Vilga:* How is it shaped when you start out?

*Gray:* I have a general outline of key words, because I'm usually dealing with a particular but loose theme. In the case of *Swimming to Cambodia*, it's about the making of the film *The Killing Fields*. In the case of *Terrors of Pleasure*, it's buying a house in the country. In the case of *Monster in the Box*, it's about the interruptions that come while trying to write my first novel. Just offhand, if, say, I was going to another monologue and ready to begin one, rarely do I know what the intention is. It could be about turning fifty and might be called *Gray's Anatomy*, and it would be about what my thoughts are about my mortality and marriage and death, what's happening in my physical body. I keep a box over there by my desk, and any time I encounter something that I think is germane to the things I've been thinking about I toss it into the box. Then I dump the box out onto the floor at the end of the year and try to put the puzzle together. Essentially a monologue is putting together the puzzle of my life publicly. Once I figure it out in front of an audience, and it's both an entertainment and an insightful piece, then I'm done with it. It's reached its fruition. It's more like a professional piece of done work that I can perform or not perform depending on when I need to do it.

*Vilga:* Do you consider what you do acting?

*Gray:* Yes, it's acting myself. You see, the difference between me and many performance artists—because I don't see myself as a performance artist at all—is that I see that what I do is acting. I've been trained in acting, and I understand how to approach a role and how to be aware of vocal intonations, rhythms, character attitudes. I'm taking myself as a character. What I do is I have a character of "Spalding Gray," which to some extent I'm stuck in. I would like to figure out ways of breaking out of it, which is why I'm writing a book now. There is a certain naive adventuresome aspect of this Spalding Gray character, like a combination of Candide and Huckleberry Finn, that keeps getting into these ridiculous situations, or to some extent creating them. When I sit down to the monologue for the first time from the outline, I'm very carefully observing myself. I make audio tapes of my performances. I'm listening back and thinking, "How would the character act now? What was the character doing now?" I'm splitting myself up in a creative way. I think the approach is very based on classical acting techniques that I had worked on in college that really feed into this work now.

*Vilga:* Is it easy to be objective about yourself in that way?

*Gray:* It has its dark sides and its problem sides, not so much in the performances as it does in my life. It becomes increasingly difficult for me to be spontaneously in the moment without the witness operating, so heavily is the writer/witness in me. Everything starts to become like a movie. Where I'm seeing myself walking down the street or seeing myself like a character in action.

*Vilga:* In order to gather more material?

*Gray:* Not necessarily. It's sort of like a job hazard where I can't shut it off. I also know that it could all potentially be material. It's just that the witness is there all the time. In the monologue it gets less and less blurry the more it gets set and the clearer I am about exactly how the material should be played. That's when the monologue really splits off and becomes a form separate from myself. I no longer identify with it, and I'm not ashamed of it or representing myself as a crippled neurotic. It has its musicality and its humor, and it becomes something else. It's usually about a year's time before that happens. I was on the road with *Monster in the Box* for a year before I'd say that when it opened at Lincoln Center it was really something separate from me, something that I'd step into, like an outfit. Like a character.

*Vilga:* Could someone else ever "do" your monologues?

*Gray:* Yes, I think so. And they have. I haven't seen them. I did write a monologue for someone to do. I was commissioned by John Houseman's Acting Company. A number of writers received short stories by Chekhov and were asked to react to them. I wrote a monologue as a reaction and saw it performed and liked it very much, although I've never performed it myself. I wrote it specifically for this other person to speak, although I didn't know who this other person was. I was writing this, I expect, for myself, but I was really consciously sitting down and writing it out for this other person based on what I was doing and reflecting on the day I received the Chekhov short story in the mail.

*Vilga:* So were they playing you, the receiver?

*Gray:* No. I'm not sure what the actor's approach was. But that's a good question.

*Vilga:* You've spoken about how you wanted to become an actor, but what about the choice to do monologues? Is acting something different, because it's often about becoming other characters?

*Gray:* I don't understand that process of the conduit, and I think there are very few actors who do it well. I think that Meryl Streep is an example of someone that seems to be able to become a self-less conduit to the material, and I think that's fascinating to watch. Somewhere along the way I realized that I wasn't one of those. I didn't want to be a mediocre character actor in regional theater who was really doing the same schtick and not getting beyond himself. I wanted to try to go deeper into myself.

I think that the impulse to go into acting came out of the fact that I would act out a lot as an adolescent and was trying to find a place for that. I was very bored with life, and I would tend to dramatize it and create dramatic situations on cue. For example, I think I was sitting in the living room with my mother when I was fifteen or sixteen, watching some fireworks go off outside, and I remember jumping up and running to the window and saying, "Mom, come quick! Russ Crumb, our next-door neighbor, is up on the roof shooting his children!" She'd run to the window and take the cue and she'd say, "Why do you have to do that? Don't do that kind of thing!" It was that kind of dissatisfaction, the humdrum of Barrington, Rhode Island, and wanting to get out of it and having a craving for dramatic situations. I'm still doing that and trying to ease down on it and give myself some rest. I'm still either finding my way into dramatic situations or creating them when they're not there. I've always had a tendency toward that. That's where I think the acting impulse came in.

I think the first crack in the traditional idea of character came when I was playing a very strong character. I was playing the role of Hoss in *Tooth of Crime* and doing that for a year.[6] That required an interesting approach. It was a very nonpsychological play; it was much more like a rock opera with wonderful made-up language. Richard Schechner, the director, asked me to shave my head for the role, and I did. That made a big difference. Putting on that leather outfit and having my head shaved, it was easier to become something other than me. I became this big, shouting, angry blowhard for a year that I didn't ever want to do again. It took me over. I felt I was being taken over by Sam Shepard's rhythms, and I began to resent that. I was beginning to think that the acting process was too claustrophobic, that it wasn't fun, that I didn't want to be that other person, that character of Hoss. I remember that there was a point after I did a very long rock-and-roll speech, about a big fight that I'd had in Bob's Big Boy in Southern California, the director told me to go neutral and to let the character that I'd developed peel off of me and then just stand there until I felt I'd come back to myself. I looked at the audience as I did this, because they were all standing around like a big street scene—there was no seating because it was an environmental production in the Performing Garage—and I can remember standing there and looking around that space and just feeling that these layers of "character" that I'd been piling up on me were peeling like an onion until I was back to myself. As I stood there it began to occur to me, "What if instead of building up the character again, I began to speak as myself?" That was the temptation, but what would I say? It was not until I started working with the Wooster Group that I, as me, spoke out to the audience.

When I was in college I was terrified. I was performing Mr. Van Dam in *Diary of Anne Frank* [Frances Goodrich and Albert Hackett] with padding and white hair. I loved to immerse myself in the illusion that I was in Amsterdam, but I dreaded looking out into the dark theater. In traditional theater you never looked out into the audience. I was terrified of Brecht and all his theories of alienation. And then working in environmental theater with Richard Schechner I was getting closer and closer to my greatest fear: the audience. I began to overcome that fear and realize that that was where I had my primary relationship. I got tired of looking into Joan MacIntosh's eyes and Elizabeth LeCompte's eyes and everyone else in the cast for a year and found it fresh to see the audience's reaction.[7] At first I was always terrified to look at the audience because I thought I would see them judging me or see them thinking, "He's just acting."

The Wooster Group, which I cofounded with Elizabeth LeCompte in 1974, was my first real audience for the work I do now. They encouraged me to perform these monologues, so that's where they started, as little autobiographic tales within a larger structure. By then the concept of acting, the drive, the need, the desire to be an actor was passing from me, not with a lot of fear—because it wasn't as if I was being left without a job or an identity—but because I was evolving. I could feel the evolution. It was still headed toward spectacle performance and a need to be onstage and present with an audience. The audience became more and more important. I related to them directly in a presentational way, with the audience's faces rather than the other actors. As soon as I started looking out, things became much more interesting.

This relationship underwent a big evolution so that my relationship to the audience is now primary. In fact, I just came back from Pittsburgh, where I was interviewing them onstage. It was a very strong event.

*Vilga:* You interviewed the audience about themselves?

*Gray:* Yes. About their lives, about living in Pittsburgh, about what they do for fun, what they think about American politics and the economy, whatever comes up. In other words, I start with one question and the answer leads to the next question, so it's a chain, an associative chain, and it goes in many directions. Often it's very strong and therapeutic for the audience. I've also been doing it with people with AIDS as a benefit for Art Against AIDS onstage in Washington, D.C., and San Francisco. I personally think that this kind of public form of confessional storytelling is very healing for me, so I think it is for other people. There was a woman that I asked to come up last in Pittsburgh that I thought was a very jolly type, that's why I chose her, to be extroverted, because there were about twelve hundred people there. In the course of the conversation, it turned out that just two years ago her daughter had been brutally murdered and burned and tied to a railroad track. She didn't get into the details of this horror, someone else did later. It was an unsolved murder, and because of all the press on it, the whole audience suddenly knew who she was and what she was talking about. She had a chance to speak very clearly and loudly on that microphone, how this horror didn't break her, how she was able to survive as an ex-Catholic, not even as a practicing Catholic. The audience gave her great applause for and great support in her extremely positive attitude. What started out to be a light, comic summer evening entertainment had this other great healing force come into it.

You never know what is going to come up and when it will be there. So that kind of thing for me is what I'm really interested in now, working with the audience or in conversations with them. Making nonagenda issues public and spontaneous, where you're just talking about living in this world. It's a dialogue, not a monologue. It's where all theater starts.

I've become more interested in people and psychology and social issues. I think if I were a playwright, I'd be working in that mode. I think it takes a lot more craft and longer to get to that. But I've found a mode that I can work in that is satisfying to me now.

**Vilga:**   When did you begin working with audience participation?

**Gray:**   1980. It was after I did three monologues, and I think I got tired of hearing myself talk. It was difficult for me in Pittsburgh because the people rushed me for autographs as soon as I arrived. I got onstage and said, "I'll give autographs afterwards if you all sit still and let me go around amongst you and choose four people." They all froze like statues and pretended they didn't notice me as I was passing through. It was the only way I could do it. Before, when people didn't know me, I could hang out in the lobby and say, "Would you come up?" "Well, what is this about?" they'd say. I'd say, "I'm Spalding Gray," and they'd say, "Oh, you are? What is it you're going to do?" And I'd say, "I just want you to come up onstage and talk to me." "Well, I don't know. Well, all right, you can put my name down." Now it's more difficult, because people want to impress me with their storytelling abilities; it's hard to get a person who's not up there with an agenda. But I was able to do it in Pittsburgh.

**Vilga:**   Are they truthful, or do you have to break something down?

**Gray:**   You have to break something down. There was one man that I didn't succeed at who was bugged by the audience, who had his shtick together. He was a teacher of business at the university, so he knew how to be public. To some extent it helps to try to throw some curve balls to those people to try to throw them off, but in most cases the people don't need breaking down, because they're not highly defended and they're not used to working over a microphone in front of over a thousand people. Mainly I'm aiming to bring the story out of the person. When I teach at workshops in autobiographical storytelling, my point is to get someone to be able to tell a highly energized personal story with structure and tell it well. If there's going to be a volatile story, it's hopefully going to be about some issue that they are passionate about in their lives. I want them to take that very strong information and find a shape for it.

*Vilga:* When you do that with an audience, are you more of a director?

*Gray:* Yes. And an editor. But most importantly, a facilitator trying to guide and just ask simple questions, giving birth to the story and letting it come out. I would say, more a facilitator than a director. A director is someone whose stamp is shaping it.

*Vilga:* How does your more traditional acting in mainstream films fit into this?

*Gray:* There's two stories that I want to tell about that. Roland Joffe approached *The Killing Fields* like the documentary film director that he was and had us do research together about what we were working on. We were there early reading books and having consciousness-raising discussions around these issues. Then he'd have me visit the man that I was playing, who was there in Bangkok at the time—he was one of the aides to the ambassadors—and use him as a study. After that, I was probably working very much from myself to develop other aspects of the character.

David Byrne in *True Stories* was interesting, in that David didn't give any direction for character development, or very little—he was more involved with mise-en-scène. I said, "David, do I need a Southern accent?" He said, "No, no, even though you're in the South, you could have moved here from New England. So do whatever you think is right for the character." I didn't know how to approach it. The first shot that we were doing was of this parade, and I was sitting in the back of this very fancy convertible with the woman playing my wife. I was like a kind of Kennedy figure, looking like a definite Wasp Brahmin in a suit, and she was sort of Dolly Partonesque with her beehive hairdo. We ride into this town, McKinney, Texas, and there's a combination of real local people there and extras, all cheering. As soon as the cheer went up for us, I went into this kind of Kennedy-Nixon thing.

That's why I like film. As soon as I get in a very naturalistic setting like that, the actual place, you just start playing around with it, and you just playact, and it's fun. You can't help but do the right thing. You find it immediately in the costumes, the props, the environment. It gives you an attitude. A character.

When I was acting in the movie *Beaches,* I didn't know what I was doing when Barbara Hershey said, "I hear you're really great in the dailies."[8] I said, "But, Barbara, I don't feel like I'm doing anything." And she replied, "Keep on doing it." Maybe that's the best-kept secret in Hollywood: you walk through as you.

I'm not a great researcher, unlike Meryl Streep, who I'm sure researches those accents. When I played a very naturalistic cop in the play *Cops,* Richard Schechner, the director, wanted me to do a Chicago accent. I said, "Why can't the character just have moved to Chicago from Boston?" He said, "No, he wouldn't have done that." All my lines were done by someone from Chicago, and I had to listen to it on tape. I got it down, but I found the process very boring. I think most actors would find that fun, the idea of the transformation and pretending, getting further away from themselves and getting closer to something very different from themselves.

I tend to keep going toward the self, whatever that is. There's a certain self-obsession there that I hope will finally turn into some form of ego-less liberation. At least, that's my fantasy. That I'll stop working and be liberated, whatever that means. That's just my propensity, to go on that route. It seems endless because of the ways, facets, and angles at which I can come at the self of so-called Spalding Gray. The novel that I'm writing is a quite different approach than my monologues.

*Vilga:* What's that about?

*Gray:* The novel I'm writing, *Impossible Vacation,* is about a kind of obsessive self-punishment that grew out of the guilt that I felt for not being present at my mother's suicide. So it's about the suicide and it's about the aftermath. It's about the absence of presence.

*Vilga:* Is it autobiographical?

*Gray:* Yes. It's an autobiographical novel, but it has fictional elements in it. The names are changed, so it's a step away from the monologues in that sense, although it's written in the first person. I'm open to doing more film work, but not stage work, because the runs are too long.

The most exciting role that I have ever played was the Stage Manager in Thornton Wilder's *Our Town* on Broadway.[9] For me that role was a go-between between the audience and the play, a kind of a Brechtian go-between. I felt that I was present, but I was minimalized. I called it New England Zen. My commentary and my attitude were so much more minimalized in the Thornton Wilder lines, and it was very refreshing for me working that way. It was like a meditation. To just learn how to simply say those lines and be of service to them, without leaning on them too much and overinterpreting or telegraphing some psychological attitude.

*Vilga:* Is any form of acting more satisfying for you now?

*Gray:* The variety is satisfying. Keeping that cultivation. I'm hoping another film will come along soon. I miss it. I'm tired of myself. My last monologue, *Monster in the Box,* because it was a hit, kind of closed in on me since everyone wants it. We've just finished shooting a film of it.

*Vilga:* Who directed it?

*Gray:* Nick Broomfield, who directed *Dark Obsession* that's just opening this week. So that's done, and the book will be published. And Windham Hill is doing the audio tapes. I'm open now to doing some more commercial film work. I might act in Dolly Parton's new film in Chicago in July. It's a good way of getting away from myself, working with someone else's words and someone else's directions. I did a pilot for ABC. I shot two days in Santa Fe in March, and that was fun. I was playing an anthropologist that was advising this student about the dangers of witchcraft. It was fun to do this role for those two days and to have someone giving me direction and seeing that I could still take it. They'd tell me, "Can you do that a little more edgy?" or whatever words they would use, and we'd do the scene again and I'd be able to do that. I would feel like I was still in touch with that method of working.

*Vilga:* Does the industry understand the different things you do? Or are they confused?

*Gray:* I'd say that they were confused. I would say that my major problem with Hollywood is this—I sometimes paraphrase Bob Dylan—Bob Dylan says, "I may look like Robert Frost, but I feel just like Jesse James." I say, "I may look like a gynecologist, an American ambassador's aide, or a lawyer, but I feel like Woody Allen." That's what the industry misses; they usually work with a kind of typecasting. What you see is what you get. My insides are not what my outsides are. I'm not who I appear to be. I appear to be a Wasp Brahmin, but I'm really a sort of neurotic, perverse New York Jew. When I was performing one year ago at this time in Israel, a review came out in Hebrew about *Monster in the Box,* and it read, "Spalding Gray is funny, sometimes hilarious, wonderfully neurotic for a non-Jew." Only the Jews can say something like "wonderfully neurotic."

What happens is that Hollywood sees my outside image and so I get cast in these rather boring, really generic roles that anyone could do. Therefore I don't have a whole lot of hope for doing something, say, like Woody Allen does or getting to the heart of who I am unless someone I know very well is directing the film and employs me. I would think—and I hate to speculate on this, because I don't know what they think—that they see me as this kind of outside oddity that they would love to plug in, if they could, in a small role so that they would attract my audiences, and then they would be able to work with me. Garry Marshall loved working with me in *Beaches* and said that he loved me because he loved my line from *Swimming to Cambodia:* "I was further out than Ivan even." He kept saying that line, over and over. I think he just wanted to have me aboard. It was a plus that I could also act, but it wasn't a crucial, large role which would make or break the film.

I don't think I'll ever do a crucial, lead role in a film because I don't think that the industry would invest big money in a nonstar. I mean, there are certain times that films come along that I feel left out and I say, "Oh, I could have done that." *Accidental Tourist* was one, the lead, I mean. After I read the book, I thought, "If that film is ever made, I could see myself in that," but I'm not part of the Hollywood club. I wouldn't be a candidate. I'm always looking at films to see where I might fit in. John Malkovich would also have been very good in the lead role of *Accidental Tourist.*

*Vilga:* Do you see types of training for other actors being valuable or any that are a waste of time?

*Gray:* I'm really out of touch with what the training is for other actors. I think that the most valuable thing for me was just acting in lots of plays, just doing it. That's all I did when I went to college. I acted in summer stock, every single summer, on the Cape and in New Hampshire, and I did plays in the winter. So in a way, by the time I ended up in college, by the time I was in my sophomore year, I had acted in quite a few plays. I was always onstage, and I learned very fast through that.

I think that constant studio scene work is fine, but if it's a substitute for the real thing it's deadly, because it's never going to go anywhere. It's too academic. It's not in the world. It's horrible to say this, because—and this is one of the reasons I would never want to be an acting teacher—how do you prepare people for the marketplace when the marketplace is so anti-quated and minimal? In the case of live theater and in the case of film, it's so competitive. It's very, very difficult.

My route into my stories came into being because I had a place to do them—the Performing Garage—and I just started performing them over and over again, every night, and just figured out the system, the method. If studio work and scene work and classes aren't balanced out with summer stock and working in the real world of theater, it's not good. To me it's a dead end.

*Vilga:* What do you think about the state of theater today?

*Gray:* Someone asked me that in Pittsburgh, actually. I said I was very discouraged about it and didn't pay a lot of attention to new plays, or as much as I should. I haven't been to see much new theater this year. I'm not sure about this, but if you look at New York City now—and I'd have to go down and study the paper and see what's on—one of the few intelligent dramas that is going on is John Guare's *Six Degrees of Separation* and that's now a white horse, a weird exception. Whereas years ago, there'd be five or six going on like that. You might go see a new Tennessee Williams play on Broadway, which I did when I first came here. I went to see *Night of the Iguana* in 1961. That's not happening now and I don't know why it's not happening. I think a lot of it has to do with the economy and fear and the way that people gravitate right to Hollywood to write film scripts and only use theater as an exercise in writing a film script.

You can see the evolution of Sam Shepard from a very theatrical, "musical," in quotes, very lyrical kind of theatrical expression heading much more toward television soap opera and psychological drama that lends itself to film. I think that more and more people write plays with film in mind, because they're writing in a depressed economy and they're fearful that they won't make enough money and they don't want to be a starving artist and all the rest of it. Theater itself as theater seems to me an antiquated museum. People just aren't really writing for the theater anymore. They're writing with the hope that it will be made into a film.

We went to see a show recently, and it was well acted and had a relatively interesting script, but the first thing everyone was talking about in my party when we came out was who was going to play the role in the film and when could it be made into a film. It's like that immediately. Of course, I'm in the same boat. I've been doing primarily just that with my monologues, but I make the monologue as a live event. The film follows if someone is interested in producing it. I don't pursue it. I need to be pursued.

**Vilga:** Do you think if an actor can do theater, he or she can do film?

**Gray:** No. It's quite different. I find that I am much better onstage, because I'm very large and I'm theatrical. I'm used to projecting, so that when I saw *Swimming to Cambodia,* the film, I thought, "My God, my face was so busy, I could have taken it way down." I can see the difference between Willem Dafoe when I worked with him in live theater, and how diminutive his presence is, versus him on film. When they say, "The camera loves you," it's really true. It makes Willem more alive; he becomes more alive in front of a camera. I think that that's his medium for whatever reason; he radiates more of everything in front of a camera. He's very intense. Onstage, somehow that intensity is encapsulated, or it doesn't happen with a live audience as much. I think that probably that's true of a lot of actors. I get in front of the camera around all the machinery, and I go flat.

The worst for me was when they decided to do *Our Town* without a live audience and film it for television. They had a Stedicam following me around, and I was talking to it like Huntley and Brinkley, like the evening news, looking close up at a fisheye lens that was reflecting my face. It made me so stiff and self-conscious. I forget about myself in front of an audience. I'm much more relaxed. I'm more relaxed in front of an audience than walking down the street. I've been in front of one for thirty years. In front of the cameras—argh! I don't know a lot about other actors, though.

*Vilga:* It's very interesting that you feel more yourself in front of the audience.

*Gray:* Absolutely. Centered, focused. An audience makes me feel smarter, more alert. I really take off of their energy and their presence. It's important for me to be in front of live eyes, to gaze at live eyes rather than a camera lens.

*Vilga:* Is that the reason you act?

*Gray:* I think it is. Another thing happened when we filmed *Swimming to Cambodia.* We had the live audience, but there were three 35mm cameras in the way. I kept looking past the cameras at the audience and being embarrassed that I couldn't see the audience and the audience couldn't see me. Jonathan Demme, the director of the film, gave me one direction the last night we shot. He said, "Be generous to the camera tonight," and at last it occurred to me that if I looked in the camera, I would be looking at the audience, because that would be the viewer in the cinema. Then I put everything into the camera. When I did the film in London of *Monster in the Box,* I just did not pay attention to the audience, I played right to the cameras, and I hated it, but I knew that the film would be better for it and I had to sacrifice that and had to let the audience witness me looking at the camera. I played it with the memory—talk about sense memory—the memory of my live performances and how I played it in live performances. I used that memory of all of those previous performances at Lincoln Center and tried to play it like that in front of the camera. Then the audience was there as a witness, as an energizer. I don't know how the audience functions, but I don't think I could have done that in a studio without them.

*Vilga:* Does it bother you that there's a final version of the performance on film?

*Gray:* No, because I can keep changing it. After *Swimming to Cambodia* was filmed, I still went on to play it live, and it did evolve. It always is open to change. The monologue is always open for change.

*Vilga:* What about working off another person in a film versus staring at the camera?

*Gray:*   I like that better because I'm not aware of the camera and I'm not looking at the camera. If you take *Beaches,* having to go to that scene where I'm jilted by Bette Midler when Barbara Hershey answers the door, that was very easy for me to play because I had all of the real stuff. The car. The house. The doorbell. And most of all, Bette. Immediately, I find film acting much easier to do than trying to act onstage.

I think that theater and film should be completely different. I just don't think that after Chekhov there should be naturalistic plays. I think that the theater should use only the conventions of theater. When I first started working in theater with Richard Schechner, we were performing an environmental version of *Macbeth,* and he had this "actuals" theory. I was Malcolm, and I was traveling with Macduff to his castle to find all of his kids murdered. Richard had us take an actual physical body route which had us crawling over and under the audience to get to the area that represented the castle, so that we had made an actual journey and when we got there we had arrived on cue. That employed a kind of theatrical device to make an actual feeling for what was missing: the horses and everything else you'd have in the film.

Richard Foreman, the Wooster Group, Robert Wilson, and the Bread and Puppet Theater and various other groups have found their own theatrical metaphors to make real theater work.[10] It's rare that you go to a theater event that is exclusively theatrical where they're working with what I think of as a theatrical language. They're usually working with a kind of naturalism that could be better done in film. I found that I knew that theatrical language when I was working with the Wooster Group. We created our own way of working in the space.

Now, if I were to be cast in a naturalistic play and I didn't have the car to pull up in and get out of, and go and ring the doorbell with Bette Midler in a real house (a scene from *Beaches*), I would find that I wouldn't know what to do. I would be very flat, I wouldn't know what to bring to it. I wouldn't know how to work in that mode. It would be foreign to me, and that's part of why I don't do a lot of theater acting. It would be interesting to try to do it, but it's difficult unless you're working with a very strong theatrical text, which is essential. I prefer film work for that reason. I love locations and all that.

*Vilga:*   Do you think that anyone can act?

*Gray:*   No. I think that you have to have that schism in there, which most writers or artists have, where there's a sense of split where you are able to be self-conscious in a good way. I mean conscious of aspects of yourself that you are working with. You are splitting yourself up, you're not just a whole unconscious person. Although I think that even though people are actually acting all the time, they're embarrassed by that fact. They would never think of it as an art form, nor would they be able to study it without shame. Essentially on some level you can look at it as a very neurotic kind of situation.

I have a tendency, because I am an actor and I know about acting, not to trust actors. I would never want to be married to an actress or live with an actress. I don't think I would trust her. It's funny to say that. It's very built-in. I certainly didn't trust Ronald Reagan for that reason. I think that people can turn sinister when they learn acting techniques, and they use the art form in life to get what they want and manipulate people.

**Vilga:** Is it just that they're better at it than most people?

**Gray:** They're better at it because they've learned how to be better at it. They practice. There are other people who do it, too, people who are not onstage but learn how to manipulate through acting. I think that everyone's acting all the time, but I think that there has to be a certain psychological disposition to be able to make that choice and turn around and make that into a profession. That has to do with lots of things, such as people needing that public eye.

I find that I am more alive with a witness than when I am alone. I find it difficult to take vacations alone, until I create dramatic scenes on those vacations in which witnesses are there. I proposed to my girlfriend in front of my therapist. I had to have a witness to the proposal. I think it has a lot to do with what my relationship to my mother was and being alive in her eyes, alive in her gaze. I think if you analyzed more actors and actresses you'd begin to see that they feel more alive when they're being seen.

**Vilga:** So you agree that there really is such a thing as star quality?

**Gray:** There really is. It's amazing. The aura, the charisma, the presence is often there in the street as well as on the camera with such performers. It's almost like a holy mystery in our culture, because we don't have any holy people really. Our stars in Hollywood are like lesser gods. They're like the minor Greek gods, a step above humanity. They do have a kind of an aura that is made from being photographed so much that their image precedes them. When you see them, you see a combination of them and the photograph. You remember. I think because actors and actresses are so extroverted and putting stuff out there, they have to be exterior—and interior as well, but they have to finally project that. Either it starts that way already or they develop it, but it puts out a kind of aura around them. A kind of extroversion that comes out of them like light. I have met Lily Tomlin in person and seen her perform sitting very close, and at both times, in person and onstage, she seems to radiate energy from her eyes. It's almost like light is coming out of her eyes. I think that's true of many people in that profession. Some politicians, but fewer. It's more than a little pagan.

*Vilga:*   Is there anything that I haven't asked you?

*Gray:*   Well, I feel a little vague on the topic of acting, because I feel as though I've slipped away from it into this weird form I do.

*Vilga:*   If you had one piece of advice to give to the young actor, what would it be?

*Gray:*   Oh, they were asking me that in Pittsburgh, too. They were coming up to me afterwards, and it's so sad when they come up. What do you say? How do you advise them?

I'd say what I said before, and that is to do it existentially. As Sartre would say, "A homosexual is one who practices homosexuality; a waiter is one who waits on tables"; and an actor is one who acts in theater and film. It's a double bind because it's hard to break into the profession. It was hard for me. I would take any opportunity, because primarily, over anything else in my life, that was what I wanted to do. I think if the passion and the determination are there to do it, it will surface, it will find a place, like water seeking its own level. That's the only advice that I can think of after all that I've been through, having been in the theater for thirty years, performing roles and performing myself.

About training, I think it's like with a therapist: you have to find a teacher you relate well to and trust so that you can find your center with them. I don't think there's any one method at all. I was lucky to have a good teacher in college. And then to find Richard Schechner afterwards. One of the things that Richard said to me that never happened in the school was, "I'm not interested in working with you on acting techniques, I'm interested in you finding out who you are and then bringing that aspect to whatever text we're doing. First do that."

No director had ever said that to me before. That was my first kind of route into autobiographical theater, because I came very stiff and unformed. I think that that's one of the problems—that I started to pursue theater before I found out who I was, because I didn't have a whole lot of places in the self to work from. At last, working with Schechner, I was touching real things in myself as much as I was going through the words of the text.

*Vilga:*   Do you think that for a lot of actors acting is a form of therapy?

*Gray:*   I suppose so. Again, it's very hard for me to speak for a lot of actors. I think that there's a piece of my pie that's missing, which is around empathy and an ability to project my imagination into what another person is really like. I've always found that very difficult. That's part of the reason why I'm not a traditional actor. I think actors and fiction writers have to be able to imagine being another. "What would Hamlet be feeling at this point?" I stopped at "What would Spalding Gray be feeling about not being able to feel about Hamlet?" That was the bottom of my iceberg.

I'm a solipsist in that way, and not an unhappy one. I mean, it's kind of the point around which I turn. I don't trust that state of "Here's what I think other people are feeling or what other actors are doing." I assume acting must be therapeutic for some actors, but mostly I think it must be something enlarging in that it causes them to be empathetic by stretching their imaginations to encompass other realities, other realms, other personalities, other ways of being and thinking. In that way it's broadening and fun and expanding in consciousness for them. I hope to be an actor again soon.

# Henry House

*Photo: Courtesy of Henry Kimsey-House*

*A former actor, Henry Kimsey-House began working as a career consultant to actors in 1983. He now runs Ontrack, a private artist's career consulting firm in Northern California through which he coaches many successful performers. He leads marketing workshops throughout the country and has begun training other "career coaches" to consult with artists on their development and marketing.*

**Vilga:**   How did you begin to work with actors?

**House:**   I was always performing, but I started really acting at eleven. I knew then that I was going to be an actor or in the theater in some way. I acted all the way through high school and college, pursuing technical theater as well. In my second or third year in college, I finally decided acting would become my full-time career.

I went to three different colleges: Lewis and Clark College in Portland, Oregon, the University of Wisconsin, and the University of Tennessee at Chattanooga. I put myself through at all those places as a theatrical technical assistant. Lighting was my particular expertise, but I did a lot of other backstage technical work. Between all those colleges I acted in thirty or forty plays while constantly doing tech work.

I really lived at the theater. I completely immersed myself in it. Even though these schools didn't have professional theater programs, I created them myself. As a result, I took no other courses! By the time I got to the second semester of my junior year at Chattanooga, all that lay ahead were the required academic courses, which held no interest for me. My advisor at the time said, "Henry, you're an actor, not a student—go to New York."

So I went to New York and began to pursue a career as an actor. I did a lot of Off-Off-Broadway theater. Then I started studying with Bill Esper at the Neighborhood Playhouse, where I really worked on the Meisner technique.[1] Right after Bill Esper, I got a job with the Alabama Shakespeare Festival. Next I did some summer stock theater in various places, then I came back to New York and got some extra work and commercials. Along with my acting income, I was supporting myself as a cab driver. Everything changed when I joined the Actors' Information Project.[2]

I began leading various workshops and doing some part-time career consulting there, and I found that I was really excited by empowering other actors. When the Actors' Information Project offered me a job as a consultant I took it. I worked there for several years before relocating to the West Coast, where I established my present company, Ontrack.

*Vilga:* How do you work with actors now?

*House:* I work primarily with actors, but I also have several nonactor clients who are writers, directors, and other artists. After I'm very familiar with each client and their work, we set up a weekly half-hour phone consultation and a longer monthly appointment. We devise strategies, brainstorm, create systems of accountability, overcome self-imposed limits, and track projects. I also conduct various workshops across the country involving different aspects of setting goals, identifying personal values and strengths, and creating effective marketing strategies based on these.

*Vilga:* How do you define your job? What do you call it?

*House:* My primary role is that of a coach. I always explain what coaching is by saying that just as any athlete who wants to make it to the

Olympics needs a coach by their side, so does any actor who's serious about having a career. Winning an Oscar or winning a gold medal; the odds of success are astronomical in either scenario. You can certainly succeed without a coach, but surrounding yourself with an informed, supportive team makes it a whole lot easier. An actor really profits from the coach's knowledge of the industry and of the client's work. Beyond personal support, a coach and a client are a powerful team for strategizing creatively, overcoming obstacles, and increasing motivation.

*Vilga:* Do you only work with private clients?

*House:* No. I also often conduct a weekend workshop which helps actors and other artists clarify their values and their purpose. After they've structured some goals that are compatible with their values and purpose, we work on identifying their personal strengths or "type."

*Vilga:* How do you do that?

*House:* Through the workshop I've come up with a system that identifies the most significant qualities successful actors market, usually falling into one of seven primary categories. Underneath those categories are dozens of other subqualities. Obviously people are complex creatures, but nonetheless most successful actors are primarily marketing one aspect of themselves with great clarity. After they become known, actors can certainly branch out and show other aspects of themselves. Yet in order to initially get work and then stand out in the public's mind, they must first market their most basic intrinsic strengths. I have to stress that this is not about finding people's limitations or pigeonholing them; it's about identifying their greatest natural strengths so they can use them to their best advantage.

After working with the person and finding their greatest strengths and their strongest three subcategories, we also isolate many of the other aspects and various colors of themselves that people witness. By the end of the workshop we've come up with a unique label for each person, one that indicates who they are in and of themselves and how they can bring that forward most clearly. We've managed to identify the strengths they have at their fingertips in a way that empowers rather than limits. Once this is clear, we develop concrete marketing strategies for each person.

*Vilga:* How necessary is that marketing?

*House:* Very. All the training in the world won't matter if an actor doesn't have a crystal-clear sense of who they are as an individual and what qualities they bring to an audition or to a role. Often most casting directors and agents make their decision as soon as the actor enters the room, before he or she even starts to perform and can demonstrate whether or not they're talented. It's absolutely vital that actors know just how they're being seen as individuals so that they can be most effective in every aspect of their presentation. This workshop lets actors identify what they have to sell about themselves, because that's a major part of getting the job, never mind sustaining the career.

**Vilga:**  But isn't that really limiting themselves, though?

**House:**  Everyone is limited in the sense that everyone is specific. Some actors like to think that they can play anything—and maybe really good ones can—but that doesn't mean they'll get hired to play everything, especially at first. You may be able to play any character, but first you've got to have a sense of who you are in the marketplace. For example, someone like Jack Nicholson has an innately dangerous quality and knows he can't afford to hide that aspect of himself. Nicholson brings danger to everything he does. If another actor with a similar dangerous quality tries to hide that, he or she comes across as bland. Sometimes a dangerous quality might not be right for a specific part, but I believe you should never hide it. I guarantee that a clear presentation to someone in the industry about who you really are will result in them calling you back for a future part which does require whatever your quality is.

To look at it another way, essentially what I try to do is get actors to identify the colors they have most strongly in their personal palette while also identifying the full combination of other colors that makes them unique. When you audition, you need to make sure they see your strongest colors. If you don't know exactly what those colors are, you're probably presenting a colorless presentation with no hues and shades clearly defined. On the other hand, trying to present every color in the rainbow doesn't work either, because then nothing stands out as vivid, memorable, or unique. You must always know and show your strongest colors. Even if your particular color isn't right for one role, a casting director or an agent is definitely going to remember a vivid color when they need it in future situations.

**Vilga:**  Are there certain kinds of training you tend to recommend?

**House:**  I think it totally varies from person to person. Different personalities tend to meld with different types of training. There are some people that work very well from a Strasberg sense memory place. Some people find that totally absurd, and for those people it's a complete waste of time. Head-oriented people, in my experience, do not function well with a lot of the Strasberg sensory stuff. They might function very well in the more British, external technique training. Someone else might be right for the whole Meisner thing, which in my mind is sort of between the two.

Personally, when I studied the Meisner technique, I felt that it actually eliminated some of my spontaneity. It's ironic because that's the opposite of the training's intentions. I realized when I came to New York and took my first technique class that I had not really learned a formalized technique. I had done thirty or forty plays in high school and college, and I was taking acting classes, but it was not really serious training. In college we had just gotten up and done some warmup exercises and the Viola Spolin stuff.³ We'd done a lot of clapping and concentration exercises, and all that was very helpful, but it was mainly just fun and games, another kind of play. Once I studied the Meisner technique, I found I really missed the play of it, so this type of training probably wasn't right for me. Having gained technique, acting became work.

**Vilga:** Do you think there are people who should not train or don't need training?

**House:** Actually, I do. I have one client who I think should never train. She's someone who is such an interesting personality with something uniquely vibrant about her that training might actually neutralize. Training might take away that spark in the name of teaching her how to re-create it. Sometimes that spark doesn't need to be re-created if it's already strongly present.

You don't always need training to deliver a good film performance. That's why you hear about film directors who don't want actors. They go and find real people. They don't want trained actors. They're looking for a spark that's real, not manufactured by good technique.

**Vilga:** Do you feel the same thing is true for stage actors?

**House:** Stage acting either requires training or a brilliant director. There are certain things that actors on the stage need to know how to do, and I think a good director can make them do that. I met a director up in Seattle who is creating wonderful theater with Eskimos that have never been trained and with people from old-age homes. This director has them create what they create in an entertaining way while making sure they aren't facing the wrong way and are speaking up loud enough to be heard and all that other kind of "technical" stuff.

**Vilga:** What about other kinds of classes such as cold reading or audition classes? Are those valuable?

**House:** I think they can be very valuable, but it depends totally on the actor. For some people, these classes can even be extraordinary. It's paradoxical, in a way. People can take many serious technique classes and learn a little something from each, but then all of a sudden they get in a cold reading class and they really blossom artistically. Maybe it's because of the teacher or because of the nature of the work, but the cold reading class might be the one they get something really important from.

With my clients, we evaluate their training needs on a case-by-case basis. We have to look together at what's really important for them right now. We examine if a class is going to contribute to their growth as an actor and to their success in the business. Or is the class going to actually just be another way to hide out. A lot of times classes are a way actors use to hide out and avoid getting into the real world and pursuing a career. That can be a real temptation, so that's why there are so many classes out there.

**Vilga:** Is there a point at which an actor can or should say, "I have had enough class" or "I have a technique?"

**House:** No. I think in any business, in any field, any master of anything is constantly developing. They say that Laurence Olivier was taking voice classes up to the day he died. Good actors are constantly studying, they're constantly developing.

To have a successful artistic career and a successful business career, an actor needs to be constantly out there, putting it on the line emotionally and putting it out there commercially in the marketplace. In my experience, the perennial student is pretty boring. I'm interested in the person who has really made the distinction between "I've got to study and develop my craft" and "I've got to put it out there in the world" and knows how to balance the two.

**Vilga:** You said that you've helped to reconcile actors with the marriage between business and art. What are the distinctions between the two, and what is the reconciliation that you help to bring about?

**House:** I don't make art and business completely distinct. I try to have people realize the business in art and the art in business. I try to collapse those two things as much as possible so that clients are not holding them distinct and calling themselves "artists" and cursing at this thing called "the business." In other words, they must realize the creativity that exists in brainstorming and forming a strategy and making a plan and going after business goals. They can experience the excitement that comes with taking a risk and facing fears, both in the business or onstage. There's a real artistry in setting a goal and going after that goal and then watching the result come in. There's actually an art and a creative charge that occurs.

I believe that Stanislavsky's father was a businessman, and a lot of phrases and terms that Stanislavsky uses come from business practices.[4] All of the skills that are taught in any Stanislavsky class are basic business skills: things like putting your attention on the other person or being prepared before a presentation. Anybody that teaches phone solicitation technique or interview technique in any business will tell you to have a script and to prepare what you want to say before you say it. You're taught to think about the preparation up to the first moment and then put your attention on the other person and work off of them. Any telemarketing person knows this stuff, and it's really just the fundamental acting technique Stanislavsky applied to the theater. I always tell actors, if they've taken any kind of acting training they've already been working on the skills which are necessary for doing business.

**Vilga:** How does an artist go out and get work? What's the traditional way, and what are ways you're trying to make this more creative?

**House:** Most actors go out to get work believing that they have to enter this stream called "The Rules of the Business." They join all the other millions of actors swimming down the middle of this stream. Basically, that traditional stream is to get a union card, get an agent, and then trust that the agent will get you work. There's one problem: that stream produces almost no results! This traditional stream is structured in a way that it will actually prevent actors from succeeding. It will keep them actively swimming in the stream but only dealing with people who are forced to reject them.

I work from a different position. Actors need to stand up and ask, "Is there a better, faster way to get to where I'm going besides following all the other actors down this same pointless stream?" The primary way that I work is to instill the idea that this is not a business of getting your union card, getting an agent, and then having the agent get you work. This is a business where the relationships that you have produce the results that you want to get. In other words, "who you know" is what really counts. You'll get work through who you know. It's that simple. This business is about establishing relationships and then looking at how to maintain and nurture them. That's the primary strategy involved in the work I do with people.

There's several ways that I have people start creating those relationships. The first way is I have them work on and nourish the relationships they've already established. Actors are notorious for their short-sightedness. They get in a play, and once the play's over no one's in touch with each other anymore. Whereas actors that I know who have stayed in touch with people who they've been in plays with are the actors who end up working a year down the road with those same people again. One of those actors becomes the star of some soap and says to their friend, "Hey, you ought to come in and read for this new character. You're right for the role. I'll call the casting director." So the first and most important strategy is keeping in touch with the people already in your life.

The second strategy is to meet more people that can help you. My clients and I figure out exactly who they need to meet. We make up lists that run the gamut from directors and producers to agents and casting directors and other actors. Then we start setting up strategies to go about meeting those people. These strategies could involve anything from sending out pieces of mail to cold-calling them, visiting them, or doing whatever's appropriate in establishing those necessary relationships.

*Vilga:* How important is it that the actor get an agent?

*House:* I don't feel it is important at all that an actor get an agent. I feel it's important that an actor get work. I think most agents will say the same thing: the actors that they're interested in are the actors with credits, which means the actors who work. Unless you're a small-time agent—one that has no clout—you're not interested in small-time actors. If you're the agent that everyone wants to work with, the reason you're that agent is because you're representing people who are working. The catch-22 for actors swimming down the traditional stream is "I've got to get an agent to get work, but I can't get work without an agent." The truth is that the agents they want to get aren't going to be interested in them because they're not working yet. First, they absolutely need to get work.

*Vilga:* Do you recommend that people concentrate on one aspect of entertainment such as film or theater or commercials? How much overlap is there between these things?

*House:* When people are starting out they absolutely should focus on one area for one reason only: they make their market smaller. If they focus on all areas at the same time, they disperse their energies, and as a result their market is much larger but they can't focus on anything strategically.

Even though you may want to do all areas of the business, have patience. Pick one and attack it head-on. If an actor decides to pursue theater for the immediate future, that decision alone cuts their market to a quarter of the size it would be if they were focusing on all areas of the entertainment industry. That's much more manageable. It's even better to pick a list of ten theaters and focus on those. Or select ten theater people. Make your list very small. Even a list of ten directors quickly grows to one hundred people who are associated with those people. In my experience, it's very difficult to handle marketing yourself to much more than a hundred people.

*Vilga:* Does mass-mailing pictures and postcards ever do any good?

*House:* Yes, but there's something important to remember about pictures and résumés for actors. In the rest of the world, a résumé is an application for a job. In this business, a résumé is an advertisement. The only function of the picture and résumé is to generate an awareness of the product, in this case you. Yes, mailings are very important, because advertising is important to any business. You need to advertise because advertising creates an awareness of you. You may actually get a result if your picture and résumé hits someone's desk at exactly the moment they're looking for someone who looks like just like you do in your headshot.

Mostly what a mass-mailing is doing, like any advertising, is it's creating a message in the brain of the person receiving it. The more they see that image, the more it's going to register there. That's what advertising's all about: keeping an awareness present. Mailings are important, but they're important as advertising, not as a job application. Unfortunately, most actors don't know this. They get disappointed when they do one mailing and don't get any response.

**Vilga:** Do you have any thoughts on how the odds are so stacked against the actor in terms of getting work? Do you ever tell people to stop or to give up?

**House:** You can't do that. You can't tell an artist not to do their art. They'll do it anyway.

What I can do is work with them to refocus their direction so that if they're beating their head against one wall—and this wall may be called "getting an agent," "getting a job in film," or something else—and they're not getting anywhere, we can work on what can they generate themselves. I think it's really important that actors create their own theater or their own film. They can produce their own work. They can make it happen rather than counting on other people to do it for them, which is how the structure of the stream has been set up.

The traditional stream that actors float down causes them to think, "All I have to do is just put myself in the stream and other people are going to do it for me." You can put yourself in that stream, but you'd better be creating your own theater and your own opportunities all the way along the line. Otherwise you're just another fish who's going to end up in someone's frying pan.

**Vilga:** Do you see actors creating their own work and producing real results from that?

**House:** The actors that I'm successful with and the actors that I'm noticing are successful are creating their own work or creating their own opportunities for work. They're not counting on other people hooking them up or other people making it happen for them. If you read biographies of contemporary actors, more and more that's what you hear about. You hear about Meryl Streep with *Sophie's Choice* and how she got that role for herself.[5] Major stars who have their pick of projects tend to have their own production companies so that they can directly control and develop the material they want. Successful actors keep creating opportunities rather than letting themselves be led, which seems to be what a lot of actors want. Nonworking actors usually want to be led, and that's always a mistake.

**Vilga:** Is there a common impulse you see behind people wanting to act, or does it really vary person to person?

**House:** I notice two common threads. One is that a lot of actors start out as outcasts. The theater community is so accepting, so very open, that it invites these deviants in with open arms. That's why you'll see so many people who are basically deviants in the theater. Theater is an instant community that accepts everyone.

Secondly, I think there is that small percentage of individuals who are truly called to acting as an art form. In other words, they have a creative need, a drive, an urge, a calling to interpret words and tell a story to other people. For them acting is the purest, most natural outlet for this urge. I think these people are only a very small percentage of actors; most are more drawn to the unique sense of community theater offers.

**Vilga:** A lot of actors are clearly seeking wealth and fame as well. Is that something you think is opposite to the real motivations to be an actor? Or is it something that can be useful?

**House:** I think anybody entering the field of acting to become rich is deluding themselves. Wealth or success based on wealth is a lot easier to do in a lot of other ways. The odds of generating great wealth are so unlikely you might as well just buy Lotto tickets. If you want to get wealthy from acting, I bet it's about the same kind of odds. The people who are drawn to it for wealth generally leave it very quickly because there's no cheese at the end of that tunnel. Very few people who stay in acting are trying to get rich.

Fame is another issue. If people are going for fame as a form of success, acting is very seductive, because when you get a job you do get acknowledgment. You may not get major fame, but the fame button gets rubbed a little bit. It may not get pushed exactly, but a little oil comes off the finger on it. Again, if you become an actor to get famous, it's almost like buying a lottery ticket, but with maybe a little bit more chance of winning.

If you enter the business for either of those two reasons, there is a delusion that is occurring. I don't try to pop the bubble of that delusion with my client, because sometimes that delusion can be very motivating. I do want them to be honest about it, though. I don't want someone who is truly going for fame to say they're doing it for the art because that's the "right thing" to say. I want them to acknowledge that what they really want is to be a star. Admitting that is important. Then we can pursue stardom wholeheartedly without deluding ourselves.

*Vilga:* Is there any acting that's affected you in some particularly strong way that you can call to mind?

*House:* Yes. Robert De Niro in *King of Comedy* was the final straw that made me give up acting. I had been thinking about changing careers for a year. I had been really wavering back and forth about whether I was committed as an artist to this art called acting or not. That film clarified things for me.

Do you know how sometimes you're not watching the performance and entertained by it but you're actually watching the work that went into creating that performance? It's like seeing the man behind the curtain. That's what happened with *King of Comedy.* I can't remember the movie for the life of me, but I remember the work that Robert De Niro put into creating that character. It made me examine things, it made me look carefully at myself. I saw the work that De Niro put into this performance, and tears started coming down my face. I realized that I wasn't personally committed to doing that kind of work. I wasn't driven in that way.

I saw the work that De Niro put into acting and I said, "I'm not willing to do that. I'm not willing to do that kind of work, that kind of research, that kind of thing." I wanted to play at it. I realized that I was drawn to acting for other reasons and I could get those satisfactions elsewhere. That performance made me let go of the need to act.

*Vilga:* What's most meaningful to you about your work now? What keeps you excited about it?

*House:* What keeps me excited about it is really the actors themselves. I just happen to love actors. I want actors to be people who are able to have lives that aren't so wrapped up in rejection and failure. I want them to have lives that are lived in a context where they can see possibility. I love being around creativity and seeing the creativity in everything. What gives me a thrill is when people have that "Aha!" experience. One of my clients will have a great idea and I'll say, "Let's play with that" and it will become an invigorating, enlivening creative experience. I love that. That's what I'm in it for.

*Vilga:* Is there something I haven't touched on about acting or actors that comes to mind?

*House:* Yes. There's something very universal about acting that often gets lost. The skills that actors have to learn in order to perform at their utmost are skills that every human being should have. Good actors have really searched their emotional life and depths and their ability to identify with other human beings. These actors have dug into themselves and their own aliveness, and they are quite evolved, empathetic individuals. That's another reason I love working with them.

***Vilga:*** Are you suggesting that everyone dabble at being an actor?

***House:*** If I could have any influence in my interview in this book, it would be to have every human being act and not have to become a professional actor. At the same time, I'd like to offer a lot of the people who call themselves "professional actors" the permission to act in their lives and not have to pursue a career as an actor. That way more community theaters will sprout up and more people will start telling stories and simply become more involved with each other. That, I think, is what acting is all about.

If all human beings could develop the skills actors have and include those qualities into their lives, then a lot of frustrated actors wouldn't have to make acting their career. Their needs—and their jollies—that almost get met as professional actors would get met far better in life.

***Vilga:*** If you had one piece of advice to give to the young actor, what would it be?

***House:*** Create your own art. Create your own career. Create it yourself. Don't wait for someone else to create it and hire you. Make it happen yourself.

# Scott Macaulay

Photo: Donna F. Aceto

*Scott Macaulay graduated from Columbia College in 1983. Macaulay was the curator at the Kitchen Center for Video, Music, and Dance from 1985 to 1992. He has produced the feature films* What Happened Was . . . *(1994), which won the Sundance Film Festival Best Screenplay and Grand Jury Prize, and* The Wife *(1996), which stars Julie Hagerty and Wallace Shawn.*

**Vilga:**  Can you distinguish the type of acting inherent in performance art?

**Macaulay:**  First, let me qualify everything I'm going to say about acting by restricting it to my area of expertise: performance art and experimental theater. The thing to keep in mind about performance art is it's not truly acting. I don't know what it is, but it's not acting. It's not informed by the same ideas that go into acting. In pure performance art, the people you'll see onstage are drawing from elements of personal history and ritual. They're trying to shape their experiences into rituals which will inform their performance. A lot of performance is concerned with gesture and symbolic actions taken with the body. Ultimately there's a kind of transformative idea operating: by using some sort of ritual, using some sort of body action, you can make an artistic piece which exists in a particular time and place and then extends into the future.

Performance really came out of a reaction in the 1970s to commodity-based art. Some artists felt frustrated by the limitations of painting and wanted to do something more immediate. Remember how in the eighties everyone had a garage rock band? Now every neighborhood will have their resident performance artist. Since the 1970s, performance art has really changed a lot, broadening to include a lot of different things. Now when people talk about performance art, they might talk about theater directors like Robert Wilson or Richard Foreman or the Wooster Group, all of which come from an experimental theater tradition.[1]

What characterizes all of these people is it's all director's theater, which is very different from a playwright's theater. Whereas a playwright might be very concerned—especially a naturalistic playwright—with psychological motivation and depth of character and things like that, a director's theater is often more concerned with an overarching directorial strategy or point of view. A lot of time the directions which are given to actors are very different from the types of directions that you would find in conventional theater. For example, I know a really interesting theater director whose only direction is "No emotion, just say it fast." And that's it. I've seen Robert Wilson direct, and he's very much concerned with body movement and gesture and completely unconcerned with psychological motivation.

**Vilga:** Does he think the actors do that on their own, or is he just not interested?

**Macaulay:** I think that actors fill in the void on their own, probably. It depends. Some people, in order to do the role, may feel that they have to. A lot of times, a lot of these directors use nonactors to try to get a very different point of view. I know that for a lot of directors, one of the most frustrating things is to have somebody who sits them down after the session and says, "So what's my point of view, what is my motivation here?" Some hate that kind of question.

The theater of performance art is very different. It's almost like it has its own anti-acting tradition. At the same time, in performance art there's certainly a relationship with Method acting. In this point in the development of both forms, you see a real crossover, particularly in the creative process as both sets of artists draw on their past history and past incidents in their work.

For example, someone like Karen Finley, when I first produced her at the Kitchen, was very committed to not having long runs of pieces, trying not to repeat the piece over and over again.[2] She was always trying to change around the material. Now she has a piece, *We Keep Our Victims Waiting,* that she tours around the country. There are sections that are loosely scripted. Even though there's a lot of improvisation within the piece, she has a script, which she actually reads from at different points of the performance. This is a real difference for her; it is more consciously—even though she would never use the word—"acted." It's a more theatrical piece. What she's done is taken the impulse behind her performance work, and used that reservoir of personal feeling and ritual and symbolic gesture, and incorporated it into a theatrically defined, evening-length performance. There are obviously some parallels there to the way Method actors work.

**Vilga:** What motivates someone to become a performance artist?

**Macaulay:** I think it's really very different in each situation. I think that the desire for attention, on the most elemental level, will certainly inform a lot of people.

With people like Vito Acconci, who was working in the early seventies, it really came out of a dedication to trying to push the boundaries of conceptual art and enlarge the boundaries of art in general. With someone like Linda Montana, who is a performance artist working for many, many years, her whole motto is "Life is Art." She's trying to use performance to change every aspect of her life into a continuing art piece. It's really about the transformative effects of art and about art leading to a higher consciousness. With someone like Annie Sprinkle, former porn star and now a performance artist, I think performance art almost plays a therapeutic role. Through performance art, she can go back and view all these different elements of her past history and transform them into something different. She attempts to transform her life into art. I think that there's something which is very healing about that for her. She would be the first person to tell you that.[3]

**Vilga:** How do you spot talent in a performance artist? Is it a measurable quantity?

**Macaulay:** By and large, I think a really good actor in one era could become a really good actor in another era. Acting styles may come and go, or they may even change drastically. People may accept a type of acting performance now which they might not have accepted a few years ago. Still, I think that good actors would merely modify their styles and technique around what's needed for their time. Whereas performance art, in terms of strict definitions, is really about the interaction of the individual artist and some sort of larger idea which exists within a very narrowly defined art world or within a larger culture as a whole.

For example, Karen Finley is an incredibly brilliant and amazing performer onstage. Yet she's also really tapping into a lot of ideas about gender politics and things like that which are very much at the forefront of intellectual thought today. That really gives her work added resonance. If she was working strictly in the field of performance art and her work didn't really have that content, I don't know if people would be as interested in it.

The person who really exemplifies the sort of crossover between performance art and acting is Eric Bogosian.[4] What's really interesting about him is that he started doing performance work that really had a specific relationship to an artistic scene in New York, typically a visual art scene. It came out of galleries like Metro Pictures and artists at the time. There's a real continuum between what they were doing and some of the things that Eric was trying to do in performance. Yet at the same time, what he was doing was—and many people thought this—very close to acting. You could evaluate it from either perspective. An "acting person" could look at what Eric was doing and really like it. The acting person might even see his work almost as a series of acting exercises. The "art person"— who doesn't know anything about acting and who wouldn't care about theater—might see Eric doing these kinds of visual, theatrical bas-reliefs, almost as contemporary archetypes or contemporary icons. In my mind, Eric is the person who exemplifies the potential for crossover in his work.

*Vilga:*   Do many performance artists want to have careers as traditional actors?

*Macaulay:*   Not really. Eric's had a number of starring roles in low-budget mainstream material. He did *Talk Radio,* a play that he wrote, that really was a play. I remember talking to Eric before that opened and he said, "I wrote this play and it's a real play." He was very careful to say it was different from his one-man shows. He acted in a TV movie, and he's done a lot of other stuff like that. So yes, Eric definitely wants to act while continuing to do his own work.

In the seventies, you saw a lot of people getting into performance and getting into a particular type of East Village, media-satire performance, which has some relationship in a lot of ways to standup comedy. Ann Magnuson, the quintessential East Village performance artist, is now a mainstream film and TV actress as well as continuing to do her own stuff.[5] With Ann that makes perfect sense. Her work was always really suited to that. I don't know whether Karen Finley now wants to be an actress. She never has before. Maybe she'll change in the future, but I don't think she's really interested.

The idea of going to a film set and waiting while the lights are getting set up, and sitting in trailers, and coming out for thirty seconds, saying a line, and then going back in, and waiting two hours and then doing something else . . . well, I really think for a lot of people the live performance is the thrill.

**Vilga:** In performance art, do you think the performer's attitude is different toward the audience than it is in conventional acting in theater or film?

**Macaulay:** A lot of performance art is very confrontational toward the audience, which is something you won't really see so much in an actor's performance onstage. You might see a type of theater, like Brecht and post-Brechtian theater, which is very conscious of the audience and conscious of confronting them in some way, but you rarely see a single performance in a play which seems calculated to annoy the audience.

Of course, a lot of performance art is about trying to get some kind of response out of the audience. Years ago, there was a guy who did a performance at the Kitchen who pulled a loaded gun on the audience. He fired into the ceiling and then chased everyone out of the space. Or another guy who did a performance where he led the audience into the theater and then had people come up and ask people to leave individually. It was a very cold day. People left their coats in the theater as they were ushered out on the street. The door was locked, and that was the end of the performance. We're talking a long time ago, and these are very extreme examples, but they really happened.

When Karen does her show, there's a line in it which is a very serious line, but occasionally she'll get crowds that will laugh at it. She says her line and people laugh, so she'll stop and explain to people that it's not funny. This is very different from what an actress would do in traditional theater. Karen is also notorious for asking coughers to leave the theater. Or if somebody's sitting on a ledge or a step or something, she'll stop the show and try to find that person a seat. She's much more interactive with the audience than performers ever would be in conventional theater.

Annie Sprinkle is the ultimate example of this as she makes the audience look up her cervix. Her work is about including the audience in the most intimate details of her life, trying to impart her brand of spiritual blossoming to them. Her range is complete—from a warm embrace of the audience to a real desire to shock and offend. There's always a direct communication to the audience that's not mediated by the material outside of an author's text.

*Vilga:*   What about charisma or stage presence? Is that as important for the performance artist as the actor?

*Macaulay:*   Very definitely. Karen Finley has it. Eric Bogosian has it. Annie Sprinkle has incredible stage presence. So does Vito Acconci, the ultimate conceptual artist. Rachel Rosenthal, a woman who performs her own shows, is sixty-five years old, and has a shaved head, is enormously commanding onstage.[6] There's something deeply compelling about these artists when they're onstage. It's an undeniable charisma the audience feels.

*Vilga:*   With these pieces, is the performer also the writer, actor, and director?

*Macaulay:*   Yes. It's always work people originate themselves and perform themselves. Some people will, for lack of a better term, describe Robert Wilson's work as performance art. It's really more experimental theater. In most performance art, the person doing it is really doing it all themselves.

*Vilga:*   How do people usually come to be performance artists versus becoming traditional actors?

*Macaulay:*   In some ways, it's hard to imagine performance artists and actors in the same basic camp. In another era, I can see performance artists doing something else entirely. There's something you see uniquely in actors, a kind of dependency that actors have on the director, that performance artists don't usually have. Traditional actors possess a weird mix of being very exhibitionistic yet also at the same time being very shy and uncertain of themselves. A lot of performance people write their own material, and while they may be scared that their own material isn't good, they're not really scared of someone else. They're not caught up into psychological issues of control, which you see in a lot of acting scenarios in the actor's field. For example, the director can wear actors down in most plays so that they're terrified of him, and that's not something you really see too much in performance, because those power relationships don't exist in the same way.

*Vilga:*   What are the satisfactions that performance artists seek?

*Macaulay:*   There are different things. They're seeking recognition by their own community, which in some cases will be a very small community of artists, in the same way that a painter might be seeking a small gallery show that's appreciated by the downtown art scene. There definitely are a few people who really view performance art as a stepping-stone to straight acting. Ann Magnuson, I think, is a little bit like that. With some people, like Karen Finley, it's just the fact that she's able to do her work. She can support herself doing it. She can write a new piece, perform her work, and do it in a way that gives her satisfaction. Karen now has a book out and has made records and all sorts of other stuff. I think she's always bemused when she's able to cross over into another medium, but she's really happy just to do her work. With someone like Annie Sprinkle, it's about positive mental health. It's being able to get on with life and have wonderful experiences and meet nice people. So there are a wide mixture of motivations and satisfactions.

**Vilga:** What do you think about the state of the art of theater today in general?

**Macaulay:** Most people in America really had no idea what performance art was until the past year. Then they saw Karen Finley on *Good Morning, America,* talking about this as her grand métier. Most people have some idea of it now, even if it's not a very clear or accurate conception. I think the political climate has given a lot of artists' work a sense of urgency with the general public, and there's an exhilaration in that.

A lot of people, like Karen, who are used to playing to a certain number of people, are right now playing to ten times more people in all these different mediums. Holly Hughes, who's a lesbian playwright, did a one-person piece, a sort of a solo theatrical work. It crossed over into the performance art category at the NEA. She got singled out for her work being homoerotic. Now suddenly there is a political charge to everything she does.[7]

A lot of the performers have a really mixed feeling about that. Performance art now is really drifting more toward standard ideas of acting and mainstream, crossover things. Some of the original avant-garde impulses behind performances with people like Vito Acconci and Chris Burden—the guy who once had himself shot in the arm or nailed himself to a Volkswagen—have faded.[8] Those sorts of people seem to be working less. There really isn't that much of a context in America for that type work anymore, although in Europe it still exists and you find a lot of people doing it. Here in America that time may certainly return, but for the moment it's past.

**Vilga:** Do you see performance as a primarily reactionary kind of art form?

**Macaulay:** Oh, no. Not in the sense of being reactionary to conservative politics.

**Vilga:** No, reactionary to the limits of the regular theater.

**Macaulay:** Oh, yes, definitely that way. All of this came out of happenings in the fifties when we had this real examination and attempt to close the boundaries between everything. You saw it with Allan Kaprow in the

1950s, and in the seventies you saw a lot of collaboration between visual artists working with choreographers, working with composers and really trying to create these multimedia but unified works.[9] It's all about pushing those creative boundaries.

*Vilga:* Do you have any thoughts on traditional acting?

*Macaulay:* I'm not an expert on straight acting, but perhaps from having worked in performance art—and I'm always speaking here in very personal terms—I always like to see people who I think are bringing part of their own personality to a role. I always like those actors who basically play themselves, like Jack Nicholson. No matter the role, he's basically always playing himself. Those are the performances I like. I'm much less interested in very technical performance. I have a love of the truly personal impulse, which motivates performance art and which you see in a lot of mainstream acting as well. I like naturalistic stage acting, but I've just never been able to really buy into the suspension of disbelief when you watch that kind of performance, especially stage acting when there's so much that's played to the audience. There's so much conscious pausing on the laugh lines and proper vocal projecting, which for me always gives those performances a certain type of distance. There are performances which I love in film, but you can't really imagine the same types of performances happening onstage. Maybe my generation is simply a nontheater generation.

*Vilga:* Why is that? What do you see happening to mainstream theater?

*Macaulay:* I'm really the wrong person to ask, but because of a loss of audience, a lack of good plays, prohibitive pricing for the masses, and a diminishing of state and government support, mainstream theater could really just fade away and completely evaporate.

Joe Papp started an artistic revival by bringing new directors and new works to the Public.[10] Even today, I know there are still people really trying to energize theater, people who are trying to work with more abstract ideas and content and staging. Who knows? Maybe some sort of innovations will amaze people and there will be a rejuvenation of theater for the masses.

I always read critics who say that in this kind of media-saturated age, this sort of immediacy, this unique personal impact of theater is something which will cut through everything else. I read something just recently saying that theater could really be a beacon to lead us on the way. It's true that theater has never had a purely escapist function, so perhaps in the twentieth century, theater could become an art form which is really about people examining their own social context and the way they live. But most theater has never really done that for me. I don't think the public sees theater as the antidote to media saturation either, or that it can counter the fact that people are subject to the social-theorist truth that immediate images don't mean anything any more. I don't know if I buy those arguments about theater's abilities to still reach an audience. Everything's flattened out now, and so I just don't know if theater still has this enlarging capacity. Maybe it does.

*Vilga:* With performance artists being seen as actors, do you see ideas of performance being incorporated into other media?

*Macaulay:* In general, no. As I've said, there is a level of crossover between, say, performance and Method. For example, there are parallels in the way that performance artists may really want to immerse themselves in a particular past physical experience as preparation or even to reenact this experience in the piece itself.

I think Chris Burden's first piece was called something like *Five by Five*. He literally put himself into this box in a bus terminal and locked himself in there for twenty-four hours. He had a bottle of water on top of the box with a thing going down and then an empty bottle underneath the box so he could pee. Twenty-four hours later, the water on the top was gone and the bottom was full. That was the piece.

In mainstream entertainment, you read about all these Vietnam films, like *Platoon* [directed by Oliver Stone], and they always hire these guys who are basically professional consultants now for "the films of Vietnam." These guys are all Vietnam vets and commanders. They take these actors, these brat-packers, and schlep them out to the Philippines and make them go through these incredibly grueling authentic army rituals. They beat them down until it's an exact reenactment of boot camp experience. There are certainly parallels in all this to the Method's practice of reexperiencing things emotionally and performance art's deliberate recreation of an event. Don't get me wrong—I don't think Oliver Stone went and saw Vito Acconci's performance. And yet there are similar ideas at work about approaching performance and creating a powerful artistic reality, usually coming from a Method source.

*Vilga:* Are performance artists ever Method trained?

*Macaulay:* I don't know anyone who's trained that way. Some people have assorted arts training, but I don't know anyone who's really had professional training as an actor. A lot of times performance artists will do the work and then, when they get to a certain point, maybe they'll go in for voice training or something. People without mainstream aspirations usually realize their limitations. For example, they've shot their vocal cords screaming, because they don't know how to project, so they get a classically trained vocal coach to help them.

***Vilga:*** Any thoughts on the future of performance art?

***Macaulay:*** Given all the media exposure to performance art, it's increasingly less alternative. That performance art has come so far is just so weird; sometimes it feels something like watching the 1950s American public examine the hula hoop for the very first time.

# *Austin Pendleton*

*Photo: Courtesy of Austin Pendleton*

*Austin Pendleton was born on March 27, 1940, in Warren, Ohio. He received a BA from Yale University in 1961 and trained for the stage at the Williamstown Theatre Festival (1957–1958).*

*Pendleton's Off-Broadway debut was as Jonathan in* Oh Dad, Poor Dad, Mama's Hung You in the Closet and I'm Feelin' So Sad *in 1962. His stage appearances include Motel in* Fiddler on the Roof, *Irwin Ingham in* Hail Scrawdyke!, *Leo Hubbard in* The Little Foxes, *Isaac in* The Last Sweet Days of Isaac, *Frederick in* The Sorrows of Frederick the Great, *and the title roles in* Tartuffe, Uncle Vanya, Hamlet, Richard III, *and* Keats. *Pendleton's film appearances include* What's Up, Doc?, The Front Page, The Muppet Movie, Starting Over, Simon, Mr. and Mrs. Bridge, *and* The

Associate. *He has directed productions of* The American Clock, The Master Builder, The Little Foxes, The Three Sisters, *and* After the Fall.

*In 1994, Pendleton became the artistic director of New York City's Circle Repertory Company. He is a member of the Steppenwolf Theatre Ensemble in Chicago. He has written the plays* Booth *and* Uncle Bob, *both produced in New York and at leading regional theaters.*

●  ────────────────────────────────── ●

*Vilga:*   How did you become an actor and a director?

*Pendleton:*   I can't remember a time when I didn't want to act. Ever. I come from Warren, Ohio, and when I was real young my mom helped to found a community theater. I was about six or seven at the time. The first few plays were put on in our living room. I wasn't in them, but I was absolutely entranced. A few years after that, when I was in junior high school, some friends of mine and I started our own theater and put on plays in the basement of our house. Also, we would go see the touring companies up in Cleveland, and that's where I first saw Geraldine Page onstage.[1] Later when I went to Yale I wasn't a drama major, but I was in every single play the Dramat did.[2] I started apprenticing at Williamstown for two years, played some supporting roles, and read all the Stanislavsky books.

All this was in a great period of American acting, the heyday of what were called the Method actors. Actually, I think we're in one right now, as well. Seeing Geraldine Page act in the theater was a big turning point for me. I told her this years later when I directed her in something. And Brando! All my friends and I went to see *On the Waterfront.* For people of my generation, you remember where you were when you saw that performance. It literally changed everything.

*Vilga:*   More than *Streetcar?*

*Pendleton:*   At that time I had not yet seen *Streetcar.* When it came out as a movie, I was too young. The community theater put it on, and I saw it there, but I didn't see the movie until years later. *On The Waterfront* was a whole new dimension of acting. I think it's like the major moment in American acting. Like Cézanne in painting, it changed everything. Brando finally brought to fruition what he'd been developing. I was also influenced by seeing some of the acting on TV that you'd see in those days: Kim Stanley and Jo Van Fleet and E. G. Marshall, people like that.[3]

I saw Geraldine Page in *The Rainmaker* [N. Richard Nash] in the theater in Cleveland, and until then I didn't think one could do that kind of acting in the theater, that kind of close-screen, immediate, real acting. She did, and it was extraordinary. I thought, "I can do that!" I mean, I couldn't do it then, but I hoped I could someday do that. The kind of acting I'd seen in the theater before then I didn't think I could do, because it was more presentational. I felt a little bit alienated by it, but at the same time I was very drawn to it. A few years after that, when I was at Yale—that was in days when the Shubert in New Haven was the big tryout house—I would see just about everything there. I came to New York to see Broadway shows. It was very easy in those days because you didn't have to pay very much.

*Vilga:* Did you train formally as an actor?

*Pendleton:* I just began to get obsessed with acting. I would read every book I could find about it, but I wasn't really trained very much. As soon as I came into New York, I began to study with Uta Hagen at HB Studios, and I got into a play, [Arthur Kopit's] *Oh Dad, Poor Dad,* which ran for about a year.

*Vilga:* You originated the role of Jonathan in that play?

*Pendleton:* Yes. It's a good play, but it was a terrible year. It's a very uncomfortable part to play, and we were all very unhappy. We weren't unhappy with each other, but we were unhappy. We all got along with each other fine. It was me with Jo Van Fleet again, whom I had idolized from afar for many years, and Barbara Harris. The play is a good play, and the audience loved it, but it was a bad year. After that I wasn't sure if I was going to act anymore. It took me a few years to get back into a joy of acting.

*Vilga:* Did you do any more training after you began acting professionally?

*Pendleton:* I returned to Uta once, and I studied with Herbert when Uta was in London with [Edward Albee's *Who's Afraid of*] *Virginia Woolf.*[4] I was in the training program for the Repertory Theater at Lincoln Center. That was for five days a week, eight hours a day, for eight months. It was in effect an eight-month audition for the company. They picked thirty of us to be in the training program, and then at the end of the year they were going to pick fifteen of us for the show. The acting teacher in that one was Bobby Lewis, and I learned a lot from him, as did everyone.[5] Back in Ohio, I had read *Method or Madness,* the book from his lectures that he'd written in the fifties. That's primarily it in terms of my training.

*Vilga:* When did you become a teacher yourself?

*Pendleton:* In the late sixties, Herbert asked me to teach here at HB Studios. I taught all through the seventies, then I stopped, but I've resumed again after he died a year ago. Uta called me and wanted me to come back, so now I'm teaching again at HB, two classes a week on Mondays and Fridays.

144 • *Acting Now*

*Vilga:*  Was your actual work as an actor or the classes you took more helpful in your training?

*Pendleton:*  Oh, it's all helpful. You really have to do both. Some actors don't get the opportunity to do both, but ideally you should. I don't think you can ever learn enough about acting. I once read an interview with Geraldine Page where she called it "The Bottomless Cup."[6] Stanislavsky was still refining his ideas and his exploration of acting in the late part of his life. The kind of actors who interest me are the ones that just keep on growing and refining. There's always something new in their work, not just recycling old patterns. You're ultimately controlled and limited by who you are—everybody is—but within that acting offers endless possibilities.

When I directed Geraldine Page, it was right toward the end of her life, and she was playing Mrs. Alving in [Henrik Ibsen's] *Ghosts*. It was an extraordinary Geraldine Page performance. It had the well-known mannerisms, but it also had a clarity and a depth to it and an immediacy and spontaneity. It was just exceptional to sit there while she worked on it. You'd help her out a little bit, but watching her work you saw that right up to the end she was endlessly curious about acting.

In this particular production, the director had to leave during previews, and then they had to replace another actor in it after the director was gone. The producers had called me just to place the new actor in it, but I said, "I'd like to redo the whole thing as a director." The producer said fine, so we started all over again.

*Vilga:*  Had the play opened by that point?

*Pendleton:*  No, it opened a few weeks later. The *New York Times* wouldn't cover it, and I still haven't gotten over that. Geraldine Page playing Mrs. Alving in New York, and the *New York Times* wouldn't cover it. They said they hadn't liked some of her recent work. Give me a break! Even if that opinion was valid—which I didn't think it was—what about the previous twenty-five or thirty years of her work? Only Clive Barnes and Michael Feingold reviewed it, and they both raved about her, saying it was one of the best things she'd ever done. They said she was one of the best Mrs. Alvings ever, but the *Times* still wouldn't cover it.

It was a big turning point in my life. I realized we were all on our own. It's a hostile environment for actors in the theater who really want to keep developing. Obviously she was a movie actress, too, and it was two years after that this supposed "has-been" won her Academy Award for *The Trip to Bountiful*. She kept working on these little productions, playing parts like the part in *Ghosts*. She kept on developing and challenging herself, which kept her work so fresh.

*Vilga:*  How do you work with people in your class?

**Pendleton:** I assign them scenes, and then I talk about them. I try to evolve over a couple of terms. I don't encourage anyone to study with me beyond a couple of terms, and then if they want to come back in three or four years, fine. People can get dependent on class in the wrong way, and it always means that other people can't get into the class. Also, through the couple of terms, I try to develop a sense with everybody of where I think an actor's problems are, and then ideally I assign them scenes around that.

**Vilga:** Artistic problems, problems with emotion, or technical problems?

**Pendleton:** All of those. And all of those are usually related, meaning there's usually a problem underlying all of those things. It's been interesting coming back to teach. I hadn't intended to. When Uta put out the call after Herbert died, I thought I'd do a term just for Herbert, because he had meant so much to me. Uta does, too. But it's been terrific to come back, because you find you've learned a lot yourself since the last time.

About three or four years ago as an actor I went underground. I think I was at least partly inspired to do that by Geraldine Page, right after she died. The last couple of things I'd done before that in the theater, I also hadn't been happy with—with my work anyway. All of a sudden, I got all these offers to do all these little Off-Off Broadway shows and play very demanding roles: *Hamlet, Richard III,* a play I'd never heard of by Sophocles called *Philoctetes,* and O'Neill's *Hughie,* which is a long tour-de-force one-act. It's a two character play, and the part I play talks almost all the time. It's one of those O'Neill things where he talks and only gradually does he become aware of what he's saying. Incredible stuff. I was asked to do all four of those things at almost the same time. They were all showcases where you just do sixteen performances—although *Hamlet* we worked on for a year, but ultimately we did sixteen performances. You don't get paid anything, or barely anything. For the whole year of *Hamlet,* I got paid eighty bucks. The idea was supposed to be that they aren't reviewed, although all of those were reviewed a little bit. *Hamlet* and *Hughie* were reviewed in the *Times.* It's wonderful, because you're in New York and you get to work in New York but essentially you're underground. I just did another terrific play called *The Sorrows of Frederick,* which I'd done before, about Frederick the Great. Really, this type of work just stretches you, and so you try to pick up whatever you can in a movie or something like that, just to pay the bills.

**Vilga:** Do you think different training is required for film and theater?

**Pendleton:** No. I don't think so. Some of the more superficial aspects of the technique are different. I could almost say you have to learn a different set of tricks for the two media, but the core of it is the same. Acting is acting.

*Vilga:* Is the class you're teaching for more advanced students?

*Pendleton:* No. I hold auditions and select students from them. I take whoever I find interesting. Sometimes there are almost complete beginners, sometimes not, but I put them in the same class.

*Vilga:* Can you tell if someone is going to be a good actor from an audition?

*Pendleton:* No. Every once in a while you'll see an audition that'll completely knock you out. But even so, you don't know how far beyond that they're going to get. In the early days of teaching, when I first taught here, I didn't audition; I accepted whoever came. The first term I taught, I only had three students. Sometimes people came in and I thought they were hopeless, and then all of a sudden something would happen. You never know. It's like when you're directing and you audition people. You see eight hours of people a day. You realize you probably saw somebody great and you didn't know it. There's just no way of telling for sure.

*Vilga:* Do you think anyone can be trained to be an actor?

*Pendleton:* I think a lot of people could act who don't act. I think for someone to act exceptionally well, it must be a gift. It almost always requires a real commitment and a certain degree of training. But I think, yes, a lot of people.

*Vilga:* Is there a particular type of training that's beneficial?

*Pendleton:* Anything, anything.

*Vilga:* Is anything a waste of time?

*Pendleton:* Well, it isn't the technique so much, but any acting that's taught by someone who doesn't know what they're doing is a waste of time.

*Vilga:* How do you avoid that kind of person?

*Pendleton:* Sometimes you don't know until it's too late. Anybody can hang up a shingle who knows the basic principles of acting. Acting is not a mystery. It really isn't. It's like practicing the piano. There are certain basic things you have to learn, but there are some acting teachers who don't even know that much. Somebody will put on a scene and they'll say, "More energy"—what does that mean? "More energy?" That's like saying, "Try to act more effectively" or "Try to act better." It's stupid. Anybody, even a plodder, who's taken the trouble to learn just the rudiments of acting can teach the basic principles in Stanislavsky. They can teach how to read a play and figure out what your character's about or the exercises for your sensory life and your emotional life. It's not a mystery. It really isn't. The kind of acting teachers to watch out for are the ones who pretend that it is. Really great acting is a mystery, but great anything is a mystery.

**Vilga:** It's interesting that there is a lot of mystery attached to many people's methods.

**Pendleton:** That's one of the corruptions that happens in teaching acting, and having taught I easily see how this occurs. Happily, my needs get answered elsewhere; I act a lot, I direct a lot. But it can become like a narcotic. Students hang on every word you say. Usually a person who's coming to an acting class is in a very hot and vulnerable period of their lives. They're trying to find themselves as an actor, and it can easily get into a kind of guru thing that you try to avoid. Some acting teachers do not try to avoid that. However, even a person like that, if they're teaching well, who cares if they insert their mystique and mystery? That's a small enough price to pay. Even if they really teach a rigid philosophy but teach in a way that is thorough and utterly professional and knowledgeably, then the very rigidity can become a source of strength. I keep saying it, but it's true: the proof is in the pudding. It doesn't matter what their philosophy is; if they teach people how to act well, then they're good teachers. The student's supposed to be a grown-up too. I don't think of actors as victims, as some actors do. Nobody puts a gun to your head to make you do this stuff.

**Vilga:** Do you think a certain amount of time is required to create a good technique? And what is a good technique?

**Pendleton:** A good technique is when you are able to more often than not produce a good piece of work. I don't think there's anybody who does fully realized work all the time. If you're able to do it more often than not, under all kinds of difficult conditions, probably you have a good technique. In other words, I think the definition of a good technique of acting is completely empirical.

When I was a young actor, you'd be appalled if someone didn't work the way you'd been taught to work and you believed was important, because you're busy defining yourself. But over time I worked with more and more actors who wouldn't do anything that I thought you needed to do, and yet their stuff worked.

**Vilga:** As a director, do you find and use each actor's technique?

**Pendleton:** I'm a big believer as a director in working with people in the way they need to work. My favorite story about that is that I heard when Elia Kazan was directing the movie of *Streetcar,* he directed Vivien Leigh in a whole other way than he directed Marlon Brando. And yet, because of that, the chemistry between them on the screen is electric. Each of them is completely allowed to come from where they come from.

When I was a young director, I would try to make everyone work the same way. The paradox is that when you try to make everyone work the same way, it doesn't come out like an ensemble. If you allow everyone to work the way they need to work, it starts to be an ensemble because everybody's coming from their own strength, and that's what makes a real ensemble. I'm a big believer in that.

A few years ago, I directed Irene Worth at Circle in the Square in a late Ibsen play, *John Gabriel Borkman*. It's thrilling, just thrilling. Very demanding roles with long, dense, complex scenes. In fact I think my favorite scene in any play I ever directed is a long scene in that between E. G. Marshall and Irene Worth. If I was in that part of town around the time that scene was playing—it's easily a half hour long—I'd go to the theater and watch it. During that production I stopped into a bookstore, and a new autobiography had come out by Sir John Gielgud, and I looked through it and said, "Irene, this book is so boring. It's just that everything he said about acting is so conventional and so superficial." Irene said, "That's the way he works." I said, "That can't be true," but she said, "It is true."

She said he would be utterly bewildered by what we were doing in these rehearsals. Yet we weren't doing anything new. All we were doing was exploring the scenes and discussing the relationships and the moments and the subtext. People have been doing that for many, many years. But Irene said, "Oh no, he wouldn't understand a word of this." I couldn't believe this was true of such an artist until Irene said, "That's the mystery of it."

I think Gielgud's work is so full of mystery, so full of reality, and charged with poetry. Yet apparently when he rehearsed—and this is according to an actress who adores him—when you worked with him, he just asked the director "Do you want this or that?" and all that stuff we were taught not to do. So if I were directing him—from my mouth to God's ears—if I were directing him, I would just try to figure out how he needed to get the job done, and I would help him to do that, because why fool with that quality of artist?

I don't know the man at all, but to me it's almost like his approach to the work contains an almost unconscious protection of his privacy. His work is so vulnerable, so exposed, that there has to be a self-protective impulse. He says that he's working superficially, using his voice and his intelligence, but that's how he gets to what's really unconscious and painful.

One of the best things I ever saw was him in Pinter's *No Man's Land* with Ralph Richardson. It's just magnificent. E. G. Marshall wants to act in that play with me, and he's trying to find a theater that will do it. Pinter said, "Do that play, because everybody's afraid to do it after it was played by Sir Ralph Richardson and Sir John Gielgud." And I reply, "I'm one of the ones who's afraid!" As an actor, I don't frighten easily, but that scares the hell out of me. It's a brilliant play. But I just can't do it. It seems like doing something very foolish.

**Vilga:**   But you've been doing Hamlet, though?

**Pendleton:**   Hamlet is not associated with just one actor. Also, I don't think that Hamlet has ever been that well played except for one actor I saw do it once some years ago named Danny Davis. Are you aware of him?

**Vilga:**   No, who is he?

**Pendleton:**   He works a lot in regional theaters, at Williamstown and even in New York. He's the only Hamlet I ever saw that I liked. When I was going to play it, I told him that there was only one performance of it that I'd ever seen that intimidates me, and he tried to figure out who from all the great actors. And I said, "No—you." I still remember him in it.

**Vilga:**   Why was he so memorable?

**Pendleton:**   Because he was playing a man. He wasn't self-righteous, which is a trap even very fine actors fall into. They take themselves so seriously that even the humor becomes self-conscious. I never wanted to play the part because I thought there was a Bermuda Triangle around it. All these excellent actors do very badly. I mean, the Olivier Hamlet is a joke. The only one who understood that this character is really screwed up was Danny Davis—he was wonderful. He's played it a lot since then in different theaters around the country. I'd love to see him in it now because I think you should play that part very well into your life. Those are very much the torments of a middle-aged man. Hamlet goes to college, but he's thirty, which is awfully old for college. People have tried to figure out why he's thirty and still in college, but I don't think there really is a reason. When Shakespeare wrote it he was about forty; he had to tell the saga of the prince who was away and came back. He was just writing right from himself, and so he just arbitrarily made the character older. You're not supposed to ask questions about it—it's just a given. If it were supposed to be logically justified, he would have done so.

   *Hamlet* is very exciting stuff to do because it feels like a first draft, partly because it's a mess. I mean, the play is way too long; you have to cut it. To do an uncut *Hamlet* is ludicrous. There's just a lot of stuff there that you just don't need. It rambles on and on and on, and it's all over the map in a structural sense. There are central questions that aren't addressed at all. It also feels like a first draft in that it feels that all the writing just came hot from the pen, like it poured out of him. It doesn't feel edited at all. It's a play about what today would be called a midlife crisis.

***Vilga:*** It's interesting to think of *Hamlet* as a first draft, because Shakespeare is just so sacred.

***Pendleton:*** I know, and yet the plays are very deeply flawed. Not just dramaturgically, either. *Hamlet* is a very sick play, a very misogynistic play. "Frailty, thy name is woman"—give me a break! There isn't anything in the play that says Hamlet might be wrong when he says that. The play just says, "No, that's the way it is. Women are corrupt and unreliable, and men have to put up with that." They're not perfect works at all, but they're so brilliantly written, so alive, and so hot. They tackle the most extraordinary themes. That's why it's so irritating when all these actors play Hamlet as this sort of wonderful man who is more sinned against than sinning. He does terrible things to people in that play. He's out of control most of the time. He is an extraordinary human being, but he's not an ideal of anything. He's certainly not a hero.

I think that Danny's the only actor I ever saw who captured that. He made it so electric it was almost painful. You thought this was a man who does not like himself very much at all, and that makes the whole play come alive. Other actors think they're wonderful human beings playing a heroic victim.

***Vilga:*** Do you feel that the star mentality hurts the work of the serious actor?

***Pendleton:*** There are good actors and not-so-good actors. If you're a good actor and you happen to have a star mentality, it's no problem. It might cause little inconveniences for people you're working with, but it's no big deal. If you're not a good actor, it doesn't matter if you're the most humble, integrated person in the world—you're still not a good actor. I think that sometimes the star mentality can throw the work out of whack a little bit, but it can also add something—a kind of danger and a kind of radiance.

***Vilga:*** Can you spot that quality in your students?

***Pendleton:*** I've always been wrong about it. I never would have guessed which of my students were going to go on to become important film stars. Sometimes I've seen people that I thought were brilliant but went nowhere. I had an actress as a student once who was so compelling that friends of mine would call me up and say, "Is she working today in your class? Is she going to do a scene?" and they'd come and watch it. She's out of the business now. I've never been able to call it.

Some of it is outward appearance, unfortunately, which is stupid. Michelle Pfeiffer is a brilliant actress who happens to be very, very beautiful, but it doesn't always work that way. She really is a wonderful actress. There's such a humility in her work. There's something unself-promoting in her acting. Yet I know magnificent actors who, just because they don't look a certain way, don't get the work that they should. I once read an interview where Meryl Streep told how before she had made it really big, she was being interviewed for a film by an Italian director. No one realized she knew Italian. While she was in the office they were saying in Italian, "Well, she's not very pretty." This is Meryl Streep! Fools, fools! So, I think unfortunately, looks have a lot to do with it.

**Vilga:**   What about stage presence or charisma? Is that something that's important to an actor?

**Pendleton:**   Sure is. After all, the audience wants to see people they want to look at. Of course, in the theater that doesn't have to do with looks at all. Some people have it and some don't.

**Vilga:**   Can it be developed?

**Pendleton:**   Yes, I've seen it happen, but some people just have it. Some people do develop it, but some people just clearly displace the air in the theater in a very interesting way. Sometimes it will make a person controversial.

**Vilga:**   Do you think people can build careers out of that alone?

**Pendleton:**   First of all, you don't build what used to be called a career in the theater at all anymore. If you're lucky in the theater, you work a lot. The idea of a theater career in the old sense of the word, ascending to the top of the theater, is a thing of the past.

**Vilga:**   Why?

**Pendleton:**   You have to make it in the movies or you're not an important name. It's simple as that. Or in television.

**Vilga:**   Aren't there any theater names?

**Pendleton:**   No, there aren't anymore. There were when I was a kid, but there aren't anymore. If a person is a name in the theater, in terms of the public, it's because the public knows them from the movies. Now, hopefully, before they got to the movies, they developed themselves in the theater, like Al Pacino. Or like Meryl Streep, if she ever chooses to go back.

**Vilga:**   Do those people go back?

**Pendleton:**   A lot of them do. Al Pacino does, George C. Scott does. Sometimes Glenn Close does. I wish Meryl Streep would, because she's so brilliant in the theater. The first time I ever saw her was in the theater. She did the season at the Phoenix. A friend of mine, Arvin Brown, directed a double bill of a play by Tennessee Williams and one by Arthur Miller.[7] I went to the first preview. This girl came out, and in each play she played this radically different character. She was way over the top, but she was so brilliant, and the contrast between the two characters she played was so striking. She had that thing, that old-time religion of star quality. Kate Nelligan has that. She can stand up there and not move, just talk and play a scene, and it's just so wonderful to watch.

*Vilga:* Have you found that the impulse to act tends to vary from actor to actor?

*Pendleton:* Yes. It's very personal.

*Vilga:* Do certain kinds of impulses lead to good or bad acting?

*Pendleton:* No. It's never pure—let me tell you that. It has to do with—I'm very aware of this in my own life right now—it has to do with being acknowledged. It's not just having people look at you but also appreciating you. I think actors tend to have a sense that "no one understands quite who I am, and I have to make it clear to the world somehow."

*Vilga:* Do you think they understand who they are?

*Pendleton:* No. Except when you're really connecting with the part—like this play I just did, *The Sorrows of Frederick*—you feel more true to yourself than you do in life. You don't know the reason why certain roles bring this out. There are plays you want people to see you in because you think that you're very good in them, and yet sometimes those roles are the ones you can take or leave. With other roles you just feel on some profound level that you're being truer to yourself than you are in everyday reality, and it just has to be acknowledged. You have this tremendous hunger to be acknowledged for what you actually are, even though the outer circumstances of the part may make no sense in terms of your life. There's this tremendous feeling that if you're not acknowledged as an actor for some of that work, that some great part of who you really are will never be acknowledged.

Some people do not have that tremendous hunger to have who they are be acknowledged, although I think everybody has it in them somewhere to a degree. To an actor, not having that acknowledgment can be truly painful. Therefore, it's vitally important that people see you in those particular roles.

*Vilga:* Acknowledgment from the audience or from the experience of doing it?

*Pendleton:* All of that. You just feel that the essence of who you are is being fully tapped in certain roles and certain pieces of work you do. Often those roles are very painful to do. Doing them can really screw you up, but you don't want to stop, because you feel it's important.

*Vilga:* Do you feel that can screw up your outside life?

*Pendleton:* Yes. It does for me, anyway.

*Vilga:* In a lasting way?

*Pendleton:* Hopefully not. You get over it. But it has a cumulative effect, which in one way kind of bends you out of shape a little bit and in another way makes you stronger, because you keep on confronting things about yourself in a very active way that you might not otherwise.

*Vilga:* Is it because you're becoming this other character?

*Pendleton:* Yes, you are becoming this other character. What it really is when you're truly connected is that a certain part of yourself is being actualized that isn't actualized to that degree in life, if at all. The only reason it's not actualized is because of the circumstances of your life. Your childhood, your patterns, and everything create a certain way that your life goes, which is not totally in tune with who you are. Everybody feels that way about something or another.

In acting, sometimes you can find a part where all that stuff that isn't actualized in the way your life has gone is suddenly tapped into. In the process of becoming another character you are becoming yourself in a way that you don't always become, perhaps in a way you wouldn't even want to. But it's still there. It's crying out to be actualized. Not just expressed, but made actual. Certain things in yourself that are usually just pure potential, a possibility for good or bad, all of a sudden come alive and make you feel deeply connected.

*Vilga:* Do you have any thoughts on the practicalities of life as an actor and the difficulties of getting work?

*Pendleton:* Well, I think it's much harder now. . . . No, it's not. It was always hard. Let's not romanticize the way it was. Agents now audition people, which they didn't use to do, so that makes it easier, if you can do a really great audition. Also, when I came to New York there weren't all these things now like showcases.[8] The play we just did, *The Sorrows of Frederick*, was a showcase and a very heavily attended one. A lot of the actors in that have picked up agents from that because it was an excellent show and they were all very good in it. Practically everyone in it has ended up with an agent.

*Vilga:* Do you think that actors are better trained now than they were?

*Pendleton:* The same. The training itself is exactly the same. There's a handful of really good teachers and some schlocks. It's always been like that.

*Vilga:* If you had one piece of advice to give to the young actor, what would it be?

*Pendleton:* Well, this is not original with me, but I would say make sure you really want to do it. Be certain that you really want to do it for its own sake. It has to do two things: it has to fulfill some real hunger in you that cannot be fulfilled any other way, and secondly, you have to have a real love of the material. In other words, it isn't just about you. It's wanting to connect with these great things that people have written. If you have that, then go for it.

If you don't have that, it becomes a very empty, emotionally brutal life. You're always being beaten up. You have to be almost absurdly lucky in a way that is not true in a lot of professions. You're at the whim of the opinions of so many people: casting directors and directors, critics and producers. No one ever went up to John Updike and said, "We're going to go a different way with who's going to write the Rabbit books." Nobody ever said to Leo Tolstoy, "With *Anna Karenina,* you don't get to write it." But that's what an actor works with all the time. "We're gonna ask another painter to do the next draft of this painting." It's a grotesque situation. It's no way to live. You have to really want to do it.

*Vilga:* Is there any way around that?

*Pendleton:* Actors come to me when I'm directing a play and they say, "I have to play this role. I just have to. I've worked for years as an actor, and now I'm ready to do it. It's exactly what I know at this moment in my life." They may be right, but still you decide not to cast them. You cast some-body else instead—I've done it myself to actors—simply because you want somebody else. You don't know whether you're right or wrong. It's just so. When I direct other actors, they are at the mercy of my whims and my subjectivity. I try to be clear with myself about it, and I try to do the right thing, but basically they're up against my opinions. That's the way an actor lives his entire life.

I also believe as an actor you have to be open and willing to go anywhere or try anything. You should be willing to act in a basement. You should do everything you can to try to keep acting, because I think it's like anything else. If you don't act for a number of years just because you don't approve of the venue, something goes out of it. Or if you always act in the same kind of role, something goes out of your work.

*Vilga:* What's more satisfying for you, acting or directing?

**Pendleton:** Acting, acting, acting. By a mile. I like directing very much. I'm about to direct *Who's Afraid of Virginia Woolf?* in Arizona with four actors I admire a great deal, and that's thrilling. But if I had to choose between acting and directing, there's no question. Acting is a very deep— I'd like to think of another word but I can't—agenda for me. Directing's a job. Sometimes it's a very exciting job, and it's very pleasurable to direct actors in really exciting material, but it doesn't keep me up nights. It doesn't make me feel that if I don't do that, a part of me will die. Acting always makes me feel that way.

# Neil Pepe

*Neil Pepe is the artistic director of the Atlantic Theater Company. He has appeared in* Trafficking in Broken Hearts, Down the Shore, The Lights, Boys' Life, Trust, Rosemary for Remembrance, *and* Women and Water, *among other plays. On TV he has appeared in* Law and Order, New York Undercover, *and* Our Town. *On film he has appeared in* Homicide, Assassination, *and the soon-to-be-released* Last Days of May.

**Vilga:** How did you first become involved with acting?

**Pepe:** I was very shy when I began high school, and I ended up taking a couple of drama classes, one with Joyce Devlin, who now teaches at

Mount Holyoke. I'm from an artsy background—my father was a composer and a jazz drummer, and my mother was a sculptor—and I grew up
in southern Vermont, where there'd been a migration of New York artists. I
took a year off between high school and college and went to England,
where I did a short apprenticeship at a place called the Redgrave Grape
Theatre outside of London. Then I went to Kenyon College thinking that I
would pursue either music or acting along with liberal arts. Kenyon had a
great undergraduate theater program, which I supplemented with an apprenticeship at the Williamstown Theatre Festival and the Circle in the
Square's summer acting program. When I got out of college, I made the
decision that I really wanted to pursue acting and that I would give myself
about five years to see where it took me.

I came to New York and just started pounding the pavement looking for
jobs. I got a money job and also did assistant stage managing jobs. I got my
first show at La MaMa. It was a performance art piece called *Return to
Sender*. Michael Chiklis, who's now "The Commish" on TV, was also in it.
It was wild and fun, just him and me and two other people. It was this 3-D
performance piece, which had all recorded music that we lip-synched to.
The audience had to wear 3-D glasses.

I got involved with the Atlantic Theater because I was working a job at
the Water Club parking cars. I met Clark Gregg, who at that time was the
artistic director of the Atlantic. He told me that he had been studying with
David Mamet, and I had always been interested in Mamet's writing.[1] I
asked Clark if there was anything I could do to help out at the Atlantic,
and I ended up assistant stage-managing a big benefit they had. I had a
great time, but I had applied to Actors Theatre of Louisville and got
accepted as an apprentice, so I left New York for Kentucky.

Louisville was my first intense exposure to what running a professional
theater really meant. I got to do a lot of acting and studying and was
exposed to great new writers, actors, and directors. The apprenticeship at
Louisville is about 80 percent tech work. If you're lucky you get opportunities to be in their shows. At the end of my time at Louisville, I got a big
agent and came to New York all set to get started in an acting career. Once
again Clark Gregg called me, asking if I wanted to come up and study with
Mamet in Vermont. I said, "Yeah, great, but I don't have the money to do
it." He said, "Maybe you could do some technical work in return for
classes." I agreed and went to Vermont that summer only to find out that I
was, in fact, the technical director for the biggest summer season they'd
ever done, something like seven plays in eight weeks. I didn't get as much
class time as I expected to, but I learned how to build a lot of sets on no
money out of cardboard boxes. That summer we did plays by Howard
Korder, Craig Lucas, Tom Dougah, and Mamet. I think John Guare may
have come up to visit that summer as well.[2]

**Vilga:**   So this was your first extended experience with the Atlantic?

**Pepe:**   Yes. It fascinated me because it was a group of students and graduates all about my age who were the hardest-working people I'd ever met. All the work they were doing was exciting, they had a common acting technique, and they were very committed to an artistic ideal, a specific way of working. Mamet and Macy and the Atlantic had a very specific technique, Practical Aesthetics, which had become a common language as well as a philosophy and a way of running a theater.[3] After that, in the fall of 1988, we came back to New York, and they took me into the company just as the company got its big start doing *Boys' Life* at Lincoln Center.

I was really excited about being part of a growing company and being involved in theater for the sake of theater, not simply for the sake of getting whatever job you could get from the exposure. I was always inter-ested in the collaborative process of theater and found I especially liked working with this group of people. Mamet and Macy are, in fact, the most loyal people I've ever met. I was also really impressed that Mamet and Mosher and Macy would take a chance on young people.[4] They taught us the strengths of staying committed to a group you believe in as opposed to getting together a disparate troop of actors every time you do a show. The payoff can be so much greater when a cohesive group creates something. We were obviously inspired by companies like the Group Theatre, the Moscow Art Theatre, and Steppenwolf.[5]

At the time the Atlantic was like a lot of young companies: we did everything ourselves. Not only did we act and direct, we ran the box office and worked in development. Once you were in the company, you were given a job depending on what you were interested in or where you were skilled. I did a lot of technical work, but I also became the development director for our summers in Vermont, establishing ways of producing and raising money for the shows there.

**Vilga:**   After performing at Lincoln Center, how did things change for the company?

**Pepe:**   *Boys' Life* at Lincoln Center was a real turning point. Up to that point the Atlantic definitely had been an experiment, more a bunch of students who were really committed to the idea of having a theater com-pany rather than developing as an institution. Because of Lincoln Center, all of a sudden we joined the union and got a lot of press and everybody was asking: "Who are these young people who are doing this hit show at Lincoln Center?"

It was a real thrill. We were all about twenty-three or twenty-four at that time. We came off of that experience and immediately went into a very ambitious summer season. We did John Guare's play *Women in Water,* which was a huge production, a play by Quincy Long called *Shaker Heights,* which we revived recently, and a play by Wendy McCleod called *Apocalyptic Butterflies.* It was a great summer, really exciting and also entirely exhausting because we were working around the clock. Yet we came out of that summer with a big, big debt and realized we needed to figure out our infrastructure, plan our long-term fund-raising, find adequate staffing, and get our own space if we were to survive.

All those questions starting coming up, so we had to pull back and reanalyze. I was very involved in this process—as were many company members—and even though I was also pursuing outside work I continued to get more and more involved in Atlantic's operations. I felt challenged artistically.

We tackled our problems one by one. We hired a new managing director. We started the process of looking for a permanent home. We continued to do big benefits. We did some small Off-Off Broadway shows. We continued to go up to Vermont and do workshops. We also continued working on the radio—that's been a fun part of what we do. Eventually, in the fall I think of 1990, we got the lease on our own Off-Broadway theater, the old Apple Corps Theater on West 20th Street.

**Vilga:**  What about the school your company runs?

**Pepe:**  At a certain point Mamet and Macy basically turned over the school to us to run. The school is a source of income as well as a way of expanding and developing this technique of acting called Practical Aesthetics. It continually reminds us where we came from and what our ideals are.

Mamet had come to teach acting at NYU in 1983 and decided he wanted to create a workshop with all of his NYU students in Vermont. Later, he was going out to Chicago to do some work with Gregory Mosher, the artistic director of the Goodman Theatre, and so he brought his students out to be interns there for a year. Those students ended up forming a company, and that's how the company and the Atlantic school started. The acting technique which those students learned continues now through NYU and the Practical Aesthetics program. Bill Macy was involved in running it, and Steven Schachter is another director who was associated with it. Now the program has evolved into a formalized three-year acting program at NYU.

**Vilga:**  Do the full-time students work in productions, too?

**Pepe:**  Sometimes. We've found splitting their focus is not good. One of Mamet's beliefs is: don't put somebody onstage before they're ready. When you're in class, you shouldn't perform much. At that point your training should be about your classes. Sometimes students help out back-stage, or they volunteer on their own time.

***Vilga:*** Can you elaborate on what technique is taught in the classes?

***Pepe:*** It's a philosophy of acting called Practical Aesthetics. It's a tech-nique developed by Mamet and Macy. Mamet had studied at the Neigh-borhood Playhouse. He began to feel that many techniques of acting that were being taught in New York and elsewhere were not effective. Simply put, they were not practical in that you didn't come away with a set of tools that you could apply performing in a play. You do all these exercises in classes and still pick up the play and realize you have no idea what to do with it. So Mamet developed this "practical" technique based in part on the theories of Meisner and on the later writings of Stanislavsky, along with ideas from Epictetus, Bruno Bettelheim, and Aristotle. It's also in-spired by Joseph Campbell's writings on myth and the role of storytelling in society.

The technique itself is all about action as opposed to emotion. It's about playing actions and working moment to moment in an improvisational way. Some people view it as a reaction to the Method, and I suppose in some ways they're right. We don't concentrate on emotion. The idea is that emotion is not something within your control. It's a by-product of action. If I'm angry, if I'm frustrated, if I'm elated, it usually has to do with what I'm trying to do in a scene and whether I'm succeeding or failing. This is opposed to walking into the scene trying to "be" elated. Your emotion has to be based on actions. It also has to do with playing off the other person. If you're concentrating on what you're trying to get done as opposed to your own feelings, it takes the focus off of yourself. You become less self-conscious. If you simply play your action, the rest will come.

***Vilga:*** How is it related to storytelling?

***Pepe:*** The general philosophy of the technique involves storytelling, per-haps because it was started by a playwright. Practical Aesthetics stresses telling the story of the play as simply and as truthfully as possible. It's a technique that gives the actor the tools to pick up a play and ask, "What's my throughline? If this is what the story is truly about, what is my role in that story? How do I personalize that? How do I get onstage and work off the other person and live truthfully under the imaginary circumstances of the play?"

As an actor you should know how to analyze a play. You need to under-stand how to pick up a play and decide what steps you'll take to bring the character to life; how to make choices as opposed to thinking about things in an ethereal way. In many ways, Practical Aesthetics is a rather selfless theory of acting. A lot of actors try to get all the focus on themselves when the focus should be on the story. The question should be: is the audience fully experiencing the story? That should be my only objective as an actor, not making myself the star.

**Vilga:** How successful have you been teaching this method to younger students?

**Pepe:** I think it's one of the most practical methods of acting that I've ever come across and also one of the best foundations for younger acting students. I think a lot of people who study acting or who talk about an acting method want to say their theory is the be-all and end-all theory. I don't believe that about any acting theory. I don't think there is only one way to study. I think there's huge value in what Stella Adler taught and in the Strasberg and Meisner work. The thing that I like most about this technique, however, is that it gives you a solid structure, which is especially important for a young student. As Macy once pointed out, it's the same idea as creating a great foundation for a house.

For us as a theater company the technique has been helpful because it's become our common language. This is not to say that everybody in the theater company has studied the technique formally, although that's how it used to be at a certain point. We realized there were many terrific actors we wanted to work with, perhaps even wanted to take into the company, who worked differently. Ultimately the company tends to find that good, skilled actors find their way to the same ends. They play objectives. They play actions. It's about doing truthful, simple work that's, above all else, telling the story of the play.

The technique itself continues evolving. Scott Zigler, the artistic director previous to me, who's now the unofficial master teacher of this technique, has done some really interesting work expanding the concepts of Practical Aesthetics. He recently got very involved with Anne Bogart's work and some Suzuki work from Japan.[6] Early on many people thought the Atlantic was just about Mamet's work, but in the past three years we've tried to establish ourselves on our own while going in new creative directions.

**Vilga:** How involved is Mamet with the company?

**Pepe:** He's still the reigning mentor of the company. He's on the board as a founding member but not as an active member. He wrote an adaptation of Chekhov's *The Three Sisters* for us, and he's constantly suggesting creative ideas. He's a great sounding board. Mamet is great at coming in and reminding us why we do what we do.

I really feel that he's one of the most brilliant teachers I've ever seen. He not only has creative input but is also constantly thinking about why you do theater and what the purpose of theater is. He has an acute understanding of this business and the history of theater and where to put your focus as an artist. He understands how you can get sucked into the whole whorish American entertainment business where everybody's tempting you to sell out. "I'll give you thousands of dollars, but you have to do it my way." Mamet is not only incredible for his sense of loyalty to those people who bravely stand by their own ideals, but also is just great in terms of gently reminding us why we're doing what we do and all the reasons not to sell out but to stick to higher principles.

*Vilga:* How many people are in the company now?

*Pepe:* Twenty-two, give or take a few. Mainly actors, some directors, a couple of writers, a casting director, and a couple of producers. What's happened in the past couple of years is people have begun—and most companies go through this—getting more and more work in Los Angeles. They get work in TV and movies and other plays. One of my focuses as artistic director has to be to find work that serves this specific ensemble. This gets more difficult when people are working all over and the available ensemble changes.

*Vilga:* How many productions do you do a year?

*Pepe:* Ideally we try to do anywhere between two and four productions a year. That always depends on how much money we can raise and how ticket sales go. We've succeeded in the past four or five years in doing at least two productions a year, sometimes three and sometimes even four. We also do late-night productions or guest artists things, or whatever we can, depending on what money we can generate.

My artistic leaning, when choosing plays, tends to be toward new plays. This is something that we've been going over a lot recently, identifying what it is exactly we're looking for in new and old plays. We're always looking for plays that are relevant, that somehow appeal to a truth that we think is important about this day and age. For instance, I wanted to do this play by Sidney Kingsley called *Detective Story* that was written in 1948. It was one of the first plays to deal with police brutality and abortion. It's about a man who's brought down by his own principles, which to me is very related to a lot of the right-wing things that are happening now. I feel the play may be very relevant even though it was written forty or fifty years ago. Also, I'm certainly looking for plays with language specifically for the theater as opposed to film or television. There are a lot of playwrights who write more for film than theater, but I'm always looking for a truly theatrical voice.

*Vilga:* Do you choose the plays the company does?

*Pepe:* For the most part, it's a democratic process. We have a literary committee and a literary manager. We get plays from agents and some that are unsolicited. When we get down to the scripts that we want to actually look at, they're usually each given two reads. If we decide we want to consider a work for production, we do a reading for the company and then I get everybody's feedback, but I make the final decision myself. It's good to have one person have the final decision, because in a totally democratic process it becomes very difficult to make decisions.

**Vilga:**  How does someone become a member of the company?

**Pepe:**  Oddly enough, I don't know exactly, because it's certainly not set in stone. It used to be you had to have taken at least four semesters of classes with the Atlantic or with Practical Aesthetics Workshop so that you had an understanding of the acting technique. About three years ago we decided that's not really appropriate anymore because there are actors we want to work with who haven't studied this method. Now it's come down to having worked with the company at some time so we have an idea of what your work is like and what your work habits are. Then somebody in the company nominates you to become a company member and it's put to a vote.

We've been revamping our company constitution over the past three months. I've been trying to get away from the things that happen when a lot of theater companies hold on to an ideal that has become stagnant. If you hold on to the past too hard, you're not going to grow. Your concerns become about protecting your vision as opposed to challenging it. I've been trying to encourage members to bring in people who will push the company in new directions and at the same time understand our philosophy. I want people who respect that it's about serving each other as much as possible and really staying committed to an ideal. Once you're in, in most cases, we're able to give people the opportunity to do good work. It's harder as the company expands, because our ability to have all our members develop on the main stage is not as easy as it used to be. But we try to, as much as possible, stay committed and loyal to our members.

**Vilga:**  How important is training to the professional actor?

**Pepe:**  I think in theater it's difficult to get by without training, especially if you're doing a run of a show that's longer than two weeks. I think in film you can get by with very little training and still be believable. There are people who just happen to be very honest, truthful individuals that can live moment to moment on film. They're not likely to be able to do that consistently for a long period of time onstage, however, and that's where technique comes in. People without technique aren't able to do things like project their voice or withstand four- to eight- to twelve-week runs or even longer.

Yet technique can kill an actor, too. Many people get too involved in the technique itself, as opposed to using the technique as a way of freeing themselves as actors. Technique should be about giving actors the ability to go onstage and act truthfully and be in the moment and have fun and improvise. Those are the reasons we do theater in the first place.

I think technique is also important to sustain an acting career. I think as a person you have to know why you're doing what you're doing and have a sense of how to analyze scripts, how to grow, and of different things you're going to try as an artist. Otherwise it's sort of hit or miss. You can perform a play and maybe you do well one night and maybe you don't the next, and you can't even determine what's behind the inconsistency.

**Vilga:** Have you ever seen training that is just a total waste of time?

**Pepe:** Yes. I've studied with some people whose work was not about training people to act. It was about the teacher and the teacher wanting to control the students. It was about whether or not people agreed with this teacher's technique. It wasn't about learning. It was extremely manipulative. Or it was about doing exercises that were supposedly to free us. I often believe in those kinds of exercises, but if they're not used in the right way, they can really throw you off. When I was younger, I walked out of a lot of classes really confused and insecure because I felt the teacher had broken me down, gotten me to this sensitive, vulnerable place, and then didn't show me why or how it translated into working on a play or a film. All these poor students are wandering around New York totally confused and not knowing why they did what they just did in class. I don't think anybody has a right to teach acting unless they understand how it really relates to getting on the stage and making scenes work. So much of it is about people making money and manipulation. I see it a lot. That's very scary and not right.

**Vilga:** Do you think that you could spot that kind of teaching more easily now?

**Pepe:** Yes, I think so. Yet there are times when I come across people who have a completely different philosophy of acting or producing theater than I do and my initial reaction is "Oh, I don't agree." Then I listen to them, and many times they convince me that it's just another way of doing theater. It turns out, in fact, that they're incredibly intelligent and just have a different approach. If they're doing it for honorable and truthful reasons and it's all about telling great, wonderful stories, it's perfectly fine.

So often, what gets produced is about the money. So much art today, so much entertainment today, is based on money and hype and fame and commercial bankability. Multimillion-dollar decisions are made that have nothing to do with whether the piece of art, the play, the movie, says anything to anyone. That's been around for a while, but I think right now many decisions are based purely on commercialism, and it creates a lot of problems for people, especially people trying to produce worthwhile theater.

*Vilga:* What do you think about the state of theater in New York?

*Pepe:* I think it's twofold. A lot of people get angry when people say this, but I think that theater as we have known it is dying—it may even be dead already. That's really depressing. On the flip side, I think that this can be exciting, because it creates opportunity for the next generation to create something new. That's what I find very thrilling and very difficult about it. People like us are trying to do plays that we believe in, however we can. We scrape together a little amount of money just so we can have the control to do pieces that speak to us powerfully and truthfully.

Theater today needs to reinvent fund-raising in order to survive. There's not a lot of government money anymore. There's not a lot of state money. Corporate money is a double-edged sword: you can get it, but then they look over your shoulder to make sure they agree with what they're sponsoring. If you want to do something controversial, they may pull the money. It's a very difficult time, but I think it's an incredibly exciting time as well because it's time to reinvent. It's an opportunity for people our age to bring out a new generation of plays, a new generation of theatergoers, and to say something about society right now.

It's exciting to be involved in theater at the end of the century, although sometimes I feel I'm banging my head against a wall. There's more money, there's more work almost everywhere else in entertainment. I get really frustrated because I've spent the past three and a half years as artistic director of a theater often getting up in the morning and wondering, "Why am I doing this? Why am I making no money? Why am I striving for something that people may or may not even come to see?"

On the one hand, I think people do appreciate what we're doing. We're producing theater and making it work. People recognize that and we get their respect, and that's an honor for me. At the same time, you constantly ask, "Do people really want theater anymore?" I think they do, it's just a very hard time to get people out of their houses. It's so heartening when they do get out of their apartments and come to the theater and see something provocative. You can sense immediately that there is a need for this, that people like to be together in a community and see things live onstage as opposed to privately on their TV sets. People are often pleasantly surprised when they do something as old-fashioned as watching a play on a stage and participating with a live audience. It's a powerful and increasingly rare feeling of community at work.

This hearkens back to one of the reasons I've made theater my career, and one of the philosophies that the Atlantic is based on, which is the role of myth and storytelling in society. I think it also goes back to why so much theater came from churches. It always had to do with a group of people gathering and a story being told that somehow got people to reflect on their lives or consider things together that maybe they hadn't considered separately. It might help their lives or it might not; it might make them laugh or it might not. It might somehow make life a little easier or a little bit richer or expose a truth that hadn't been exposed before. My artistic checkpoints are always "Is it truthful? Do I believe in it? Am I seeing something that I really believe in, or are people lying?" I think the opportunity and unique power of theater to expose and share these truths are still there if we keep trying to push forward.

**Vilga:** Are there certain modern career traps you see actors falling into?

**Pepe:** Yes, I think there are a couple of them. I was talking before about how in this day and age there's a temptation for young actors to want to make it right away. Young good-looking men and women want to be scooped up by the film business to make movies. Sometimes those movies will be great and sometimes they'll not be. In some ways it's great for people to have the opportunity to have success so early. I think the thing that is difficult is for them to recognize is that it's important to train in order to sustain a long career.

It's painful sometimes for me to watch young people do a couple of movies and then realize that they don't have any technique or the skills to take on anything large. All of a sudden they're twenty-six, they've exploited their niche, and they have no work. They're left with nothing. You need to have a clear idea of what you're getting into this business for, always challenging yourself further to learn and develop your craft.

It's difficult, because you can't expect to make a living in the theater. I know so many wonderful actors who want to be doing theater but can't. They have to do television or films to pay the rent. Some television and some films are great, and we all want to do them. The difficult thing is that sometimes people are forced to compromise their beliefs or their talent because they need to make money.

The paradox is either you're making tons of money in California or you're making nothing in New York. Even Broadway actors are hardly earning a living. I'm seeing a lot of decisions, as difficult as they are, made solely on the idea of money and fame as opposed to really stepping back and making a conscious personal choice about the artistic reasons for doing something.

Another thing is the need to have the ability to look yourself honestly in the mirror and say, "This is who I am." That's a longer process which everybody should go through, not just actors. The constant inquiry must be "Who am I, really?" Whether you need to go to a shrink to do that or explore it through your acting class, the better idea you have of who you are—an honest self-perception of what you look like, how you're perceived, what your strengths are, what your weaknesses are—the happier you're going to be. It's really sad, but I meet a lot of people who have a perception of themselves that differs entirely from how they actually come across to the world.

It sometimes happens to actors as they get older. They perceive themselves to still be young leading men or women when they're not. It's hugely important to have a strong sense of who you really are, and it's a lifelong process. If we watch all of the great artists that we've admired, that's their constant pursuit. Whenever they have a success, they immediately turn inward to reexamine "What am I? Who am I? What am I trying to do?" They continually look at themselves as realistically as possible, which is extremely hard to do. It's really nice if somebody comes up to you and says, "You're just great; you're going to be a star." We all love compliments, but the more I meet people that I really respect, I find that self-inquiry, humility, and openness of ideas are what make fulfilling lives.

*Vilga:* If you had one piece of advice to give to the young actor, what would it be?

*Pepe:* Take your time. Be honest. Be brave. Stick to your goals and principles at all costs. Everybody's going to tell you something different, but the clearer and more honest you are about who you are, the more satisfying your life and work is going to be. Have goals that you believe are honorable and are for the good and that you can bravely pursue. Don't let anybody take them away from you, especially when you get into situations where you're being offered lots of money or being told that you're wrong because you're not doing the commercial thing.

When push comes to shove, I always feel when you get to the end of your life you're going to turn back and ask, "What am I proud of?" I'm proud of those decisions I made that I knew I wanted to make, when I stood by what I believed in and didn't compromise. People who live on throughout history are those people who, like van Gogh, may never have realized any success in their own lifetime but stuck by what they believed in. That's difficult sometimes, yet I think that kind of commitment really pays off for the artist. You'll have much more fulfilling relationships if you're able to do that, because you'll surround yourself with other people who believe in something and who are honest people who stick by their word and are loyal. That's the kind of support an artist really needs if he's to truly discover and reveal himself in his work and in his life.

# *Juliet Taylor*

*Following her graduation from Smith College in 1967, Juliet Taylor joined the staff of producer David Merrick, remaining there until the spring of 1968. At that time she went to work as a secretary to Marion Dougherty, who was opening a motion picture casting office in New York. Taylor ran Marion Dougherty Associates from 1973, when Marion Dougherty left casting to produce films, until 1977, when Taylor became director of East Coast casting for Paramount Pictures. She left that position in 1978 to cast motion pictures independently.*

    *Films Taylor has cast include* The Exorcist, Taxi Driver, The Front, Network, Marathon Man, Julia, Close Encounters of the Third Kind, Annie Hall, Pretty Baby, Interiors, Manhattan, Arthur, Terms of Endearment, Broadway Danny Rose, The Purple Rose of Cairo, Hannah and Her Sisters, Big, Working Girl, Mississippi Burning, Dangerous Liaisons, Crimes and Misdemeanors, Postcards from the Edge, The Grifters, Sleepless in Seattle, Schindler's List, Wolf, Interview with the Vampire, Bullets over Broadway, Mighty Aphrodite, *and* The Birdcage.

●————————————————————————●

***Vilga:*** How did you become a casting director?

***Taylor:*** That's actually an interesting question, because I certainly didn't plan to become a casting director. I'd always enjoyed performance. When I was a child I always loved the theater. I acted throughout grade school, and when I was in high school I'm sure I had acting fantasies. By the time I got to college the competition was already too stiff for me, so I started to back off. Clearly I didn't have the temperament for an acting career.

***Vilga:*** Did you train as an actor?

***Taylor:*** No, just the usual active high school drama club, that kind of thing. As I say, I started to give up any performing aspirations in college, but I majored in theater nonetheless. I spent most of my time studying literature and criticism, which I enjoyed tremendously. At the same time, I really decided not to pursue a scholarly route. It became sort of problematic because I clearly was in theater but didn't, in my opinion, have any apparent talent. (*Laughs*) I certainly couldn't design, and I really didn't have whatever the stuff was that was going to get me up on a stage unless I was asked. I didn't want to have to audition for anything.

I didn't even know what producing meant, because I came from a totally untheatrical family. Everybody was afraid that I would get in with a rough crowd, but still I just blindly came to New York to look for a job. I literally started pounding the pavement. I was very fortunate, because I got a job working for David Merrick, the theatrical producer. This was in the fall of 1967. He was extremely prolific and had seven or eight shows running on Broadway at the time. My first day working there, in fact, was the morning after Pearl Bailey debuted in *Hello, Dolly!* It was a very, very active and exciting office, and I was really in the thick of it. I was just a secretary-receptionist there, but it was very thrilling.

A woman who worked for David Merrick as a casting director had left to become a casting director for someone else. She went to work with Marion Dougherty, who was the primary film and television casting director in New York, in fact in the country, at that time. She had done all the live television in New York. When films started coming to New York, she was the one who everybody turned to for movies. Marion was so busy then because when Mayor Lindsay came in he suddenly made it very attractive to make movies in New York, which had never happened before.

She started an office with a staff and asked if I wanted to come and be a secretary. I had heard of casting directors before, and I'd even heard one speak once when I was in college. I thought it was sort of an interesting way to combine one's interest in theater and performance and also to maintain an emotional involvement with a production. I hadn't really thought about it too much more than that, and so it was just by chance and good fortune that I fell into it.

*Vilga:* When did you first realize that you were particularly good at it?

*Taylor:* I think that there's a general terror among casting directors that they aren't really particularly good at it, so I'm not sure. (*Laughs*) I'm a little insecure about it. It may be that it's the carrot of fear that keeps you doing a good job. I think almost every good casting director is full of self-doubt at times.

*Vilga:* Having arrived at this career indirectly, was there a moment where you thought, "I am a casting director, and this is exactly what I'm going to do?"

*Taylor:* I think I was extremely attracted to it from the beginning and really wanted to do it. Once I got there I never doubted it. I loved and still do love working with directors. This part of the process really thrills me still. Not only is it a fun thing to think about—obviously which actors might play what roles is a thrilling thing to think about—but you're always part of the beginning of every project, when people are at their most optimistic and most enthusiastic and nobody's angry at anyone yet.

Also, one of the things that makes it so interesting is that because it is the beginning, it's often part of the process of figuring out who the characters are. You settle into a project thinking you're just going to be casting the role, and then you realize that you spend an enormous amount of time really trying to figure out what the story's about and who the characters are. You really do feel like you add a dimension to things because you are there trying to sort it out and hammer out what the movie's about, then figuring out what actors you approach for the roles.

*Vilga:* How much do directors tend to rely on casting directors for things? Do they ever let you cast certain parts, or is everything ultimately up to them?

*Taylor:* Ultimately the choice of actors is up to the director, but I do think that film directors rely on casting directors quite a bit. Directors rely very much on their creative team. I think that's why casting directors have become more visible over the years. They've emerged as an important part of the team. If you have a long-standing relationship with the director, you find that they rely on you for a lot more than simply who's going to play Waiter Number Two.

I find with most directors I work with now, with whom I have a long-standing relationship, that I start talking with them very early, especially when they write their own material like Woody Allen does. We start talking before he has even written his script. He'll talk about what his next idea's going to be. Sometimes he'll be sure of an idea or debating between a couple of different ones. We'll talk about casting while he's writing the script, before I've even read anything. It's a very exciting feeling to make a contribution that goes beyond just the day-to-day aspect of casting.

*Vilga:* It sounds very collaborative.

*Taylor:* I think it is. I'm not the only casting director who feels this way. All of us tend to have people with whom we have that kind of relationship. But finally, to answer your last question, which was about how much responsibility do they let you take, we are really there to provide alternatives. Almost every director will make the decision down to the one-line roles. Directors, truthfully, are very good at listening to what people who work for them have to say in different areas. In my experience, they listen carefully to what you have to say but they don't always agree with you.

Certainly they might say to you, "That person doesn't bring to the part what I feel somebody else could bring to the part" or maybe isn't even talented enough to play it. Then you keep looking for alternatives. You can't persuade a director to hire someone that they have reservations about even if you feel terrific about someone. You could certainly push it. But if they have reservations, they're the ones who have to work with them in the end. However, if they like someone and you don't . . . I find at least directors will feel like they've gotten an adequate warning.

*Vilga:* What kind of warning would you provide?

*Taylor:* It's a funny thing when you think of it from a director's standpoint. They live all over the world, and they come to New York or they come to Los Angeles, and they're seeing actors out of context. They're relying a lot on what we say about the actors. They can't just rely on a single five-, ten-, fifteen-minute audition totally out of context. They have to be prepared by us for what they can expect on the set. It's very important for us to give accurate information, such as that someone has certain strong areas and certain weak areas. Maybe they're good at auditions, maybe they're bad at auditions. Perhaps what you see in an audition may be all you're going to get from them. All those pieces of information are very important to the director who doesn't know the actor's work.

***Vilga:*** How great a sense do you have to have of an actor, then? Would you be able to send people in after meeting them once or twice, or do you have to have seen them in a lot of work?

***Taylor:*** It varies. In the first case you described I would say, "You know, I've never seen this person do anything, but he read for me in my office and I thought he had an interesting quality." I'd explain what the qualities were that I thought he might bring to a role.

***Vilga:*** Does it vary how many people you'll send for particular roles? Do you try and limit it, or do you try and send a lot?

***Taylor:*** I was brought up by Marion to be very selective and to usually not bring in more than two or three or four people for a part, all different, so that you weren't just repeating yourself. You were actually giving the director a choice of different ways to attack a role. That's my approach. Then there are always parts for which you do a larger search where you have to see many people.

***Vilga:*** Was there a particular part that springs to mind that you found very difficult to cast, one where you just couldn't get the right person?

***Taylor:*** Sometimes you feel at the time that maybe the people you really would have liked aren't available. I guess there are a couple of times when I feel we have fallen short. Then sometimes fate will really take a good turn. You'll feel disappointed going into it and it will turn out okay.

***Vilga:*** When an actor comes in to see you, how important is your first impression?

***Taylor:*** It's pretty important in movies. What a person is when they walk in the room and how they hit you immediately often is representative of the impact they're going to have on film. Of course you hope they can back it up with talent. There are people who surprise you by not moving you particularly in one-on-one meeting situations who then are just wonderfully talented. Those situations come less frequently because there are only so many people who are really that gifted.

***Vilga:*** Do you think you can tell if someone is going to be a good actor from a meeting? Can you tell from an audition?

***Taylor:*** From a meeting you can't really tell talent, but you can tell if they're going to be interesting. You can tell what kind of impact they might have on the screen visually and charismatically. An audition can tell you that someone's really talented, but that alone isn't necessarily the final word on talent either.

***Vilga:*** How much attention do you pay to someone's acting training? Do you care if actors have studied with certain people or at certain places?

*Taylor:*  If someone is well trained it means a lot to me. There are people who graduate from some of the finest drama schools who aren't that talented, yet you're more hopeful for someone who's had good training. You say, "Gee, this person studied with so-and-so or has gone to this or that drama school and so they must be good"—or so you say to yourself. You sometimes find yourself disappointed, but the odds are in those actors' favor, as certain drama schools are very selective.

*Vilga:*  Have you seen that certain programs or certain methods tend to work better than others?

*Taylor:*  No.

*Vilga:*  It really just varies person to person?

*Taylor:*  It may be the case that there are certain methods that make better actors. I'm not remarkably informed on different methods and their effectiveness. I don't know whether certain drama schools produce some of the better actors because of the kind of training they're getting or because they just have the cream of the crop available or it's just the rigor of the program. People tend not to be very trained in this country; if anyone goes through a conservatory program for three or four years, he or she is going to be ahead of the game.

*Vilga:*  Do you think that training is vital to the actor? Are there people who can get by without it?

*Taylor:*  I think 99 percent of them need it, because I think they go through their resources very quickly if they're not trained. There will always be an exception, a Jack Nicholson or someone who seems to have emerged as a natural. There will always be that exception, but I think it's very rare. I think you have to be exceptionally gifted and resourceful and disciplined without training.

*Vilga:*  Sometimes directors approach you very early on, but what's the traditional process of casting a film?

*Taylor:*  In general, the usual time we work on a movie is about ten to twelve weeks before the start date for filming. You receive the script and break it down by every role. A principal casting director like I am is responsible for casting every part that speaks, no matter if it's one word. Obviously the leading roles in your movie come first if they're not already cast. Even that can be done through discussion if it's required.

*Vilga:*  Are those often done in advance? Do people come attached to projects?

*Taylor:*  Yes, that does happen, but again, because I tend to start earlier on, less and less. Oftentimes I'm part of that process. There certainly are lots of pictures that are fully packaged with stars. The New York films are not as much that way.

Next all the supporting roles are cast. We have a reading and discussion, and depending on how well you know a director, sometimes you can decide on someone without seeing them. Most of the time you have people in to read. There's always a part or two for which you have to do an unusual kind of a search.

*Vilga:* Is it common that people read for the second leads in a film?

*Taylor:* It's common if the person isn't well known or if the director is important. An actor might read even if he or she is well known. For example, if the actor wants to play a part that's a departure from anything they've done before and they want it badly. For instance, Michelle Pfeiffer offered to read for *Dangerous Liaisons* because she had never done anything like that before. She understood that everybody wanted to see what she would be like. She was wonderful, and it took—it takes—a lot of guts to do that. There are good actors who are really great about this step, and there are other ones who would never do it. It's completely a question of personality. There are actors who wouldn't even meet with you or wouldn't even consider a role until they've been officially offered it. All the hierarchical nonsense does go on.

*Vilga:* Do you bring in five actors for a director to see for Waiter Number Two?

*Taylor:* If it were just somebody saying, "More champagne, please" (*laughs*), then I might bring in just one person. The director would say, "That's fine," or he or she might say, "Well, actually I was thinking of someone older," and then I might just bring in another one or two.

*Vilga:* Do you meet a lot of actors for general meetings to see their work?

*Taylor:* On a daily basis.

*Vilga:* How do those people come to you?

*Taylor:* Our biggest source is the theater here in New York. People we've seen in plays. We get pictures in the mail every day, and we try to go through them very carefully when we have time. Sometimes some agents will be very excited about someone new. Or they'll say someone up-and-coming is in town and they're only here for three days, so you meet them. Or we'll see people we feel have good faces or people we feel look very interesting and have good credits. I think all casting directors are a little remiss about unsolicited photographs because we're always busy.

*Vilga:* Is it possible, then, for a young actor to send a casting director such as yourself a photo and then actually get an interview? That happens?

*Taylor:*  Yes, but it's very tough unless they happen to be exactly right for the role I'm casting at that exact moment. Many casting directors, I am convinced, never look through their unsolicited photographs. I know people who don't. It takes a lot of discipline to do it.

We do it out of conscience, but we're slow. Really slow. Right now, we've been extremely behind for the last couple months, and we have a big sack of unsolicited photographs. Initially the person who opens the mail goes through them to make sure there isn't anything for what we are working on at the moment. Then we put them aside, and then they sit for a couple of months. We've just gotten out from under an important project, and today we're going to go through them. It takes time. Some people, as I say, throw them right in the wastebasket, particularly people who don't have sit-down offices like we do. They just don't have the space. It's a huge headache.

Also, because we work for Woody Allen, we always have to go find new faces and new interesting people. About every four years Woody does something outrageous, so we pick unusual funny faces. We need special styles for him when he does something like *Radio Days*.

*Vilga:*  When you say that you look at photos for people that have good faces, is there something specific that hits you? What would make you pull a photo and say, "Maybe we should look at this person?"

*Taylor:*  Actors who don't look too much like actors. That "real" look that suggests real life is particularly difficult to find. Looking like an actor sometimes means looking a little bit too pulled together. It's especially hard to find interesting middle-aged men to play mid- to small-sized roles. All the actors that are available seem a little bit too graying at the temples.

*Vilga:*  Is there an advantage to being in New York as opposed to Los Angeles? Or do you go back and forth?

*Taylor:*  I don't. Most of my friends do. I made a choice not to for family reasons. I have this great situation where I do one Woody Allen movie a year. That's really a gift to have that here. He never leaves, of course, and I never leave, but most people do. Casting in New York is a lot juicier than casting in Los Angeles.

*Vilga:*  Why is that?

*Taylor:*  On movies that I've done that have been based in Los Angeles, someone from my office goes out there to pick up some of the smaller parts, but the main parts come out of here. It's very difficult to get people to play small roles in movies out there. People in New York want to be in the theater. They're happy to work in a small role in a movie just to get the experience. There's a different attitude about it.

*Vilga:*   In New York there tends to be more of a commitment to theater and perhaps to acting in general.

*Taylor:*   Yes, but I don't know why that is. We found that casting what they call day players—somebody who works for a day on a project—casting them in Los Angeles is a very difficult thing. Agents don't represent that many people who want to do that type of work.

   Here in New York they're all thrilled to get the job or just to work with a good director. There are plenty of people working who don't even have agents. I think it's significant that in L.A. there are two separate unions, the Screen Actors Guild and the Screen Extras Guild.

*Vilga:*   That's not true in New York?

*Taylor:*   No. We have one union. Here good actors will play the silent part that might get upgraded and become the more interesting focus part. It's a different ball game out there. In L.A. it would be unthinkable, I'm sure, to an actor to do a silent bit part, because that would put them into a whole different caste system. Certain stars earn a certain amount of money, and they don't want to work for less. In L.A. people won't work for less money on a picture than they are used to earning, because they feel they're jeopardizing their careers.

*Vilga:*   On the other hand, there is much written about big stars coming to do New York theater. So I guess maybe there is a reverse trend as well.

*Taylor:*   I think that there is. I think that some of these actors still want to do good work. They just want to validate themselves in some way. A lot of the movies that are being made aren't all that interesting.

*Vilga:*   Do you think that theater acting and film acting require different training? Or if you can do one, can you do the other?

*Taylor:*   There has always been a debate that certain people work onstage but don't work in movies. You have this old argument, but I think that that's been bashed a little bit. I think finally if you really a wonderful stage actor, if you really have got something very special, you're going to have it with movies, too, with the proper guidance. It might be different, though.

   There are people who can play leading men onstage but who aren't going to necessarily be leading men in movies. It has to do with the intimacy of movies. If they're that gifted, there's going to be a place for them in movies that's going to be effective.

*Vilga:*   Is there a real star quality that certain actors have?

*Taylor:*   I think there definitely is a star quality. Some people are just fun to watch. I'm not sure that doesn't happen onstage, too. I think there are some actors—this is getting really down to a fine point—but there are some actors who never let you know who they are in movies. There is something general about them and not specific. They never expose themselves. It keeps them, in a way, from being the person who can emotionally carry a movie. They can be a wonderful character actor or play a wonderful off-beat person, but they might not be the person who gives their emotions out to the audience. Sometimes onstage it won't be as apparent to everyone, because you're creating such a large character that there's a part of you that's hidden. It might not make that difference onstage but it's very clear in the movies.

**Vilga:** Does a casting director negotiate fees for actors?

**Taylor:** That's a very, very important part of the job. They say that anyone could cast a movie if they have all the money in the world, but we have to do it within a specific budget. Every movie has a different budget. Sometimes it's easy and there's money to burn. Sometimes you work on movies where you can't pay anyone more than the minimum. It's a very hard part of the job. It's a challenge to make it all come out right.

**Vilga:** Do they have a general budget for the actors, or do they say, "We can only pay so much for a certain role?" Or do you hire someone first and later negotiate?

**Taylor:** It's usually based on the budget for a movie. The lower budget the movie has, the less money the actors get paid. For instance, *The Grifters* was a low-budget Hollywood movie. It wasn't so low budget, but it was low budget for Hollywood. Our three stars got much less money than they ordinarily would have, and then everyone else in the cast got scale.[1] That was what it was across the boards. That's how we did it.

**Vilga:** Do people accept that in order to work with an important director like Frears?

**Taylor:** Yes, but not everybody does. There were some people who turned it down. Woody Allen's movies don't pay actors terribly much money. Now it's become okay. It's become fun and fashionable. People have always been more game for him than for other people, but there are people who have said no.

**Vilga:** Is there any common mistake actors make in approaching directors or casting directors?

**Taylor:** It's a two-part answer. I think that the best thing always for actors to do is to trust themselves when they go into an audition situation. They should realize that everybody's very anxious for them to do a good job, because that would solve a lot of problems for everyone. They should know that nobody's against them, that everybody wishes that things go well for them. Oftentimes when they don't get the parts, it's not that personal.

That's the foundation of my second point, which is that sometimes I feel like actors come in and try to alter themselves in some way rather than presenting themselves as just who they are. There are times when it can be appropriate to move themselves gently in a particular direction if the part calls for it. But it's always upsetting to me when I meet someone and I read them for something and they do a nice reading, and then I call them back and suddenly they come in all dolled up in the way they think is necessary for a particular role. Whatever was really nice and interesting in the first place is now behind this new facade. They should really trust themselves to come in bringing themselves. I always think to be natural is the best choice.

*Vilga:* What can you expect when you go into an audition as an actor for a casting director? Do you get the script? Do you get it in advance? How does an audition usually work?

*Taylor:* It can be any number of things. I'll ask them to read cold, in the sense that I'll let them go out and sit in our waiting area with a scene. Very often I'll ask them to read just for quality mainly, not expecting a finished performance. Usually it will be a short scene but it'll be pertinent to what I'm doing to see if they are going in the right direction at all. If I'm having them back to see a director, I always provide the material for them. Except with Woody Allen.

*Vilga:* Oh, really, because of his secrecy thing?

*Taylor:* Yes. I always try to give actors as much information at the time as possible so that they're informed. Sometimes for me, if I know exactly what I'm looking for, I'll let them read the part right away.

*Vilga:* In an audition can actors say, "I want to try it a different way," if they aren't satisfied with a reading they've given?

*Taylor:* Almost every director will respond to that. If an actor says, "I'm not sure that was quite right. Is there anything you can tell me that would improve it?" a director might say, "No, no, it sounds fine to me." But they'll usually add, "If you're unhappy, go in another direction." Or the director will give them a note. Even if the director felt they weren't correct for the part, they almost always will give them another opportunity if they ask for it.

*Vilga:* How much do actors play themselves, exploring their own emotions through themselves, versus becoming and transforming into other characters?

*Taylor:* That's such a tricky question. I think most roles are going to be cast close to who the actor is in life. The truth is, of course, we all know that great performances are about transformations. That happens more frequently on the stage. When somebody who's onstage forgets who they are, it's amazing. That's great acting. It happens less in film. There are very few actors who are given the privilege to play a role where there is a radical departure from who they are. In film, actors don't often get that opportunity. Part of it is just the demand of the medium: you have to realistically convey what you are playing.

*Vilga:* Do you think that there are many actors who have a problem identifying their type? Do you find them thinking too much or too little about what kind of type they are?

*Taylor:* I think that many actors feel that they can play anything. "Just because I am a twenty-five-year-old man doesn't mean I can't play an eighty-five-year-old woman." (*Laughs*) They'll practically tell you that. Onstage it might be possible, but film is all about reality. The opportunity to make really big departures is onstage. In film, they're usually small departures. Every once in a while, we're given the opportunity to really take that leap, to find someone to play something that's just very far from who they are in life.

*Vilga:* Do you ever suggest that maybe acting is not the right path for someone?

*Taylor:* No. It's not really my role to do that. If it were someone I knew very well and they asked me, I might say something. But I wouldn't hurt someone's feelings in that way if I didn't know them. I hear there are people who do counsel very strongly, though.

Sometimes you'll have someone come in and they have attended some competitive, prestigious university, they're bright, but unfortunately their work is intellectual and not compelling. Still, I think they have to figure it out for themselves.

*Vilga:* That's probably true of most things.

*Taylor:* You have to come to it yourself. Maybe they'll end up going into another field in the same business. There are several casting directors and agents that I used to call in for parts years ago when they were actors. Sometimes when I was younger, I used to find it very hard to interview men who were older than I was, who obviously were taking small, bit parts when I knew they were married and had families to support. For me it was a very painful thing.

*Vilga:* You don't find it that way anymore?

*Taylor:* No. Because I figure they are doing what they want to do. They're making a living by hook or by crook. They're not just acting in film. They're doing commercials. They're doing industrials. They're doing a little print work. They're doing whatever they do, and the fact that they're willing to come in and do a couple of lines or whatever isn't necessarily a sad thing. They made the choice to do that. They'd rather do that than be a middling white-collar executive somewhere or a factory worker or whatever. They made a decision, and they're making ends meet somehow. Everybody thinks that to be an actor, it means you've got to be a star or a big success, but there are lots of people for whom it's a job. Maybe they originally dreamed it would be more than that, but they'd rather do it than not. They almost don't have a choice if the calling is there.

*Vilga:* Have you ever thought someone was talentless only to find yourself reconsidering your impression years later?

*Taylor:* When somebody walks in the room, your first impression is almost always borne out. I would say I can think of maybe two or three people who I thought were kind of bland in the meeting but who turned out to be wonderful actors. They just came to life on the stage.

On the other hand, some people have walked in the room and just knocked me out but then turned out not to be that talented. You tend to realize that fairly quickly, but not always, because those kinds of people can sustain something for a long time. People keep giving them chances and chances and chances, but gradually you learn there's not much there.

*Vilga:* Should actors who are starting out head for New York or head for Los Angeles? Does it depend on what they want to do, or can they do anything anyplace?

*Taylor:* I think that New York is a much, much better place both artistically and practically. I think there's much more going on here for people who have no money and no paying jobs. There's a huge amount of Off-Broadway and Off-Off-Broadway workshops. An actor would find a young sympathetic community here of people who really want to do good work which gives them a chance to grow. Work, work, work, and do something to pay the bills. Wait tables if you have to.

There's such drive here among young actors. It's still the Big Apple, it really is. I think that it's a great place to start. I also think that, from a more practical standpoint, Los Angeles respects New York actors more than they respect their own. If someone has accomplished something in New York, they're regarded highly out there. When a New York actor goes to L.A., they arrive with a certain status immediately. In L.A. they believe New York actors are better than Los Angeles actors. And in New York, we think London actors are better than ours.

*Vilga:* Who does London think is better than they are?

*Taylor:* They used to say Paris. I don't know if that's true or not. They're slightly intimidated by Paris. The Parisians don't admire anyone else.

*Vilga:* Is a showcase a valid opportunity for an actor to be seen?[2]

*Taylor:* Definitely. Certain venues are better known and get more attention than others, but casting directors certainly go to all sorts of things. That's what we have to do. That's what makes us better than the next person. We're always seeing as much as we can.

*Vilga:* On an average do you go out once a week or twice a week to see theater?

*Taylor:* When I started out, before I had children, I used to go every night. Sometimes on the weekends, there would be two things in a night. Midnight shows at La MaMa. I used to go every night, but now I don't. Also, there is not as much theater to see as there used to be.

*Vilga:* One thing I've asked everyone is if you had one piece of advice to give to the young actor, what would you tell him or her?

*Taylor:* Try not to get distracted by how people perceive them or by the pursuit of wealth and fame. I think that many, many people are rewarded for mediocre work, and that's a big distraction for actors. They see people doing ridiculous things on television and making a fortune at it. It has to turn their heads around in a bad way. I think it isn't good for an actor's soul.

Most importantly, I would tell them to work as much as they possibly can. Just get out there. Work and study and eventually, I think, they'll succeed. I hate to even say it that way. because it makes me sound naively optimistic, but it's true. To become really good, actors simply have to work.

# Nela Wagman

*Wagman received her BA* cum laude *from Harvard University, where she was the first woman to major in dramatic literature and the first undergraduate to appear professionally with the American Repertory Theatre. She has acted in over sixty New York and regional productions and starred in a Broadway presentation of* Tomorrow Was War *directed by Vanessa Redgrave, at the Marriott Marquis Theatre.*

*Nela Wagman directed the premiere of* My Left Breast *for the 1994 Humana Festival and for Watermark Theater in New York, where it won an Obie, Off-Broadway's highest award. Other New York directing credits include the world premieres of David Simpatico's* Waiter, Waiter, *Neena Beber's* Acts of Desire, *Patricia Scanlon's* Just beneath My Skin *(as director and cocreator),* Blaming Mom *by David Edelstein, and* The Arrangement

*by Susan Kim and the American premiere of Lucinda Coxon's* Waiting at
the Water's Edge. *Regional credits include Harold Pinter's* Old Times *and
Rena Potok's* Eleh Ezkera: I Will Remember. *Wagman founded Watermark
Theater in 1993, serves as its artistic director, and yearly coproduces the
WordFire Solo Performance Festival. In 1995, Watermark was awarded*
Encore *magazine's first annual Taking Off Award for groundbreaking
theater.*

● —————————————————————————————— ●

***Vilga:*** How did you begin working with actors?

***Wagman:*** I was an actor myself. I started acting when I was a very small
child, and I continued acting even after I began directing in college.

***Vilga:*** Was acting a career you'd chosen for yourself?

***Wagman:*** Yes. I never questioned that choice until the end of college,
when it began to dawn on me that I had more to say about the play as a
whole than I could express as an actor. An actor gets only one little corner
of a play. I wanted to form the whole.

***Vilga:*** What was your training as an actor?

***Wagman:*** I took classes as a kid, I studied at the Lee Strasberg Institute
when I was twelve, and I studied at Carnegie-Mellon for a summer, and at
Arena Stage, where I was blessed with the instruction and generosity of
actor-teacher Mark Hammer. As a teenager I apprenticed in a lot of theaters over summer vacations, then I went to Harvard as an undergraduate.
With the arrival of the ART in Cambridge, there were a few drama courses
for credit beginning to be offered, which I took.[1] I created an independent
major in dramatic literature with Professor William Alfred, which included biology, sociology, anthropology, and history as well as theatrical
literature and history. But basically my acting training was to be in as
many plays as I could. Obviously that's the very best training: be in as
many plays and act as much as you can.

 After college, I did some directing regionally but was invited to become
an actor with the Cornerstone Theater Company, which traveled the
country doing residencies in Kansas and other communities. I toured with
them for one year. My only formal full-time training program came after,
at the Circle in the Square Professional Training Program.

***Vilga:*** This was after you had performed in all these other productions in
college and touring companies?

***Wagman:*** Yes. I already had been acting professionally for almost ten
years.

*Vilga:* What made you decide to pursue formal training at that point?

*Wagman:* A combination of things. I wanted to be in New York. I wanted to settle down somewhere where I knew the theatrical environment would offer me growth and opportunity. Artistically I wanted to solidify what I was already doing. At the time I was at a crossroads between directing and acting. I wanted to clarify my notion of procedure and my notion of technique so that whichever I chose as a full-time occupation would have a background that was rooted in a foundation, something concrete, a method. As it turns out, the training I got was rooted in the Method.

*Vilga:* How did your level of acting experience compare with the other students?

*Wagman:* There's always a varied range of talent and accomplishment. In general I think perhaps most of the students weren't as experienced as I was, but nonetheless I learned an enormous amount studying at Circle. It gave me a chance to explore a lot of different things, to feel more consistent and more expert before I launched myself out into the world again. In a sense, it was a kind of an edifying rest although, God knows, it was not restful per se. It was grueling—something drama school always is. It gave me a chance to learn that there were concrete concepts and steps to follow and a chance to employ them.

*Vilga:* Do you ever see actors who can succeed without training?

*Wagman:* Occasionally you find that rare someone who seems to be consistently able to act well without training. Generally it's the consistency that suffers. Again, I think that the bulk of one's training, if one is smart and perceptive, comes from the doing. That's really the only way to learn to do anything. It's like roller skating; you can read all you like about roller skating, but you have to lace up the roller skates to really do it. In acting school you learn to act by acting round the clock. I also recommend observing and talking to older actors so you can learn different ways one can create with consistency.

*Vilga:* Do you see a difference in various methods of training and the results they produce in actors?

*Wagman:* I always feel that various methods catch the blame for various kinds of bad actors. The best actors often learn techniques to explore and be consistent from more than one method. Obviously certain methods speak more forcefully to some people than others, just as different kinds of literature are more fun for some people than others. One method may touch something powerfully within the actor, perhaps through something which other methods don't emphasize. In the end it's an individual's vulnerability and courage that makes him or her a good actor. The method they choose and are trained in can either enhance that natural affinity or not.

*Vilga:*  Do you find yourself using different methods? Or do you find that you don't really deal with how actors create the performance as much as shaping the overall work?

*Wagman:*  As a director I am very involved in how my actors work and with how my actors achieve their final product. I know that there are directors who are less concerned with getting involved with the inner workings of their actors' journeys than I am. As an actor I've worked with some who seem to be that way.

*Vilga:*  Do you discuss an actor's method of working?

*Wagman:*  I don't generally discuss their process of working, but there is a certain common language amongst all the methods that you can usually get to. For example, asking, "What does this character want here?" is something that every good actor can answer, whether they've been trained to answer it formally and as a matter of course or whether they have to stop for a second and think about it. Most of them have been trained to do that as the axis by which they guide their performance. It's certainly how I go about things, because I find it the most effective way. Sometimes I'll ask the actor what the character is trying to do at a particular second or overall, both broken down in a scene and as a whole.

*Vilga:*  Do you ask them what the character wants, or do you tell them? Or do you do both?

*Wagman:*  I guess you'd say I do both. I always start by asking. Oftentimes they'll know a lot more than I do. If they come up with something that I don't agree with, I will suggest my thought. It's very hard to get an actor to do what you want them to do if they don't agree with you. I think in the end it often comes down to a couple of basic human impetuses: people want to be loved, and people are afraid and want to protect themselves. Some permutation of those two things is usually what it's about. A "Yes" or a "No," as I like to say. You can usually isolate it to a "Yes" or "No" and then decorate it after that.

*Vilga:*  Do you think that different training is required for film than theater?

*Wagman:*  Yes. In a sense, training is an external application of technique to enhance the truth of what you're doing. The techniques that you use to enhance the truth in film are different because the ways in which you tell the truth in film are different.

In film your face is huge and the details can be incredibly tiny. We read great meaning into the visual image we see. Whereas the details onstage have to be a different size to be visible. I think if you're going to get trained you need to train to employ those details that are appropriate to the medium. I think that in all acting, film or stage, you need to be capable of portraying the truth.

*Vilga:*   How has your own acting experience shaped you as a director?

*Wagman:*   I think it's affected me a great deal as a director. There are often differences between directors who have acted versus directors who have not, although sometimes directors who haven't acted understand the actor's process quite well. Directors who have acted do tend to have a better sense of where the work comes from, what part of the psyche generates it. This often means they can help an actor produce more specific and focused work. Certainly for me as a director, I come at the material completely as an actor first, and then I bring other things to it.

Of course, my approach to the material and the way I work changes and evolves the more I direct. I'm sure it will continue evolving for the rest of my life. In general, I'm attracted to more psychologically driven plays. I like to manifest what themes exist first and foremost within the psychology of the character. Then I focus on the set and the costumes, the overall design concept. All of these are important, but my experience as an actor definitely informs my every breathing moment as a director in rehearsal and in performance. I focus most on obtaining an honest performance, because an honest performance makes whatever good kind of literature you've got come alive. A dishonest performance camouflages whatever truth that playwright might have up his sleeve.

*Vilga:*   What do you mean by "honest," and "dishonest?"

*Wagman:*   By "honest" I mean where we the audience sense both the character's and the actor's emotional presence and vulnerability. By "dishonest," I mean when the audience can sense an actor faking to the point of avoiding any real emotional experience, and expecting the audience not to notice.

*Vilga:*   Why did you start a theater company instead of just pursuing a career as a director?

*Wagman:*   I wanted to make a place for a certain kind of play in New York. I didn't feel that there was a specific home anywhere in the city for the kind of aesthetic that I found most interesting and most inspiring. Watermark produces only new plays because I feel that's the most necessary focus. We need to encourage the creation of new American theater literature to ensure that the theater continues. Obviously there are other companies in New York that do new plays, but not necessarily plays I feel take the greatest risks. I seek to direct productions that are truthful and daring and professionally well put together at a level where certain kinds of risks can be taken: risks in new authors, in collaborations with other artists, and in methods of presentation. I wanted to make a theater where these works would be produced well, with insight and care, for not a lot of money.

That way, you can more easily take these kinds of risks when you're smaller. You can remain true to your vision without worrying about cruder commercial viability or mass audience appeal. Although Watermark has gained a great deal of attention, we're still at a level where we can produce an unknown writer because we don't have a huge subscription audience to please. I trusted that there would be a segment of the theatergoing community that wanted to come and see the work of writers of a certain kind of vigor and integrity and honesty. We're finding that audience and that audience is finding us. Now, because we've built such a strong early reputation, we can program an exciting total unknown and still get reviewed by all the major New York press while attracting strong houses.

*Vilga:* Watermark is producing Off-Off-Broadway. Why?

*Wagman:* On the most mundane level, it's the most affordable. Having said that, however, beyond financial concerns, Off-Off is extremely liberating because there's just more opportunity and more freedom. I like the feeling of being able to do what I want artistically. Off-Broadway theaters are far more expensive, and so everything is dictated by the amount of money they have to generate.

I would love to have something I direct be moved to Off-Broadway so that more people could see it and the respect due these playwrights and actors would be afforded them. I would love to create some sort of a bridge between Off-Broadway, Off-Off-Broadway, and, in a perfect world, even Broadway itself. But right now, I think Off-Off is both the most affordable and the most creatively free place to be.

*Vilga:* Do you think there is a big difference between Off-Broadway and Off-Off-Broadway?

*Wagman:* Yes and no. Yes, if only from a financial standpoint. The union contracts that you work with Off-Off versus the ones that you work with Off are vastly different financially. It's a huge monetary leap between Off-Off and an Off-Broadway show. Consequently what happens Off-Broadway is sometimes but not always, for lack of a better word, "safer." Off-Broadway has to please a much broader range of people because it's more dependent on raising large amounts of money. So yes, I think there is a big difference.

Don't get me wrong. I think there are wonderfully courageous forays into nonconventional, nonsafe theater done Off-Broadway. In fact, I think there's a great focus on Off-Broadway now because Broadway itself is so extravagantly expensive to produce that extremely little theater of a non-surefire nature gets produced there. For playwrights like Edward Albee and Terrence McNally to be producing Off-Broadway first and not directly on Broadway is a sign that that's where they feel comfortable and that's where their work is welcomed.[2]

Since Off-Broadway has become a more focal (and expensive) place, it's harder for Off-Off-Broadway companies to move there than it might have been ten or twenty years ago. On the other hand, it also means that Off-Off-Broadway itself is now perhaps the most important place in American theater to see the truly exciting new work.

**Vilga:**   What is the experience like for actors Off-Off-Broadway? Do you have trouble getting them?

**Wagman:**   I don't have trouble getting actors to work Off-Off-Broadway for what are unfortunately ridiculously small quantities of money. It's even possible to get really wonderful actors to work on exceptional plays for no money. When smart actors find good literature they usually want to do it, because there's not a lot of good literature getting done. In fact, often you find actors who are or who are becoming commercially successful who want to work on this kind of new material just because it's so challenging and compelling. I can't afford to pay them the little I do, and yet I wish I could be paying them so much more.

**Vilga:**   How would you contrast the state of New York theater and regional theater?

**Wagman:**   They are both shifting. Certainly New York theater is shifting toward the Off-Broadway and the Off-Off Broadway. Regional theater is becoming more important as a theatrical voice in America, as a trendsetter, and as a standard. Where New York used to be looked at exclusively, regional theater has now become the establishing point for many of the most important new works because it's become too risky to premiere them in New York. It's very exciting to see that happen, to think that these theaters across the country are establishing a place for themselves in the formation of literature and drama. There are a lot of voices that don't come to New York that we need to hear.

**Vilga:**   Why does Watermark Theater present a solo performance festival every year?

**Wagman:**   The WordFire Festival that Watermark Theater produces each year is dedicated to the solo performer and the amazing and singular art of the spoken word. It's particularly important to me because in a sense it's essential theater. It is like the theater before there was any kind of enhancement. No stage or lights. One person speaking words at a campfire.

It's quote-unquote "theater." It's the act of a single person re-creating a world through words, a world that is not physically, tangibly present in any other way at that moment. To me, it's extremely important because it's the ultimate test of the human imagination, both on the part of the teller and on the part of the listener. I just find it fascinating how far one person speaking can take you; to any part of the world or galaxy, at any time, in any emotional state, just through a word. It makes words amazingly powerful in a way that perhaps we don't realize they are, in a way that perhaps they always are, but one that deserves highlighting because we take it for granted the rest of the time when we're just talking.

***Vilga:*** What are the unique difficulties of a one-person show?

***Wagman:*** In order to create dramatic conflict, one usually has at least two people to represent the two sides of the conflict. When you work with one person you have only one person and whatever else you can think of to create both sides of the conflict. Sometimes it's within the person, sometimes the person creates many people, and sometimes the conflict is a social situation or a tragedy or any number of things. One has to be rather creative about where that tension is coming from since it can't come from two people. That makes it challenging but also thrilling.

***Vilga:*** This year's and last year's festivals both had pieces that dealt with women's health issues. Is that a coincidence?

***Wagman:*** It's a choice. Women's health issues have always been incredibly important to me because I'm a woman and because we have half the population of the planet whose health has been considered less important.

I felt very lucky to be exposed to Darci Picoult's *My Virginia* and to Susan Miller's *My Left Breast.* I selected these pieces because they are extraordinary pieces of writing and because they address issues I feel are decidedly underaddressed. At one fell swoop I could present a piece of really enthralling theater for all theatrical and quote-unquote "artistic reasons" while simultaneously bringing to light social issues that are beneficial to anyone who hears them. It's so important to talk about health issues in public, a subject which people normally tend to avoid. If you can create an artistically invigorating piece out of an issue, theater is a wonderful medium to begin the discussion.

***Vilga:*** Why do you think theater is a particularly good way of doing that? There are easier ways to reach more people.

***Wagman:*** Theater is a great medium because it's something that you can do relatively independently. You don't need a huge studio to give you permission to go out and present something. Theater is a particularly beautiful medium because it is about an actual live person communicating with a group of people. You can tell you're reaching people immediately by the living, breathing, unrepeatable audience response. When you're sharing an experience with a women's health issue or any personal, traumatic, or even comedic issue, and you share it amongst people, there's a special enhancement of the experience. Theater seems uniquely appropriate for this kind of personal sharing made public and yet remaining very personal.

*Vilga:*   What's been the hardest challenge of starting an Off-Off-Broadway theater?

*Wagman:*   Of course there is the perpetual challenge of raising funds, but now it's also about getting the word out, letting people know what kind of a product you have to offer. We've been lucky, and we've worked very hard to let people know what we're doing and with what values we do it. If those are the values that appeal, and they seem to, people come in droves.

*Vilga:*   What about when people say theater is dead?

*Wagman:*   All I can say is, I've been kept very busy. (*Laughs*) There are still a lot of stories to tell, a lot of playwrights who tell them beautifully, and a lot of actors who bring them to life beautifully. There's a large audience who want to see that done. As long as those elements exist it seems to me that the theater is not dead.

*Vilga:*   Now that you've been directing and have your own theater company, what's changed for you in the way that you look at acting or actors or the whole process? What do you know now that you didn't know then?

*Wagman:*   I used to feel—at least I remember this very vividly, particularly in college—that I could do anything as an actor. "I can do any part. Just give me that part and I can do it. I can make this person completely unlike what you think I am. Even though you don't think I am right for it, I know I can make you believe it." As a director I have come to learn and understand more about what it means to be right for a part. It's something that I will probably always battle with, because I have found actors who I think are amazingly talented but were not right for something that I was casting.

I think that the way that I value the rightness of an actor may be different than other directors. What another director may find in an actor that makes him or her not right for a given character is often exactly what I think makes that actor right for the character. It may be unconventional, but that's interesting to me.

*Vilga:*   Can you give an example of that?

**Wagman:** Actors can be amazingly versatile, and I have gone very unconventional in a lot of casting choices, and I'm proud of that. For example, I cast Patricia Scanlon as the femme fatale in David Edelstein's *Blaming Mom*. Patricia had begun making a name for herself as an explosive, comedic solo performer, usually playing someone downtrodden and on the edge. She's not model pretty, so everyone assumed she'd be reading for one of the male lead's insecure girlfriends. Instead, I cast her as the gorgeous femme fatale, and she was absolutely brilliant. Both Ben Brantley and Vincent Canby at the *Times* singled her out, as did the *Village Voice* review. If you just met Patricia casually you might not have thought she could have ever played this totally glamorous woman, but she did. She understood the character's specific type of self-possession and infused it with her own inimitable energy. Through her talent she was able to transform herself into something utterly compelling to watch. In the end it was a gut response that I trusted which led me to offer her the part.

**Vilga:** How clear a sense of the part do you have when you start auditioning? Are you looking for someone who's right, or are you looking for someone who surprises you?

**Wagman:** I'll read a play and I'll say, "I've got a feeling that character wants to be loved in a particular way that I recognize." I'll look for an actor who has that understanding, which is often unspoken. An actor comes in and just yearns in a certain way that I feel when I read that character or that I yearn when I imagine myself with that character. It's almost ineffable, but it is specific. Sometimes an actor will come in and will make some sort of choice that I've never thought of before and find I totally love. It educates me on the spot. I'll go with it because I love it and I hadn't thought of it. So in a sense it's either something that I am looking for or something that I'm shown for the first time. The only thing that's consistent is the intensity and the depth of commitment. I cast based on the intensity of what someone's doing—whether it's something that I thought of before or something I've never thought of—an intensity which hits me as truthful.

**Vilga:** How much of your decision is made from the moment an actor walks into the audition?

**Wagman:** It's funny, but a lot of the decision is made as they walk in the door. Not so much "Are they right for the character?" although that has even happened, but certainly you ask and often decide, "Do I want to work with this person?" It's a hiring situation and you immediately ask, "Is the person on time? Is the person well kempt?" As an actor, I probably never even thought about that. I assume I was on time and that I was well kempt, because it's very important to come to any job interview in a way that shows one wants to be respected and respects others.

*Vilga:*   What's the biggest professional mistake you see actors making?

*Wagman:*   The biggest business mistake I see actors make is attitude of some kind or another: being sloppy, having a sloppy résumé or dishonesty on a résumé that you can track, and most importantly, bad attitude. For example, an actor once came into an audition after he had been very rude on the phone about picking up a script. He came into the audition, and I introduced myself, and he said, "Oh, you're the woman I spoke to. Well, if I'd known you were the director I would never have spoken to you that way. I thought it was just an assistant on the phone." I immediately thought to myself, "Never again will I see this person." How he would speak to me and how he might speak to my assistant oughtn't to be very different if he is a decent person.

*Vilga:*   Can you tell right away if someone has talent? How easy is it to spot?

*Wagman:*   I usually get a sense of whether the actor is available to me, whether the actor wants me in his brain and heart, or whether an actor is closed off to me and is trying to fake me out. I'm not interested in being faked out. Even if I'm looking for someone to play someone who fakes people out, I want to see *that* working. I want to see the honesty behind it, the honest need to fake people out. If an actor walks in and she feels real to me, then she's usually got some talent.

*Vilga:*   Have you seen people who have auditioned well and some people who have auditioned badly and still been able to identify talent?

*Wagman:*   Yes, I think so. It's still very difficult, though, to cast someone who auditions badly even when I get a sense that it might just be a bad audition. It may only be a bad audition, but you can't be sure. Sometimes their nervousness is so large that you don't quite know what is behind the nervousness. You can't know whether it's great talent that would become freer in rehearsal, or a great talent that would never become freer, or just a lot of intelligence.

*Vilga:*   Is star quality or charisma a part of talent, or is it a separate phenomenon?

*Wagman:*   I guess each director, each person on earth, has their own sense of what star quality is. To my mind they are linked, although I can imagine how some people see them as separate. Part of what I think star quality is is a kind of occupation of space which is compelling. Sometimes people have that occupation of space which is compelling and that's all they have, or that's all they need, or that's all the person watching them perceives. I particularly enjoy watching someone with that kind of compelling occupation of space who also is interested in telling me a truthful story. Such actors use their "largeness" not just to attract attention but to convey some kind of truth. I have met actors who do that, and they're the ones that fascinate me the most.

***Vilga:*** How good is the audience at telling what's true or false?

***Wagman:*** I always like to think that in the end they can sense it, whether they know it or not, and they respond to it. They respond to lots of things that surprise a director or that surprise an actor. They respond to what they feel is truthful based on something that just strikes a chord in them. The thing I fall back on is that I tell what truth I perceive and hope that other people see that as truth as well. Sometimes something that I'll put up at a particular moment will ring wildly falsely to me but will speak volumes of truth to audience members.

***Vilga:*** You would put on something you thought was untruthful?

***Wagman:*** Oh, it would only be a brief moment; I'm certainly not going to put up anything I don't believe in. I'm speaking about some little moment, some brief interchange which I've always tried to fix but can't get the actors or playwright to change. Sometimes that moment will just seem like the truest thing on earth to other people.

***Vilga:*** Do you think with a certain amount of training anyone can become an actor?

***Wagman:*** No. There's so many elements which go into making an effective actor: honesty, the desire and the entitlement to share themselves in one way or another, and some elements that just can't be taught.

***Vilga:*** Such as?

***Wagman:*** An actor needs to honestly recognize what is within them that they want to share and then have the courage to share that thing. They have to share it in such a way that is not indulgent but offers their own humanity and their own experience to others in a way which includes them, rather than excludes them. It's a certain kind of imagination combined with a willingness to be open; a capacity to be undefended and to imagine. Those are things you can encourage but you can't teach.

***Vilga:*** Is this what you look for in auditions?

***Wagman:*** Yes. I search for a capacity to share and imagine without defense and with precision. It's about successfully matching my sense of actors who seem to be able to share themselves in the same ways the characters in the play do. That makes a good chemistry in the cast, and therefore the truths of the play get told with precision, with elegance, with craft, and with honesty.

*Vilga:*   Is there anything else that you can think of about acting or training that we didn't talk about?

*Wagman:*   I think it's important for actors to remember not to use acting as some sort of loud therapy.

*Vilga:*   Do you see a lot of that?

*Wagman:*   I see a certain amount of it in performance. I certainly see enough of it in auditions. There's something excluding about what they're doing that makes it be about themselves, not you. It's supposed to be about *us*.

*Vilga:*   How can you guide an actor to make that differentiation?

*Wagman:*   That's hard. I think an actor has to be very true to what the character wants and needs in a given circumstance or moment. They have to be true to that and not to what they the actor need from that moment— which is a funny thing to say because, of course, you have to make the character's need your own. Yet the actor can't bring his needs to the character. He must take the character's need and make it his own in order to bring it to life to serve the character and the playwright's truth.

*Vilga:*   Do you see a wide variety of reasons why people become actors?

*Wagman:*   I see a wide variety, and yet in a sense I would venture that the wide variety represents some basic constant, some basic need. It's clearly a very strong need, because you have to go through a great deal to become an actor. I've always felt there's no way to make it as an actor unless you truly need to be an actor. What that need is made of is probably far more difficult to say and it probably varies from person to person, yet it's always some sort of need to share oneself and it's always some sort of need to have others see what you're sharing. There's nothing wrong with that. In fact, it's a thing of great beauty because it brings meaning and pleasure into many people's lives.

*Vilga:*   Did you have a sense of your talent? Did you name it, or did someone else name it for you?

*Wagman:*   I always felt a need to make stories. People seemed to like it when I did. It has always been tremendously gratifying to me to sense the emotional connection of an audience. When the audience identifies with the events onstage, I feel as if we know each other, that the group or even the world is a community. That we are not alone. I feel this both as an actor and as a director.

I'm more tangibly aware of what faculties of mine are involved in directing. I trust those and I can identify them. With acting, you channel your creative energy through a filter which asks you not to use your identifying skills after a certain point. In performance, the best actors don't identify, they just trust.

**Vilga:**   Anything else?

**Wagman:**   Yes, and this is important. I would tell a young actor: "Don't be selfish. Don't overprotect yourself on stage. Use yourself to expose as much of yourself as possible." I think that's the highest accomplishment, and it makes everyone else's work better, too.

**Vilga:**   If you had one piece of advice to give to a young actor, what would it be?

**Wagman:**   Know who you are and tell the truth.

# Notes

● ——————————————————————————————— ●

## Preface

1. Toby Cole and Helen Krich Chinoy, editors, *Actors on Acting* (New York: Crown Publishers, 1970).
2. Ibid., page xvi.
3. Stella Adler, *The Technique of Acting* (New York: Bantam Books, 1988); Sanford Meisner and Dennis Longwell, *Sanford Meisner on Acting* (New York: Vintage Books, 1987); Lee Strasberg, edited by Evangeline Morphos, *A Dream of Passion: The Development of the Method* (Boston: Little, Brown, 1987).
4. Eva Mekler, *The New Generation of Acting Teachers* (New York: Penguin, 1987).

## Harold Baldridge

1. Sanford Meisner's seminal repetition exercise consists of actors initially repeating an observation mechanically again and again. After purely verbatim repetition, the actor incorporates an individual point of view. According to Meisner, the goal of the exercise is to use repetition to free the actor and restore his or her connection to inner emotional impulses.
2. Lee Strasberg (1901–1982) adapted Stanislavsky's system into an American "Method." In 1931, with Harold Clurman and Cheryl Crawford, he founded the Group Theatre, where he directed plays and began to develop his system of actor training. He became the artistic director of the Actors Studio in 1951, continuing to direct on Broadway and off. Strasberg taught acting to Al Pacino, Paul Newman, Dustin Hoffman, Marilyn Monroe, and Joanne Woodward among many others.
3. Harold Edgar Clurman (1901–1980), one of the founders of the Group Theatre, was a noted director and teacher.
4. Alexander technique is a method for improving human functioning by re-educating the kinesthetic sense to appreciate the relationship of the head, neck, and back. The technique was developed by Frederick Mathias Alexander (1869–1955), who thought that habitual reactions, beliefs, and patterns of tension caused tightening of the muscles of the neck, back, and spine. Actors and others study Alexander work to correct kinesthetic habits that produce tension that might inhibit a performance or interfere with normal physical movement.
5. Sanford Meisner and Dennis Longwell, *Sanford Meisner on Acting* (New York: Vintage Books, 1987).
6. Jerzy Grotowski (1933–), famed Polish director of the Institute for Research into Acting in Wroclaw (formerly called Theatre Laboratory). He is the author of a book detailing his method, called *Theatre Laboratorie* (Wroclaw,

1967). Kabuki is a type of popular Japanese theater derived from the older No theater. In Kabuki, the actors, primarily male performers, wear elaborate costumes and perform stylized movements, dances, and songs in both tragedies and comedies.

## Tanya Berezin

1. Judd Hirsch (1935–) has acted on stage, screen, and television. Off-Broadway, Hirsch won an Obie Award for Lanford Wilson's *Talley's Folly* (1979) and received a Tony nomination for his performance when the show moved to Broadway. On Broadway, he won Tony Awards for his performances in *I'm Not Rappaport* (1985) and *Conversations with My Father* (1992). His performance in the 1980 film *Ordinary People* garnered him an Oscar nomination. Hirsch's television credits include *Taxi* (1981 and 1983 Emmy Awards) and *Dear John* (Golden Globe Award).
2. La MaMa E.T.C. was founded in 1961; the company works out of four theatrical spaces in New York City and produces dozens of shows each year. La MaMa's shows often have a downtown, avant-garde sensibility.
3. Rob Thirkield, actor-director and cofounder of Circle Repertory Company. Lanford Wilson (1937–), playwright awarded the Pulitzer Prize for *Talley's Folly* (1979). Other credits include *The Hot L Baltimore* (1973), *Burn This* (1986), and *Redwood Curtain* (1992). Marshall Mason (1940–), director of various Wilson works, including *The Hot L Baltimore, Talley's Folly,* and *Fifth of July* (1979).
4. Berezin resigned her position in November of 1994.
5. The Linklater technique was created by Kristin Linklater (1936–), a Scottish actress trained at the London Academy of Music and Dramatic Art. Linklater began teaching vocal technique in New York in 1963 with numerous companies and university programs. The Linklater technique seeks to liberate the natural voice of the actor based on two assumptions: first, that everyone has a voice inherently capable of expressing complex emotions and thought; second, that the stress of living in the modern world often diminishes this capacity. The technique seeks to remove blocks that inhibit the vocal instrument, so that it comes in direct contact with and is inspired by emotional impulses. Linklater is the author of *Freeing the Natural Voice* (New York: Drama Books, 1976).
6. Swoosie Kurtz (1944–) received a 1980 Tony Award for Lanford Wilson's *Fifth of July* (1979). Her film credits include *The World According to Garp* (1982) and *Dangerous Liaisons* (1989); on TV she appeared as Alex on *Sisters*. The London Academy of Music and Dramatic Art (LAMDA) is an independent drama school founded in 1861 and dedicated to training actors, stage managers, and technicians.
7. Eve Arden (born Eunice Quedens, 1912–1990), comedienne who debuted in the Ziegfield Follies of 1936 and created the title character in *Our Miss Brooks* in television and film. Arden won a 1953 Emmy Award for *The Mothers-in-Law*; her film credits include *Stage Door* (1937) and *Mildred Pierce* (1945).
8. Royal Academy of Dramatic Art (RADA), founded in 1904 by Sir Herbert

Benson. The school offers three training programs: one for the actor, one for the stage manager, and specialist diploma courses. For LAMDA, see note 6 above.

9. Maureen Stapleton (1925–) originated the roles of Serafina in *The Rose Tattoo* (1951 Tony Award), Lady Torrance in *Orpheus Descending* (1957), Carrie Berniers in *Toys in the Attic* (1960), three separate characters in *Plaza Suite* (1968), and Eva Mears in *The Gingerbread Lady* (1971 Tony Award). Stapleton has also received an Oscar for her work in the film *Reds* (1981) and an Emmy for *Among the Paths of Eden* (1967).

10. Anna Magnani (1907–1973), Egyptian-born Italian actress who appeared in Roberto Rossellini's 1945 *Open City;* she was Rossellini's companion until Ingrid Bergman entered his life. In 1955 she won an Oscar for her work in the film version of Williams's *The Rose Tattoo.*

11. Alan Schneider (1917–1984), director who won the 1963 Tony for his production of Edward Albee's *Who's Afraid of Virginia Woolf?* Other credits include Samuel Beckett's *Endgame,* Albee's *A Delicate Balance,* and Harold Pinter's *The Birthday Party.*

## André Bishop

1. TCG, the Theatre Communications Group, founded in 1961, is a national organization that provides a forum and communications network. According to TCG's mission statement the organization "serves theatre artists and non-profit professional theatre organizations by: recognizing and encouraging artistic diversity, providing a forum for the open and critical examination of issues, standards and values, fostering interaction among theatre professionals . . . and serving as the principal advocate for America's nonprofit professional theatre." TCG has over seventeen thousand individual members, and the three hundred theaters affiliated with it entertain over twenty million people a year. Among its many activities, TCG offers grants, fellowships, and awards to individuals and to institutions, produces workshops and roundtable discussions, and publishes many plays, books, and periodicals about the theater.

2. Peter Evans (1950–1989) won the Clarence Derwent Award and a Drama Desk Award as Outstanding Actor, both for David Rabe's *Streamers* in 1976. Evans graduated from Yale University in 1972. David Rounds (1930–1983) was an actor who won a 1980 Tony Award for his work in *Mornings at Seven.* Ron Rifkin (1939–) plays a recurring role in the TV drama *ER.* His film credits include *Manhattan Murder Mystery* (1993), *Silent Running* (1971), and *The Sunshine Boys* (1975).

3. *Career,* a play in three acts by James Henry Lee, opened on April 30, 1957, and ran for 232 performances.

## Robert Brustein

1. Clifford Odets (1906–1963), playwright associated with the Group Theatre whose works include *Waiting for Lefty* (1935), *Awake and Sing!* (1935), and *The Flowering Peach* (1954).

2. Robert Lawrence Benedetti (1939–) was chairman of the acting department at the Yale School of Drama from 1970 to 1971 and dean of the School of Theatre Art at California Institute of the Arts from 1974 to 1982. Director Robert Lewis (1909–) is a well-known acting teacher and author of the book *Method or Madness* (New York: Samuel French, 1958). Lewis was a member of the Group Theatre and, with Elia Kazan and Cheryl Crawford, founded the Actors Studio in 1947. Biographical information on Stella Adler is contained in the headnote to her interview in this volume.

3. The Group Theatre was founded in 1931 by Harold Clurman, Cheryl Crawford, and Lee Strasberg as a permanent company of actors and directors whose goal it was to maintain regular New York seasons. The Group was the first company in America to use Stanislavsky's ideas to train its actors and as an artistic approach for its theatrical productions. Often producing highly political works, it was the first company to present the works of Clifford Odets. The company disbanded in 1940.

4. Andrei Serban (1943–), the Bucharest-born director who was associate director of the Yale Repertory Theatre from 1977 to 1978. Lee Breuer (1937–), American playwright and winner of two Obie Awards, for his plays *Shaggy Dog Animation* (1978) and *A Prelude to Death in Venice* (1980). Breuer directed *Earth Spirit* at the Yale Drama School in May 1977. *Earth Spirit* is the first part of Frank Wedekind's *Lulu; Pandora's Box* is the second.

5. Fredric March (1897–1975) won the 1956 Tony Award for his performance as James Tyrone in Eugene O'Neill's *Long Day's Journey into Night*. His film work includes *Dr. Jekyll and Mr. Hyde* (1931), *Anna Karenina* (1935), *Nothing Sacred* (1937), *A Star Is Born* (1937), *The Best Years of Our Lives* (1946), and *Inherit the Wind* (1960).

6. In 1996, the acting-directing training was largely revamped under the direction of institute director François Rochaix and associate directors Marcus Stern and Scott Zigler.

7. *The Idiots Karamazov*, by Christopher Durang and Albert Innaurato, opened at the Yale Repertory Theatre on October 31, 1974; the cast included Meryl Streep and Durang. The play was performed by the Yale Drama School in the spring of 1974; however, it premiered a year earlier, in Silliman College at Yale. The production was directed by Innaurato and titled *The Brothers Karamazov, Starring Dame Edith Evans*.

8. Robert Brustein, *Reimagining American Theatre* (New York: Hill and Wang, 1991).

### Ellen Burstyn

1. Under the name Ellen McRae, Burstyn made her Broadway debut in *Fair Game* (1957), written by Sam Locke. Paul Roberts directed. Sam Levine was her costar.

2. Actor Jeff Corey (1914–) has appeared in numerous films, including *Butch Cassidy and the Sundance Kid* (1979) and *Clear and Present Danger* (1994).

3. Peggy Feury was an actress and teacher. She attended Barnard College, followed by Yale Drama School and the Neighborhood Playhouse. She was a founding board member of the Actors Studio, the artistic director of the

Actors Studio West in Los Angeles, and a teacher at the Lee Strasberg Institute in California. Her Broadway roles included *Enter Laughing*, *Peer Gynt*, *The Grass Harp*, and *The Turn of the Screw*. Her film appearances included *All of Me*, *Crimes of Passion*, and *The Last Tycoon*. With her husband she founded the Loft Studio in Los Angeles in 1973 and the Loft Theater in 1984. Feury was killed in a violent car accident on November 20, 1985.

4. Bruce Dern (1936–), actor whose film credits include *Marnie* (1964), *They Shoot Horses, Don't They?* (1969), *The Great Gatsby* (1974), and *Family Plot* (1976).

5. The musical *Pretty Belle*, starring Angela Lansbury, was staged by Gower Champion and produced by Alexander H. Cohen. The show was a tremendous flop; it has the distinction of being one of the shows included in the gallery of failed-show posters in New York City's Joe Allen's restaurant.

6. Sense memory exercises are used to strengthen an actor's ability to recall past sensations when creating a character. Lee Strasberg in *A Dream of Passion* describes these exercises at length and says they lead the actor to "realize that acting is not just make-believe; the imagination of the actor cannot only conceive but recreate an experience" (New York: Penguin, 1987, page 137).

7. Paul Berliner's *Thinking in Jazz: The Infinite Art of Improvisation* (Chicago: University of Chicago Press, 1994) astutely observes the process of musical improvisation.

8. Sarah Bernhardt (1844–1923), legendary stage actress, appeared in film versions of some of her best-known theater roles, such as *Tosca* (1908) and *Queen Elizabeth* (1912).

### Robert Falls

1. John Cassavetes (1929–1989), actor and director, appeared in such films as *Rosemary's Baby* (1968) and *The Dirty Dozen* (1967). His directing credits include *Big Trouble* (1985), *Gloria* (1980), and *A Woman under the Influence* (1974). He was married to Gena Rowlands.

2. Second City is a Chicago-based theatrical troupe that was founded on December 16, 1959. Six or seven actors, using few props or costumes, fill an empty stage with topical comedy sketches. Second City performances consist of improvisational skits. These are based on ideas suggested by the audience during sets held nightly after the regular show. By refining, culling, and amplifying these ideas during rehearsals, finished pieces become the next revue. Second City also has a well-known national touring company. Performers such as Bill Murray, Betty Thomas, James Belushi, Chris Farley, Mike Myers, and Julia Louis-Dreyfus have all been members of the touring company. Second City takes its name from a derisive profile of Chicago by A. J. Liebling in *The New Yorker*.

3. Viola Spolin originally used her theater games as problem-solving exercises for the children in her Young Actors Company; however, since their inception in the early 1960s, these exercises have been recognized as a legitimate approach to theater for people of all ages. The Spolin theater games are detailed in Spolin's book *Improvisation for the Theater* (Evanston: Northwestern University Press, 1983).

4. Shirley Knight (1936–) received the 1976 Tony Award for *Kennedy's Children.* Her film credits include *Sweet Bird of Youth* (1962) and *The Rain People* (1969).
5. F. Murray Abraham won an Oscar for his role in the 1984 film *Amadeus,* as well as the 1985 Golden Globe and Los Angeles Film Critics Awards. His stage roles include Vanya in *Uncle Vanya* (1984 Obie Award) and Roy Cohn in *Angels in America* (1992).

## Marilyn Fried

1. Peggy Feury was an actress and teacher. She attended Barnard College, followed by Yale Drama School and the Neighborhood Playhouse. She was a founding board member of the Actors Studio, the artistic director of the Actors Studio West in Los Angeles, and a teacher at the Lee Strasberg Institute in California. Her Broadway roles included *Enter Laughing, Peer Gynt, The Grass Harp,* and *The Turn of the Screw.* Her film appearances included *All of Me, Crimes of Passion,* and *The Last Tycoon.* With her husband she founded the Loft Studio in Los Angeles in 1973 and the Loft Theater in 1984. Feury was killed in a violent car accident on November 20, 1985. Lee Strasberg (1901–1982) adapted Stanislavsky's system into an American "Method." In 1931, with Harold Clurman and Cheryl Crawford, he founded the Group Theatre, where he directed plays and began to develop his system of actor training. He became the artistic director of the Actors Studio in 1951, continuing to direct on Broadway and off. Strasberg taught acting to Al Pacino, Paul Newman, Dustin Hoffman, Marilyn Monroe, and Joanne Woodward, among many others.
2. Headshots are eight-by-ten-inch photographs of an actor, often just of the actor's face. A résumé of professional acting experience and training is attached to the reserve side. Traditionally, headshots are an aspiring actor's calling card, which he or she circulates to potential employers within the industry.

## Spalding Gray

1. Tom O'Horgan (1926–) has directed many La MaMa E.T.C. productions. He has also directed the original productions of *Tom Paine, Futz, Hair, Lenny,* and *Jesus Christ Superstar.*
2. Antonin Artaud (1896–1948) wrote the seminal work *The Theatre and Its Double* (1938), translated by M. C. Richards (New York: Grove, 1958). Artaud argued for a revolution of Western theater by including rituals, kinetics, and mysticism and leaving reality and narrative behind. He was deeply influenced by the trance and frenzy of Balinese theater, in his manifestos calling for a rebellious avant-garde "theatre of cruelty." Bertolt Brecht (1898–1956), playwright and director, developed what became known as epic, or nondramatic, theater. Brecht, perhaps the major German dramatist of the twentieth century, believed theater should not imitate reality or try to convince an audience they are watching an actual event. Rather, theater should produce "the alienation effect" in which the audience is constantly aware that they are watching a theatrical performance. Thus Brecht conceived the actor's role as

an instructor of the audience, showing the meaning of the actions. Although often in conflict with Stanislavsky's ideas, Brecht did share some of his concerns, particularly with the "superobjective." The Wooster Group was cofounded by Elizabeth LeCompte (1944–) and Spalding Gray in 1976 and has its origins in the Performance Group (1967–1980) founded by Richard Schechner (1934–). The Wooster Group took over the Performance Group's SoHo theater space, used many of the same performers, and often followed a similar tradition of creating theater pieces that adapt and weave in and out of classic texts.

3. Jerzy Grotowski (1933–), famed Polish director of the Institute for Research into Acting in Wroclaw (formerly called Theatre Laboratory). He is the author of a book detailing his method, called *Theatre Laboratorie* (Wroclaw, 1967). The Open Theatre (1963–1973), founded by Joseph Chaikin, began producing plays but soon focused upon more radical and alternative physical performances that were developed by the group as a collective. For example, *Terminal* (1969), an exploration of death, involves chanting the word "dead" and using simple props that serve as beds, embalming tables, and graves. The piece ends with increasingly incoherent performers sprawled on the floor.

4. Paul John Austin (1937–) is a director, teacher, and writer who has appeared on stage, screen, and television. He currently operates the Image Theater on West 42nd Street in New York City.

5. Michael Chekhov, *To the Actor* (New York: Barnes and Noble Books, 1985).

6. *Tooth of Crime* is a rock drama by Sam Shepard, written in the early seventies while the playwright was in London. The show was produced at the Performing Garage in 1973.

7. Joan MacIntosh was an actress with the Wooster Group. Elizabeth LeCompte is the artistic director of the Wooster Group and the recipient of a MacArthur Foundation fellowship. For the Wooster Group, see note 2 for this chapter.

8. *Beaches* (1988) is a film directed by Garry Marshall and starring Bette Midler, Barbara Hershey, and John Heard.

9. Gray refers to Lincoln Center's production of Thornton Wilder's *Our Town*, which ran from December 1988 through April 1989. Gray played the Stage Manager, Penelope Ann Miller played Emily, and Eric Stoltz played George.

10. Robert Wilson (1941–), famed theatrical artist whose awards include several Obies, countless international citations, and a 1986 Pulitzer Prize nomination for his work *The Civil Wars: A tree best is measured when it is down* (1983–1985). Richard Foreman (1937–), director and playwright, won a 1976 Obie Award for *Rhoda in Potatoland* and a 1987 Obie Award for *Radio Is Good*. He recently directed Susan Lori-Parks's *Venus Hottentot* at the Public Theater in New York. The Wooster Group was cofounded by Elizabeth LeCompte (1944–) and Spalding Gray in 1976 and has its origins in the Performance Group (1967–1980) founded by Richard Schechner (1934–). The Wooster Group took over the Performance Group's SoHo theater space, used many of the same performers, and often followed a similar tradition of creating theater pieces that adapt and weave in and out of classic texts. The Bread and Puppet Theater was founded in 1962 by Peter Schumann, a German refugee living on the Lower East Side of Manhattan. The first

performance was about rats, rents, police, and other neighborhood problems. The company derived its name from its use of puppets and from the home-made bread they shared with the audience after performances. The puppets are often quite large and require several people to control them, and performances incorporate sculpture, music, and dance. Although the core group disbanded in 1974, Bread and Puppet Theater continues today in Glover, Vermont.

## Henry House

1. Bill Esper (1932–), well-known director and educator who founded his own studio, William Esper Studio for Actors, Inc., in 1965. In 1986, Esper became chairman of the Rutgers University theater arts department in New Jersey. The Neighborhood Playhouse was founded in 1915 as an amateur repertory company; it turned professional a few years later and then disbanded. However, the company's offshoot organization, the Neighborhood Playhouse School of the Theatre, survives to this day. The Meisner technique, an acting technique developed by the actor and director Sanford Meisner (1905–), focuses on "being in the moment" and truly listening to one's acting partner; Meisner invented the famed "repetition exercise" and was fond of saying, "The foundation of acting is the reality of doing."

2. The Actors' Information Project in New York City was founded in 1979 by Jay Perry, a writer and producer, Susan Perry, an actress, and David Rosen, an agent. Designed to provide career guidance and a support system for actors, AIP offered a variety of workshops and programs to enhance the marketing and employment skills of actors. AIP closed in 1991.

3. Viola Spolin originally used her theater games as problem-solving exercises for the children in her Young Actors Company; however, since their inception in the early 1960s, these exercises have been recognized as a legitimate approach to theater for people of all ages. The Spolin theater games are detailed in Spolin's book *Improvisation for the Theater* (Evanston: Northwestern University Press, 1983).

4. Konstantin S. Stanislavsky (1863–1938) was born in Moscow to a wealthy merchant family.

5. Meryl Streep won an Oscar for her portrayal of a Polish concentration camp survivor in *Sophie's Choice* (1982), based on the novel by William Styron. According to one (unconfirmed yet published) story, Streep fell to her knees before director Alan J. Pakula to insist she play the coveted part of Sophie. Streep perfected both Polish and German dialogue for the role.

## Scott Macaulay

1. Robert Wilson (1941–), famed theatrical artist whose awards include several Obies, countless international citations, and a 1986 Pulitzer Prize nomination for his work *The Civil Wars: A tree best is measured when it is down* (1983–1985). Richard Foreman (1937–), director and playwright, won a 1976 Obie Award for *Rhoda in Potatoland* and a 1987 Obie Award for *Radio Is Good*. He recently directed Susan Lori-Parks's *Venus Hottentot* at the Public Theater in New York. The Wooster Group was cofounded by Elizabeth

LeCompte (1944–) and Spalding Gray in 1976 and has its origins in the Performance Group (1967–1980) founded by Richard Schechner (1934–). The Wooster Group took over the Performance Group's SoHo theater space, used many of the same performers, and often followed a similar tradition of creating theater that adapts and weaves in and out of classic texts.

2. Karen Finley (1952–), writer and performer whose theme is usually anger about the exploitation of women by men in contemporary society. When conservative journalists strongly objected to her National Endowment for the Arts award because of her controversial work—deemed vulgar and offensive by many—Finley's artistic visibility greatly increased. Her published works include *Shock Treatment* (San Francisco: City of Lights, 1990) and *The Truth Is Hard to Swallow* (New York: Pow Wow 069, 1990).

3. Vito Acconci (1939–), poet and visual artist. His poetry often borders on conceptual art: one 350-line poem was printed with only a single line per each of the 350 pages, and his self-published *Book Four* (1968) consists of a series of entirely self-reflexive statements. Acconci's performance pieces include one where he confessed genuine personal secrets to individuals in a quasi–confessional booth and another, *Seedbed* (1972), where he claimed to be masturbating under a wooden floor, allowing spectators to hear his activity. Linda Montana is well known for works like *Art/Life One Year Performance 1983–84*, for which she spent an entire year tied to her partner Teching Hsieh with an eight-foot rope. Annie Sprinkle is a self-described "feminist porn activist."

4. Eric Bogosian (1953–) is the author of *Drinking in America* (1986), *Men Inside* (1982), and *Voices of America* (1982). Oliver Stone directed Bogosian in the film *Talk Radio* (1988), based on Bogosian's play of the same title.

5. Ann Magnuson's (1956–) TV credits include the role of Catherine Hughes on *Anything but Love* with Jamie Lee Curtis (1989–1990 and 1991–1992). She starred in the 1986 film *Making Mr. Right,* directed by Susan Seidelman.

6. Rachel Rosenthal's (1926–) performance texts can be found in the book *Scenarios* and in journals including *Performing Arts Journal* and *High Performance.*

7. Holly Hughes (1955–). The work Macaulay is referring to is Hughes's *World without End.*

8. Chris Burden's (1946–) other works include *Through the Night Softly* (1973), *Trans-Fixed* (1974), and *White Light/White Heat* (1975).

9. Allan Kaprow (1927–) began working with assemblages that used materials found in public places in 1956. Kaprow then began making "Environments" or artistically contained spaces. He is most famous for his "Happenings," mixed-media pieces usually involving people following directions but attaining surprising results. Kaprow's Happenings often took place in public spaces. Kaprow is the author of *Assemblage, Environments & Happenings* (New York: Abrams, 1966).

10. Joe Papp (1921–1991), theatrical producer who created the New York Shakespeare Festival in 1954 and founded the Public Theater in 1967. The Public has premiered such works as *Hair!, A Chorus Line,* and Savion Glover's *Bring In 'Da Noise, Bring In 'Da Funk.*

### Austin Pendleton

1.  Geraldine Page (1924–1987), American actress acclaimed most for her portrayals of Tennessee Williams characters and recipient of the 1985 Academy Award for her role in the film *The Trip to Bountiful.*
2.  The Yale Dramatic Association is the largest undergraduate theater organization at the university and the second oldest college theater association in the United States.
3.  Kim Stanley (1925–) was nominated for an Academy Award for her 1959 performance in *The Goddess.* Jo Van Fleet (1919–1996) won a 1954 Tony Award for her performance in the play *The Trip to Bountiful* and a 1955 Oscar for *East of Eden.* E. G. Marshall (1910–) is an Emmy Award–winning actor and has acted in such films as *Twelve Angry Men* (1957), *The Caine Mutiny* (1954), and *Nixon* (1995).
4.  Uta Hagen (1919–) is a German-born actress whose honors include two Tony Awards, for her performances in *The Country Girl* (1951) and *Who's Afraid of Virginia Woolf?* (1963). She was married for more than forty years to Herbert Berghof, the noted director and founder of the acting school HB Studios. She is the author of *Respect for Acting* (New York: Macmillan, 1973).
5.  Director Robert Lewis (1909–), well-known acting teacher and author of the book *Method or Madness* (New York: Samuel French, 1958). Lewis was a member of the Group Theatre and, with Elia Kazan and Cheryl Crawford, founded the Actors Studio in 1947.
6.  The interview Pendleton refers to here can be found in the anthology *Actors on Acting,* edited by Toby Cole and Helen Krich Chinoy (New York: Crown Publishers, 1970), page 635.
7.  Arvin Brown (1940–) has been the artistic director of the Long Wharf Theatre in New Haven since 1967. Arthur Miller (1915–) is the author of more than thirteen plays, among them *Death of a Salesman* (1949) and *The Crucible* (1953). The plays of Tennessee Williams (1911–1983) include *The Glass Menagerie* (1944), *A Streetcar Named Desire* (1947), and *Cat on a Hot Tin Roof* (1955).
8.  Showcases are theater productions in which all actors work without salary; under Actors' Equity Association guidelines, showcases can run no more than sixteen performances in a six-week period, and actors must be reimbursed for transportation to and from rehearsals and performances.

### Neil Pepe

1.  David Mamet (1947–), American playwright, is the recipient of the 1984 Pulitzer Prize and New York Drama Critics Circle Award for his play *Glengarry Glen Ross.* He won an Obie Award for Best New Playwright in 1975. He has written and directed several films including *House of Games* (1987), *Things Change* (1988), *Homicide* (1991), and *Oleanna* (1994).
2.  Howard Korder wrote and directed the 1988 production of *Boys' Life* at Lincoln Center for the Atlantic. Craig Lucas (1951–), playwright whose credits include *Missing Persons* (1981), *Blue Window* (1984, 1986 Los Angeles Drama Critics Award), and *Prelude to a Kiss* (1990 Obie Award and Outer Critics Circle Award). John Guare (1938–) is the author of such plays

as *The House of Blue Leaves* (1971), *Six Degrees of Separation* (1990), and *Four Baboons Adoring the Sun* (1992). Guare received the 1972 Tony Award for Best Book of a Musical for his adaptation and lyrics to *Two Gentleman of Verona*. David Mamet is mentioned in the previous note.

3. William H. Macy is an actor and director who has appeared in the films *Homicide* (1991), *Searching for Bobby Fischer* (1993), *Oleanna* (1994), *Mr. Holland's Opus* (1995), and *Fargo* (1996).

4. Gregory Mosher (1949–), originally a stage director, became the artistic director of the Goodman Theatre in Chicago at the age of 27. He became the artistic director of Lincoln Center Theater in 1985; during his successful tenure there he produced such plays as *House of Blue Leaves, Six Degrees of Separation, Anything Goes,* and *The Front Page.* In 1991, he left Lincoln Center to direct theater and produce film. In 1996, he was appointed producer of Circle in the Square in New York City.

5. The Chicago-based Steppenwolf Theatre Company was founded in 1976 by Jeff Perry, Terry Kinney, and Gary Sinise. Steppenwolf produces older American plays, European classics, and new works. The company has developed such actors as Glenne Headly, John Malkovich, and Sinise. The Moscow Art Theatre was founded and led by Konstantin Stanislavsky (1863–1938). With the Moscow Art Theatre, Stanislavsky presented over fifty plays by authors such as Chekhov, Gorky, Ibsen, Tolstoy, and Ostrovsky while he developed his system of actor training.

6. Anne Bogart, American theater director, winner of two Obies and a Bessie Award, founded the Saratoga International Theater Institute with Japanese director and theorist Tadashi Suzuki (1939–) in 1992. Using primarily American subjects, Bogart's pieces include "Going, Going, Gone," which layers conversations about quantum physics onto the basic scene structure of Edward Albee's *Who's Afraid of Virginia Woolf?* (1963). Another of Bogart's signature pieces is a production of Tennessee Williams's *A Streetcar Named Desire,* in which eight different actors play the role of Stanley Kowalski. Tadashi Suzuki developed his own, very physical, training method for actors while making his reputation as a director of adaptations of classical theater such as *The Bacchae, The Trojan Women,* and *Clytemnestra.*

### Juliet Taylor

1. *The Grifters* (1990), a film directed by Stephen Frears, starring Anjelica Huston, John Cusack, and Annette Bening, based on a novel by Jim Thompson. Screen Actors Guild (SAG) scale salary for film actors was set at $540 per day and $1876 per week as of July 1, 1996.

2. Showcases are theater productions in which all actors work without salary; under Actors' Equity Association guidelines, showcases can run no more than sixteen performances in a six-week period, and actors must be reimbursed for transportation to and from rehearsals and performances.

### Nela Wagman

1. The American Repertory Theatre was founded in Cambridge, Massachusetts, in 1980. Under the artistic direction of Robert Brustein, the performing,

touring, resident, and educational programs of the ART work out of the Loeb Drama Center. The ART Training Institute was founded in 1989.

2. Edward Albee (1928–) is the author of more than twenty plays, including *Who's Afraid of Virginia Woolf?* (1962) and the Pulitzer Prize–winning works *A Delicate Balance* (1966), *Seascape* (1975), and *Three Tall Women* (1991). Terrence McNally (1939–) is the author of such plays as *Lips Together, Teeth Apart* (1991), *Frankie and Johnny in the Clair de Lune* (1987), the book for the musical *Kiss of the Spider Woman,* for which he won the 1993 Tony Award, and the Tony-winning plays *Love! Valour! Compassion!* (1994) and *Master Class* (1995).

# Index

# About the Author

Edward Vilga is a writer, director, and producer. *Acting Now* is his third book. He has produced numerous Off-Broadway theater productions. Vilga is a Yale graduate.